Statistical Modeling

STATISTICAL

APPLICATIONS IN

MODELING

CONTEMPORARY ISSUES

William S. Mallios

 IOWA STATE UNIVERSITY PRESS/AMES

William S. Mallios is Professor of Information Systems and Decision Sciences in the School of Business and Administrative Sciences at California State University, Fresno.

© 1989 Iowa State University Press, Ames, Iowa 50010

Manufactured in the United States of America

First edition, 1989

Library of Congress Cataloging-in-Publication Data

Mallios, William S. (William Steve), 1935–
   Statistical modeling : applications in contemporary issues / William S. Mallios. — 1st ed.
     p.   cm.
   Includes index.
   ISBN 0-8138-0307-1
   1. Social sciences—Statistical methods—Mathematical models.
   2. Regression analysis.   I. Title.
HA31.3.M35   1989
300'.1'5195—dc20   89-31303
                                                           CIP

Dedicated to
Richard L. Anderson and Evan J. Williams

CONTENTS

PREFACE

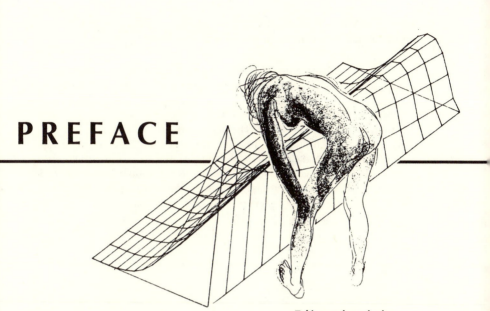

Taking a closer look.

I ssues of the late twentieth century are given added perspective through statistical modeling. Such issues include terrorism, drunk driving, discrimination, gambling, currency fluctuations, and the adequacy of the jury system. Objectives are to reexamine each issue, to define relevant problems, and to provide problem resolution through exploratory models. Modeling results are intended to form working hypotheses for future studies.

As it relates to recent issues, the technology of data acquisition portends vast assemblages of data containing varying degrees of information. The purpose of data analysis is to develop models that extract information. No doubt many of the emerging and existing data sets will remain unanalyzed for years. The National Aeronautics and Space Administration recently reported a 10-year backlog of unanalyzed data. (Indeed, knowledge of the hole in the ozone layer would have been uncovered years earlier had available data been analyzed.) Burgeoning cancer registries and financial data bases contain untapped sources of information. Unfortunately, the number of qualified statisticians willing to undertake these analyses is limited.

Caveats should accompany the term *problem solving*. For the issues under study, modeling results are exploratory; there is no finality of a grand solution. It is axiomatic that the situation can only deteriorate when dogma dictates that problem resolution is at hand.

> Let us imagine an Intelligence who would know at a given instant of time all forces acting in nature and the position of all things which the world consists; let us assume, further, that this Intelligence would be capable of subjecting all these data to mathematical analysis. . . . Nothing would be uncertain for this Intelligence. The past and the future would be present to its eyes. . . . All efforts of men in search for truth have the aim of approaching closer and closer to the Intelligence, but man will remain forever infinitely far removed from it. (P. Laplace, *Introduction to Theory of Probability* [1812]; quoted and discussed in P. Frank, *Philosophy of Science* [Englewood Cliffs, N.J.: Prentice-Hall, 1957], p. 263.)

Statistical Modeling

Introduction

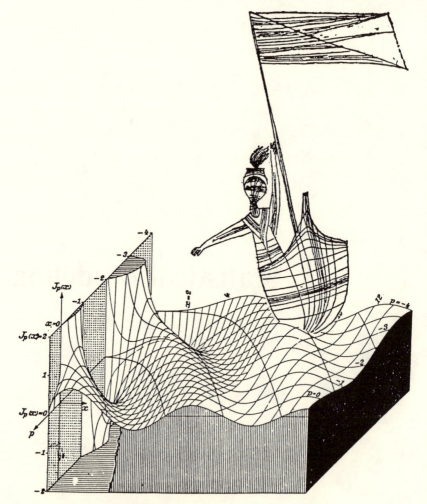

An odyssey of experiments: oh for Leucothea.

Experiments, Data, and Models

1.0 Experiments versus Observation

What's an experiment? According to the *Encyclopedia Americana,* an experiment is an operation designed to establish or discover some truth, principle, or effect. It differs from observation in that the phenomena observed are, to a greater or lesser extent, controlled by human agency. Watching the moon's eclipse of the sun is thus an observation. Capitalism and communism are experiments.

Based on the above definition, it is a contradiction to describe an experiment as uncontrolled, since lack of human control renders the act an observation. Accordingly, classification of experiments could be in terms of the amount of control imposed by human agency. This book focuses on experiments toward the nearly uncontrolled end of the spectrum. Even though these experiments will be termed uncontrolled, the contradiction is understood.

2.0 The Pivotal Role of the Experiment

The experiment plays a critical role in any cycle of inquiry. In this cycle, (1) a hypothesis is formulated (i.e., some truth, principle, or effect is hypothesized), (2) the hypothesis is tested through experimentation, and (3) the hypothesis is accepted, rejected, or modified. In theory, the cycle is repeated until the problem is resolved. In practice, constraints often limit the number of cycles: for example, the operational test and evaluation of a weapon system must be terminated at some point before the system becomes obsolete; a new antibiotic must be marketed before

3

it become ineffective against new, mutant strains. Other experiments—political systems—are dynamic. For these, problem resolution may be ongoing.

The pivotal factor of the cycle is the experiment, in which controls are imposed. In the classical, controlled experiment, the experimenter deliberately introduces changes in certain independent (exogenous) variables within the process being investigated to evaluate their effects on one or more dependent (endogenous) variables. The makeup of the independent variable—or so-called treatment—defines the experiment (such as the specification of soil nutrients in crop yield experiments). Other exogenous variables—termed *concomitants*—may be measured to increase efficiency and decrease biases. All other variables—termed *extraneous variables*—are ignored, controlled, or neutralized through randomization.

When the intent is to compare treatments, the experiment is termed *comparative*; otherwise it is *absolute* (such as estimating the unemployment rate in Los Angeles). However, the experiment may change in intent when it provides unexpected results. This is common in uncontrolled experiments, where serendipitous effects may dominate outcomes. Such effects may emerge when some concomitants are found to be endogenous and possibly affected by treatments and/or when extraneous variables are included in the analysis "to see what happens." For example, when tested, evaluated, and subsequently marketed, a drug to reduce hypertension was found to have the side effect of stimulating hair growth. After further test and evaluation, the drug was marketed as a remedy for baldness.

3.0   A Controlled Experiment

The classical agricultural experiment, as set forth in design and analysis by R. A. Fisher, epitomizes the controlled experiment. We will paraphrase Mahalanobis[1] in contrasting agricultural experiments pre- and post-Fisher. Suppose the intent is to compare effects of six kinds of soil nutrients (treatments) on crop yield. The experimenter prior to Fisher would divide the field into six blocks and each block would receive one of the treatments. Fisher's reaction to this method was that "the treatment giving the highest yield would of course appear to be the best, but no one could say whether the plot [block] would not in fact have yielded as well under some or all of the other treatments."[2] How can we be sure that the observed differences in yield are due to differences in treatments and to soil heterogeneity—a factor that can account for most of the total variation in crop yields? Fisher solved the problem by subdividing each block into a number of plots of smaller size and by assigning one plot to each treatment at random—the well-known randomized block design. This subdivision of blocks provides treatment replication, which is the source of the error estimate. Randomization neutralizes effects of extraneous variables (such as variations in the technique by which treatments are applied) and ensures that treatments are unbiased. Blocking is a control imposed to reduce the effect of soil differences; that is, blocks are constructed such that soil differences are minimized within blocks and maximized between blocks. (Needless to say, one has recourse to higher-order or incomplete block designs in the event of soil heterogeneity within blocks.) Finally, Fisher's analysis of variance gives a convenient and valid method of extracting the information contained in the data.

Since our studies deal with uncontrolled rather than the classical, controlled-type experiments, there is room for considerable improvisation in modeling. Why? Statistical methods developed for controlled-type experiments tend to be inadequate for uncontrolled experiments. For the latter, modeling is often exploratory and tentative and may fall short of desired goals; for example, in modeling futures prices of currencies, one may have to be content with disproving random walk and developing a forecasting model that lacks the precision necessary for daily investments in puts and calls. For studies herein, our intent is to understand the experiment and its objectives, to tap existing data bases, to design data collection techniques when existing data are inadequate, to tailor the analysis to meet the objectives (rather than manipulating the objectives such that they conform to a prescribed analysis), and to make sense out of the analysis results.

4.0 The Experiment's the Thing

The following questions pertain to uncontrolled experiments:

Why must there be unanimity among 12 jurors for conviction?
Is bank X guilty of sex discrimination?
Can one identify likely recidivists at first offense?
Can the winning point spread for National Football League games be predicted?
How does marketing affect the odds of winning bids for contracts?
Which loan applicants are likely to declare bankruptcy under Chapter 7?
What are effective tactics against terrorists who are attempting to steal a bomb from a nuclear facility?
What are the odds that the near-term futures price of the British pound goes up, down, or remains about the same?
What is the return in sales dollars per dollar spent on advertising?

These questions have common themes. They refer to human encounters and to experiments within experiments. Football, for example, is an experiment in masculine fortitude. Each game is an experimental unit, the entity upon which controls are imposed and variables are measured. Controls by human agency include team strategies and the rules and regulations under which the game is played. The imposition of new rules and/or variant team strategies create subexperiments conducted in hopes of achieving desired results. The overriding dependent variables are the final score and the profit margin.

Monetary systems are experiments evolving within other experiments: political systems. The short-term fluctuations of currency futures reflect a blended influence of machinators and supply and demand. Models should reflect both influences, if possible, and random walk should be rejected except as a last resort. A classic example of manipulation ocurred in 1815 with the fall of Napoleon at Waterloo. Through his swift couriers, Nathan Rothschild was the first London financier to learn the battle outcome. Arriving at the stock exchange, Rothschild did not invest as logic would suggest but instead sold heavily. The implication? Wellington must have lost. The result? The price of British bonds plummeted. Just seconds before Rothschild couriers made public the announcement that Napoleon had been crushed, Rothschild bought a huge parcel of bonds for a song.

Terrorism is, like football, a force-on-force encounter, though with considerably fewer constraints. The drug scene, an experiment with its own evolutionary track, has historical ties to terrorism. In the eleventh century, Hassan Ben Sabbah indoctrinated a following of political killers by drugging them and then taking them to a secret garden patterned after the paradise described in the Koran. Compared with the squalor they knew, the drugged individuals indeed found the garden a paradise. Afterwards, Ben Sabbah told them they had been dreaming and that Allah had given them a view of the hereafter. Drugged by hashish, not only when taken to the garden but during their subsequent missions, Ben Sabbah's followers became known as hashishim, or assassins.

In the context of alcohol abuse and drunk driving, the recidivist encounters himself, others, and/or society in violation of laws and mores imposed by society. The Albuquerque, New Mexico, screening, referral, and tracking program for drunk drivers is a subexperiment (an intervention) intended to alter the course of the drunk-driving epidemic. Another intervention, the women's equality movement, results in class-action, sex discrimination suits—against Bank of America, Chase Manhattan, and Allstate.

One way or another, judicial recourse threads its way through all experiments. In fact, judicial systems are experiments themselves. Contrast, for example, the procedure under Anglo-American law—where prosecutor and defense counsel are adversaries and the judge acts as arbiter—with that under the Continental law of Russia and France—where prosecutor, defense counsel, and judge are all charged with the task of finding the truth. In the Continental system, the prosecutor assembles all the evidence both against and in favor of the accused and presents it to an examining judge, who then decides whether the accused should be brought to trial; if the judge rules in the affirmative, the judge is, in effect, finding the person guilty, and proof of innocence then rests with the defendant. (Thus, when the case goes to trial, the Continental system reduces the chances that a guilty person goes free—the probability of a type II error—while the Anglo-American system reduces the chances that an innocent person is convicted—the probability of a type I error.) The two systems do not blend easily. During the Nuremberg Trials, the systems were melded in the international military tribunal composed of Americans, British, French, and Russians. The Russian concept of the trial so shocked Robert Jackson, U.S. Supreme Court justice and American prosecutor, that he suggested that the best thing might be for each nation to try the Nazis it held in custody according to its own customs.[3]

Scientific testimony seems better suited to Continental law. Why? Under the adversary system, the scientist is usually tasked with discrediting his counterpart's testimony. The problem is that discreditation too often supersedes the truth. Add to this situation proficient attorneys and a judge and jury unfamiliar with matters scientific, and the situation can border on the irrational. The studies presented here on statistical depositions demonstrate the need for revisions from a scientist's viewpoint.

5.0 The Model

Football is multifaceted. Those using the game for profits extract information from existing data (which may range from numbers to nonnumeric, past experiences) in making decisions. The gambler decides which way to bet, the coach formulates and revises the game plan, and each player is allowed some degree of improvisation. The extent to which each is successful depends on the worthiness of their model.

A model is used to extract information from existing data and predict the outcome about which a decision is to be made. Generally, a model is any device that enhances (rapid/nonrapid) extraction of information (under stress/not under stress) for purposes of making (critical/noncritical) decisions. Descriptors in parentheses may vary between individuals for a well-specified situation requiring a decision.

It is important that prediction be distinguished from decision making. The experiment provides the data, the model converts the data into a prediction, and the decision is based, to varying degrees, on the prediction. For example, based on data gleaned from a psychological questionnaire, a model predicts that a convicted drunk driver, at first offense, is likely to become a recidivist. The judge makes the decision to direct the defendant to a rehabilitation program. The decision is based on the perceived or demonstrated validity of the prediction model and on the risk of each incorrect decision. These risks may be defined monetarily in terms of the specific consequences of no rehabilitative treatment, given the defendant is a problem drinker, and of mandated treatment, given the defendant is not a problem drinker.

This book focuses on statistical models used for prediction in decision-making processes. Too often, such models play minor roles because the people concerned believe statistical models cannot incorporate ad hoc information relevant to the decision. Such opinions are usually based either on total ignorance of Bayesian inference or on associations with inept modelers. Perhaps the measure of the statistician is the role his model plays in the decision support system.

Any general discusion on models warrants comment on the principle of parsimony. "The grand aim of all science . . . is to cover the greatest possible number of empirical facts by logical deduction from the smallest number of hypotheses or axioms."[4] Einstein's words prompt emulation. However, the premature application of the principle can be damaging. In many studies, knowledge is in its infancy. Too often scientists present as truths results derived from overly simplistic models—whether knowingly or unwittingly, whether for purposes scientific or otherwise. To oversimplify is to mold the problem into something it is not in order to solve it. This should not be the aim of science.

References

1. Mahalanobis, P. C. "Biography of R. A. Fisher." *Sankhya* 4, pt. 2 (1938).

2. Fisher, R. A. *The Design of Experiments*. Edinburgh: Oliver & Boyd, 1935. (Quotation, p. 271.)

3. Conot, R. E. *Justice at Nuremberg*. New York: Carrol & Graf, 1984.

4. Einstein, A. *The World as I See It*. New York: Covici, Freide, 1934.

Statistics in Judicial Proceedings

Sinking.

'esterday, Today, and Tomorrow

This study sets the stage for the next three chapters. In addressing the theme statistics in judicial proceedings, we begin with a standard: the jury system under Anglo-American law. The premise is that such standards are not indefeasible.

Next, differences in philosophical views between scientists and jurists are discussed in terms of hypothesis testing. It is argued that statistical depositions are better suited to Continental law than to Anglo-American law.

Finally, recent cases involving statistical testimony are discussed, and the future role of statistics in jurisprudence is examined. Litigation is perhaps the nation's fastest growing industry, and statistical depositions are becoming indispensable. Thus, the objectives of statisticians should be twofold: (1) to uncover whatever truths exist in sets of data and (2) to make these truths understood by all parties concerned. These objectives form recurring themes in subsequent studies.

1.0 The Jury System

1.1 Views on the Jury System

In 1785 the French mathematician-philosopher Condorcet became the first to subject to mathematical investigation the correctness of judgments determined by a majority of votes. He believed he showed the English jury system—forced unanimity among 12 jurors for conviction—to be bad. What was his alternative? For civil cases he proposed a court of 25 judges to decide by majority; for criminal cases, a court of 30 judges in which a margin of at least 8 was required to condemn the accused. Subsequent events—the French Revolution—may have changed Condorcet's mind. Louis and Marie were beheaded; appeals were made to George Washington to intercede in behalf of the imprisoned Lafayette. Meanwhile, the aristocratic Condorcet was caught while changing hiding places. "Who are you?" demanded a dark figure. "A carpenter," replied Condorcet. "Show me your hands." Condorcet's upturned palms bore no calluses. "You're no carpenter." Condorcet died by poisoning in prison.

Nonetheless, Condorcet's 1785 essay, "Essai sur l'applicition de l'analyse à la probabilité des décisions rendues à la pluralité des voix," influenced other French mathematicians, including Laplace and Poisson. Based on lectures given in 1795, Laplace wrote, "The probability of the decision is too feeble in our juries, and . . . in order to give sufficient guarantee to innocence, one ought to demand at least a plurality of 9 votes in 12."[1] In his 1837 treatise, *Recherches sur la probabilité des jugements en matière criminelle et en matière civile,* Poisson wrote, "Among the applications of this calculus, one of the most important is that which concerns the probability of correctness of judgements," and then commended Condorcet for his "ingenious idea."[2]

Writing on the history of probability, the Englishman Todhunter was not so impressed with Condorcet's pronouncements: "Condorcet seems really to have fancied that valuable results could have been obtained from any data, however imperfect, by using formulae with an adequate supply of signs of integration."[3]

If optimal solutions were sought from current-day statisticians regarding the number of jurors and judges making up a tribunal and the proportion required for guilt determinations, those coming up with a solution unanimity among 12 jurors for conviction would likely be branded inept. On the other hand, there are aversions to mathematical opinions on such matters. Indeed, many consider our jury system a venerable institution. Witness the nonmathematical explanations for the number of jurors: the 12 tribes of Israel, the 12 patriarchs, the 12 officers of Solomon record in the Book of Kings, and the 12 apostles. Not all of these give a happy connotation to the number 12: "The first implies that there may be . . . juror(s) who got lost somewhere in the corridor and the last that there is a Judas on every jury."[4]

1.2   Thoughts on the Probability of Conviction

We begin with the erroneous but convenient premise that the probability of conviction, denoted by p_c, can be determined through the binomial probability density function (pdf); that is,

$$p_c = \sum_{x \geq x^*} \binom{n}{x} p_v^x (1 - p_v)^{n-x}$$

where n is the number of jurors, x is the number of guilty votes, x^* is the number of guilty votes required for conviction, and p_v is the probability of a guilty vote. Table 2.1 presents values of p_c for varying values of n, x, x^*, and p_v. It is interesting to note that under the English jury system, the probability of conviction is slightly greater than .50 (actually, .54) when $p_v = .95$. Under Laplace's suggestion of a plurality of at least 9 votes in 12, p_c increases to .980 when $p_v = .95$.

The problem with the binomial probabilities is that the underlying assumptions are invalid. Namely, juror votes are not independent, and p_v is not likely constant between members of the same panel. Consider first the question of independence. The writer's experience in jury duty is that, usually, no more than 3 jurors express independent views; others are merely followers. Table 2.1 shows that for unanimity among 3 jurors the probability of conviction is .857 when $p_v = .95$. In effect, then, p_c is much higher than .54 when there are three "leaders" and nine "followers" in a panel of 12.

There is good reason for the lack of independence. Under the English jury system, "twelve men and women are to be selected at random; they have never before had any experience of weighing evidence and perhaps not of applying their minds judicially to any problem; they are often, as the Common Law Commissioners of 1858 tactfully put it, 'unaccustomed to severe intellectual exercise or to protracted thought.'"[4] It has been observed that most individuals accustomed to "protracted thought" either are eager to avoid jury duty or are not selected as jurors owing to peremptory challenges. These circumstances may lead to juries that are inept

TABLE 2.1 The Probability of Conviction (p_c) as Determined by the Binomial Probability Density Function

	x^* for $n = 12$						x^* for $n = 3$	
p_v	7	8	9	10	11	12	2	3
.80	.981	.927	.795	.558	.275	.069	.888	.512
.90	.999	.996	.974	.889	.659	.282	.967	.729
.95	1.000	.999	.998	.980	.882	.540	.993	.857
.99	1.000	1.000	1.000	.999	.994	.886	1.000	.977

Note: $p_c = \sum_{x \geq x^*}^{n} \binom{n}{x} p_v^x (1 - p_v)^{n-x}$

x = number of guilty votes, x^* = numbers of guilty votes required for conviction, n = number of jurors, p_v = probability of a guilty vote.

in understanding the issues at hand; for example, in its 3 September 1979 issue, *Time* magazine reported that at the 14-month trial of *SCM* v. *Xerox*, a \$1.5 billion antitrust suit, the jurors' average educational level was 10th grade.

Next, consider the value of p_v per independent juror. The value of p_v is primarily determined by the juror's perception of the evidence and the interpretation of "reasonable doubt," both of which are highly subjective. Mathematically, p_v may be expressed as

$$p_v = \int_D^1 f(p; \mathbf{a}) \, dp$$

where p is the probability that the accused is guilty, $f(p; \mathbf{a})$ is the pdf of p, $\mathbf{a}$ denotes a vector of parameters for the pdf, and D is the borderline value between reasonable and unreasonable doubt regarding guilt; $0 \le D \le 1$. The beta pdf is a logical choice for $f(p; \mathbf{a})$ because of the flexibility of its shapes:

$$f(p; \mathbf{a}) = p^{a-1} (1 - p)^{a^* - 1}/B(a, a^*)$$

where $B(a, a^*)$ denotes a beta function. The parameter vector $\mathbf{a} = (a, a^*)$ is written as $\mathbf{a}(e)$ to indicate that its values are determined by the evidence. Through the beta pdf, effects of $\mathbf{a}(e)$ and D on p_v are illustrated as follows:

a	a^*	$E(p)$	$(D,$	$p_v)$	$(D,$	$p_v)$
2	.5	.800	.90	.468	.99	.159
5	.5	.909	.90	.753	.99	.499
10	.5	.952	.90	.871	.99	.712
20	.5	.976	.90	.934	.99	.845

where $E(p) = a/(a + a^*)$ is the expected value of p. In each case, values of $\mathbf{a}(e)$ are chosen such that the $E(p)$ are high. Changing reasonable doubt from .90 to .99 is seen to have a pronounced effect on p_v. This should be of some concern because of the ambiguity of the legal definition of "reasonable doubt." (Note that a shortcoming of this formulation is that D and $\mathbf{a}(e)$ are assumed independent. In reality, the juror may formulate D and $\mathbf{a}(e)$ in nonindependent fashion.)

Based on these thoughts, questions arise. (1) How should the number of jurors and the concept of unanimity change as the number of independent jurors increases or decreases? (2) How should the jurors be chosen to ensure maximum understanding of the evidence? (3) How can evidence be presented so that it is more uniformly and properly understood? (4) What are proper definitions for D and the relation between D and the evidence? (5) Is there a role for the juror who is both a follower and not accustomed to "protracted thought"?

2.0   Conflicts between Scientific and Judicial Views: Hypothesis Testing

Regarding unanimity among jurors, consider a statement by Laplace: "Has the proof of the offence of the accused the high probability necessary so that citizens would have less reason to doubt the error of tribunals if he is innocent and condemned, than they would of the unfortunate ones who would be emboldened by the example of his impunity if he were guilty and acquitted?"[1] Associating "innocent and condemned" with a type I error and "guilty and acquitted" with a type II error, we find a possible genesis for the Neyman-Pearson lemma, which provides the foundations for classical, statistical hypothesis testing. The two types of error usually have different philosophical meanings to scientists and jurist.

Consider the null (H_0) and alternative (H_a) hypothesis as viewed by the scientist.

H_0: The state of knowledge does not go beyond the status quo.
H_a: The state of knowledge has been advanced.

Since H_0 can only be disproved, not proved, H_0 is a statement on the status quo. The objective is to disprove H_0 and show that the state of knowledge has been advanced—if, in fact, H_a is true. Possible outcomes of hypothesis testing are as follows:

	Decision	
State of nature	Do not reject H_0	Reject H_0
H_0 is true	Correct decision	Type I error
H_a is true	Type II error	Correct decision

The scientist strives to minimize the chances of a type II error so as not to retard the advancement of knowledge. Conceptually, statistical hypothesis testing is predicated on choosing the test that minimizes the probability of a type II error. In application, however, the circumstances may dictate minimizing either or both probabilities.

Next consider null and alternative hypotheses for the accused under Anglo-American law, where prosecutor and defense counsel are adversaries with the judge acting as arbiter:

H_0: The accused is innocent.
H_a: The accused is guilty.

Possible outcomes of the trial (hypothesis testing) are as follows:

	Decision	
State of nature	Do not reject H_0	Reject H_0
H_0 is true	Correct decision	Type I error: an innocent person is convicted
H_a is true	Type II error: a guilty person is acquitted	Correct decision

Anglo-American law is philosophically bound by Lord Blackstone's comment that it is better that 10 guilty men go free than 1 innocent man be convicted. (Blackstone did not provide a cost-benefit analysis.) Clearly, the avoidance of a type I error should be paramount to the jurist—which is contrary to the scientist's objective of minimizing the chances of a type II error. The difference may be explained in terms of emphasis. Judicial emphasis is on the individual while scientific emphasis is on society.

Although this difference in emphasis may lead to little, if any, difficulty, another difference does. The scientist seeks to establish a scientific truth, while the lawyer seeks to win a case under an adversarial system. What is the implication of this difference when scientist and lawyer meet in the latter's bailiwick? The scientist may have to choose between finding truths in a set of data and formulating results toward winning the case. The two may well be in conflict. Because of this conflict, scientific depositions seem better suited to the Continental system of law, where prosecutor, defense counsel, and judge are all charged with finding the truth. All the evidence is then presented to an examining judge, who then decides whether the accused should be brought to trial. If the judge rules in the affirmative, the accused is, in effect, guilty unless proved innocent through the trial. Null and alternative hypotheses are thus

H_0: The accused is guilty.
H_a: The accused is innocent.

As a logical setting for scientific depositions, Continental law gives equal emphasis to the individual and society.

3.0   Directions

3.1   Recent Cases

In 1935 the decision in *Norris* v. *Alabama*[5] opened the door to mathematical applications in jury discrimination cases.[6] A criminal identification case,[6] tax cases,[8] and a case study of an antitrust suit[9] used statistical evidence, as have suits in race discrimination[10] and equal opportunity.[10] Nonetheless, usable methodologies are far in advance of their application. Why should this be so? With the uncertainties that often surround innocence and guilt, it seems natural that recourse be given to the science of uncertainties: statistics. Herein lies a dilemma. On the one hand, there is the widespread acceptance of probability theory and its application. On the other hand, there is the moral abhorrence of convicting an innocent person and the mystique of mathematics. "Mathematics, a veritable sorcerer in our computerized society, while assisting the trier of fact in the search for truth, must not cast a spell over him."[11]

Since mathematical arguments cannot be totally avoided, even by those wishing to do so, judicial recourse has been to accept mathematical arguments that are deterministic, as illustrated in the following case. A gross misuse of probability theory led the California Supreme Court to overturn the conviction of *People* v. *Collins*[11] (see Exercise 2). In illustrating a proper application of mathematics, the majority opinion referenced *People* v. *Trujillo*:

> Clothing belonging to Trujillo was subjected to a test by an expert for the purpose of matching fibers with those found on the scarf and other pieces of apparel from Odom's body. [Odom was a police officer whom Trujillo was accused of slaying.] Eleven sets of matching fibers were found. . . . [The expert witness] testified that the chances were one in a hundred billion that this number of matches would be in coincidence; therefore he concluded that these articles had come into contact with one another.[7]

Also referenced as proper were applications by Finkelstein in jury discrimination cases. For example,

> in [*Swain* v. *Alabama*[12]] . . . venires with five or fewer [blacks] appeared in thirty consecutive cases. The probability of this occurence . . . is . . . 4.63×10^{-21} [assuming that black males constituted one-quarter of the adult population of Talladega County, Alabama]. This means that . . . if thirty venires were selected at random in Talladega County every day of

the year, the daily selection would correspond to the facts of Swain only one day, on the average, in thousands of trillions of years.[6]

The odds in these applications leave no room for doubt; they represent certainty. The unknown is whether less certain probabilities would have been admissible as testimony. For example, suppose that, in *Trujillo*, the probability was .10 instead of near 0 that "this number of matches would be in coincidence" or that, in *Swain*, the probability was .05 instead of near 0 that venires with five or fewer blacks would appear in 30 consecutive cases. Is such testimony misleading or uninformative? The answer is yes only if the validity of the probabilities is suspected. Accordingly, the majority opinion in *Collins* states that probabilities used in testimony should have proven standards of validity. As precedent, the New Mexico Supreme Court is quoted: "We hold that mathematical odds are not admissible as evidence . . . so long as the odds are based on estimates, the validity of which have not been demonstrated."[13] Unfortunately, in elaborating on the validity of estimates, the majority opinion in *Collins* includes statements on statistical estimation that are incorrect (see Sigal[8]). The statistical testimonies of a statistical incompetent in the *Collins* case and those of a statistical opportunist in *State* v. *Sneed*[3] had the effect of blemishing statistical testimony in judicial proceedings.

3.2   The Future

Statistics in jurisprudence: what's in store? The answer is obvious given the growth of the litigation industry. For discrimination cases in particular, statistical depositions are often a mainstay of the evidence. There are problems, however, that should be addressed and resolved. First, statistical testimony is generally not understood by most jurors; after all, the jurors are "unaccustomed to severe intellectual exercise or to protracted thought." Moreover, the statistical expertise of lawyers is usually limited to elementary statistics—though this appears to be changing. Second, there are often diverging issues of truth and triumph. And the reality is that money overshadows all else.

I will address these issues indirectly. In the next three chapters case studies are presented wherein difficulties are exposed and exploratory statistical models are part of the decision support system. It is only after such difficulties are exposed that resolutions may be forthcoming. The first case study, a class-action sex discrimination suit, applies to the preconviction phase; that is, is the bank guilty of sex discrimination beyond reasonable doubt? The second case study deals with the postconviction phase, where statistical modeling is used to establish compensation in a labor-managment dispute. The third case study, also in the postconviction phase, deals with identifying problem drinkers among convicted drunk drivers and with establishing a program for resolving the drunk driver epidemic. These studies do not address the "jury problem." However, some of the discussions might supply some ideas for making statistical depositions comprehensible.

Exercise 1

Under the English jury system, there must be forced unanimity among 12 jurors for conviction. (In 1974 the British amended their trial procedures to permit non-unanimous verdicts in certain criminal cases.) Suppose you are a soothsayer at a point in time when innocence or guilt is based on the outcome of mortal combat. You are asked to evaluate the existing procedure. Would you retain the existing method of mortal combat? If so, why? Would you advocate the English jury system? If so, why? If neither of these systems appeals to you, what system would you devise? Defend your answer. (I have included this question on graduate examinations for a number of years. Less than 5% of all students defended the English jury system.)

Exercise 2

Consider the case of *People* v. *Collins*.[11] On a sunny afternoon in Los Angeles, Mrs. Juanita Brooks had been shopping and was returning home with groceries. Suddenly she was pushed to the ground by a person she neither saw nor heard approach. Looking up, she saw a blond woman running from the scene. Immediately following the incident, Mrs. Brooks discovered that her purse, containing $35 to $40, was missing.

About the same time, John Bass, a resident of the neighborhood, saw a woman run out of the alley in which the incident had occurred. The woman, described as Caucasian with blond hair in a ponytail, entered a yellow automobile driven by a black with a beard and mustache.

The defendants—Malcolm Collins and his wife, Janet—were questioned several days later. She had blond hair in a ponytail. Malcolm had no beard but he was known to have worn one prior to the crime. A yellow Lincoln, known to have been driven by them, was parked outside their home. Although Malcolm was unemployed and Janet earned not much more than $12 a week, Malcolm had paid a $35 traffic fine the day following the crime. He said the money had been won gambling.

During the interrogation, Janet said, "If I told you that [Malcolm] didn't know anything about it and I did it, would you cut him loose? I just want him out, that's all, because I ain't never been in no trouble. I won't have to do much [time], but he will. What's the most time I can do?"

The conversation was recorded, introduced in evidence, and played to the jury over objections based on *Escobedo*[14] and *Dorado*.[15] Mrs. Brooks could not identify Janet, and Bass's identification was incomplete. There was evidence that Janet had worn light-colored clothing on the day in question, but both the victim and Bass testified that the girl they observed wore dark clothing.

In attempting to bolster their identificaiton, the prosecution called an instructor of mathematics at a state college. This witness explained the product rule, which states that the probability of the joint occurrence of a number of mutually independent events is equal to the product of the individual probabilities that each of the events will occur. Without presenting any statistical evidence whatsoever to support the probabilities used for the following characteristics, the prosecutor proceeded to have the witness calculate the probability that the defendants were innocent and that another couple having the same distinctive characteristics committed the robbery.

Characteristic	Individual probability
Partly yellow automobile	1/10
Man with mustache	1/4
Girl with ponytail	1/10
Girl with blond hair	1/3
Black man with beard	1/10
Interracial couple in car	1/1000

Applying the product rule, the witness concluded that the probablity of any couple other than the defendants being at the scene was 1 in 12 million. The defense objected to this testimoy on the grounds that it was immaterial, invaded the province of the jury, and was based on unfounded assumptions. The objections were temporarily overruled, the evidence was admitted subject to a motion to strike, and the motion was denied at the conclusion of direct examination. The couple was found guilty. Malcolm appealed, citing as reversible error the admission of Janet's conversation with the arresting officer and the admission of statistical testimony. The California Supreme Court reversed the finding.

Was the prosecution's use of the product rule valid? Describe alternative methods for obtaining the probability in question. Find the probability that at least one other couple has the same characteristics as the Collins couple by using southern California as the population base.

References

1. Laplace, P. S. *A Philosophical Essay on Probabilities*. Translated from 6th French ed. New York: Dover, 1951. (Quotations, pp. 139 and 133.)

2. Poisson, S. D. *Recherches sur la probabilité des jugements en matière criminelle et en matière civile*. Paris: Bachelier, 1837. (Quotation, p. 2.)

3. Todhunter, M. *History of Mathematical Theory of Probability*. New York: Chelsea, 1949. (Quotation, p. 410.)

4. Devlin, P. *Trial by Jury*. London: Stevens, 1956. (Quotation, pp. 10 and 5.)

5. *Norris* v. *Alabama*, 294 U.S. 587 (1935).

6. Finkelstein, M. "The Application of Statistical Decision Theory to Jury Discrimination Cases." *Harvard Law Review* 80, no. 1 (1966): 338–76. (Quotation, p. 357.)

7. *People* v. *Trujillo*, 32 Cal. 2d 105, 109, 194 P. 2d 681 (1948).

8. Sigal, P. "Judicial Use, Misuse, and Abuse of Statistical Evidence." *Journal of Urban Law* 47 (1969): 165–90.

9. Lozowick, A. H., Steiner, P. O., and Miller, R. "Law and Quantitative Multivariate Analysis: An Encounter." *Michigan Law Review* 66 (1968): 1641–78.

10. Kaye, D. "Statistical Evidence of Discrimination." *Journal of the American Statistical Association* 77 (1982): 380–88.

11. *People* v. *Collins*, 66 Cal. 497, 438 P. 2d 33 (1969).

12. *Swain* v. *Alabama*, 380 U.S. 202 (1965).

13. *State* v. *Sneed*, 76 N.M. 349, 414 P. 2d 858 (1966).

14. *Escobedo* v. *Illinois*, 378 U.S. 478 (1964).

15. *People* v. *Dorado*, 42 Cal. Rptr. 169, 393, P. 2d 361 (1965).

3

Sex Discrimination: Statistica

Portrait of woman, circa XXI.

A class-action suit was filed against a central California bank, claiming sex discrimination in the bank's managerial levels. Partially as a result of statistical analysis, the case was settled out of court. The focus of this chapter is on the interpretation of statistical analyses and issues related to probabilistic evidence in class-action discrimination suits.

Employee data were obtained from subpoenaed personnel files. The variables under study were as follows: starting and current salaries, current managerial position, number of years of formal education and related experience prior to current employment, number of years of current employment, and gender. Regression analyses, with both current and starting monthly salaries as dependent variables, showed significant effects of employee gender on each of the dependent variables after adjustment for concomitants. Average male salaries exceeded those of female counterparts by $200 to $400 per month.

Do the significant effects of gender constitute sex discrimination? Bank counsel argued (1) that women are more likely to interrupt their careers to care for home and family and that this likelihood is reflected by the significant sex effects, (2) that inequities in starting salaries are a result of previous higher salaries for men, and (3) that previous salaries are positively correlated with current productivity. Counsel for the plaintiffs countered by referencing testimony in the Allstate sex discrimination case that past salaries and current productivity are uncorrelated.

Major disputes could have been avoided through the analysis of employee data on current productivity (as measured from performance appraisals), absences, and salary history prior to current employment. Accordingly, general guidelines are presented for probabilistic assessments in class-action discrimination cases.

1.0   Introduction

1.1   Background

Title VII of the 1964 Civil Rights Act, as amended in 1972, addresses unlawful employment practices by employers (with 15 or more employees) who discriminate against any individual because of race, color, religion, sex, or national origin. Regarding sex discrimination, the act states that "the employer is further forbidden to classify applicants or employees in any way that would tend to deprive any individual of employment opportunities because of the individual's sex" (Sec. 703[a][2]).

For many years, the act fell on deaf ears, as illustrated by the status of women in the banking industry. In 1973 the Council on Economic Priorities conducted a study to assess the status of minorities and women in banking. The study sampled 18 banks representing a cross section of the industry. Conclusions were that (1) employment discrimination against women and minorities is endemic to commercial banking, (2) commercial banks are unwilling to permit public scrutiny of their employment practices, and (3) secrecy and discrimination are perpetuated by federal law, policy, and complacency. Women were found to hold 73% of all clerical jobs and only 15% of official and managerial positions.

Conditions changed from 1973 to 1981. In 1981 the Equal Employment Opportunity Commission reported that women represented 39.5% of the officials and managers in half of the largest banks in the country. Why the change? In 1974 class-action sex discrimination suits were filed against Bank of America and eventually settled for $3.75 million. Part of the settlement required the bank to improve the management skills of its female employees. In 1976 a suit was filed by 10,000 women against Chase Manhattan. To settle the case, the bank agreed to spend about $2 million over a three-year period.

1.2   The Present Study

The present study deals with a class-action suit against a California bank located in the San Joaquin Valley. The suit claimed sex discrimination in the bank's managerial levels and was eventually settled out of court. Employee data were obtained from subpoenaed personnel files. Table 3.1 presents the number of women employed in each of four levels of management: upper, upper-middle, middle, and lower.

Several approaches can be used to define sex discrimination. One approach is with reference to Table 3.1, where women appear to be underrepresented in the three highest management levels and overrepresented in the lowest. Consider the proportions of women in a relevant

TABLE 3.1. Number of Women Employed per Management Level

Management level	No. of employees	No. of women	Women (%)
Upper	13	1	8
Upper-middle	17	0	0
Middle	55	21	38
Lower	57	52	91

population—say, the San Joaquin Valley—who are available, qualified for the respective management levels, and desirous of employment. If a comparison of these proportions with those in Table 3.1 shows women to be underrepresented in all but the lowest level, then one might argue the existence of sex discrimination.

There are several problems with this approach. (1) It might be argued that even though an individual was available, desirous of employment, and qualified, they might not have applied for the position, which, presumably, was properly advertised. Hence, underrepresentation of women could occur through no fault of the bank. (2) It is difficult to establish reliable estimates of the proportions in the relevant population. Inferences based on these estimates may thus be in jeopardy. (3) Even if women were properly represented in each of the management levels, there may be blatant sex discrimination with regard to salary. For these reasons, the approach taken in the following sections evaluates effects of employee gender on present and starting salaries.

2.0 Regression Analysis in the Estimation of Sex Effects

2.1 The Variables under Study

The writer was presented the data package after the fact—in the sense that the variables and data under study were selected by lawyers without statistical consultation. Moreover, there was an unwillingness to augment the data package with additional variables that were critical in problem resolution. This issue will be discussed in section 3.2.

For each employee file, the following variables were measured:

PSAL = present salary;
SEX = 1 for male,
    = 0 for female;
YRS = number of years employed by the bank;
SSAL = starting salary;
ED = years of formal education when hired (e.g., ED = 16 for an undergraduate degree);

EX = 1 for five or more years of related experience when hired,
   = 0 for less than five years of related experience when hired;
M = 0 for lower-level management (which includes loan officers
      and supervisors),
   = 1 for middle-level management (which includes project and
      operation managers),
   = 2 for upper-middle-level management (which includes branch
      coordinators and general service managers),
   = 3 for upper-level management (which includes executive, ad-
      ministrative, and senior vice presidents).

Since only one woman appeared in the two highest management levels, all data for M = 2 or 3 are discarded in the analysis.

For the 112 individuals in lower or middle management, PSAL averaged \$1,844.28/month with a range of \$900 to \$3,390. ED averaged 13.97 years with a range of 12 to 18 years. When hired, 40% of the sample had more than 5 years of related experience.

2.2   Direct and Indirect Sex Effects

Regression analysis is applied in estimating effects of employee gender on salary. Of the variables listed above, SSAL and PSAL are considered endogenous so as to establish which of the following is the case: (1) There were no sex inequities in SSAL and there are none in PSAL. (2) There were inequities in SSAL and these inequities have increased, diminished, or remained the same in regards to PSAL. (3) There were no inequities in SSAL, but there are in PSAL. Only in situation (1) is there no evidence of discrimination regarding salaries.

To present an overview of the analysis, we first discuss effects of SEX on PSAL and SSAL, disregarding the other variables. Consider

$$\text{PSAL} = f_1(\text{SEX}, \text{SSAL}) = c_{11}\text{SEX} + c_{12}\text{SSAL} + e_1 \qquad (3.1)$$

and

$$\text{SSAL} = f_2(\text{SEX}) = c_{21}\text{SEX} + e_2 \qquad (3.2)$$

where the unknown functions f_1 and f_2 are assumed to be adequately approximated by the given first-order expansions; e_1 and e_2 are model errors. (For convenience, intercepts are excluded.) The coefficients c_{11} and c_{21} are, respectively, the direct effects of sex on PSAL and SSAL; for example, c_{11} quantifies the average sex inequity in PSAL after adjusting for differences in SSAL; see Chapter 14, Methodological Overview, for definitions of effects and their estimation through regression systems. Similarly, c_{12} is the direct effect of SSAL on PSAL. The expansions in (3.1) and (3.2) form a structural regression system. In general, structural systems quantify all direct effects of exogenous variables on endogenous variables and of endogenous variables on one another.

If the right-hand expression in (3.2) is substituted for SSAL in (3.1), we have

$$\text{PSAL} = (c_{11} + c_{12}c_{21})\text{SEX} + (e_1 + c_{12}e_2) \qquad \text{(3.3)}$$

The coefficient $(c_{11} + c_{12}c_{21})$ is the overall SEX effect on PSAL. This effect aggregates the direct (c_{11}) and the indirect $(c_{12}c_{21})$ SEX effect on PSAL; that is, $c_{12}c_{21}$ is an indirect effect in the sense that it arises indirectly through the direct SEX effect on PSAL and the subsequent direct effect on SSAL and PSAL. In general, the overall effect of a variable U on a variable V is the sum of the direct and all indirect U effects on V. (Note that in [3.2], the direct effect c_{21} becomes the overall SEX effect on SSAL since there are no indirect SEX effects on SSAL.) The expansions in (3.2) and (3.3) form a reduced regression system. In general, reduced systems quantify overall effects of each exogenous variable on each endogenous variable.

2.3 Analysis Results

Aside from PSAL and SSAL, all other variables are considered exogenous and are utilized in a reduced system through expansion of the following functions: PSAL = f_1(SEX, ED, EX, YRS, M) and SSAL = f_2(SEX, ED, EX, YRS). Note that YRS identifies the year in which the individual was hired because all employees in the sample were current as of 1983. Hence YRS is used to account for effects of inflation on salaries.

In the expansion of the f's, all first- and second-order terms are scanned for significance through stepwise regression. Reduced equation estimates, given by equations (1) and (2) in Table 3.2, are based on the following ground rules. All first-order terms are included in the model whether significant or not. A second-order term is included in both equations if it is significant in either equation.

Except for M, ED is the only variable not having interactive effects. ED has a direct effect on SSAL (i.e., with each additional year of formal schooling, SSAL increases by an average of $44.05 per month) and a significant effect on PSAL at the 10% level of significance. Since the

TABLE 3.2   Ordinary Least-Squares Estimates of Reduced and Structural System Parameters

Dependent variable Predictor	Equation (1) SSAL Coefficient estimate	$|t|$	Equation (2) PSAL Coefficient estimate	$|t|$	Equation (3)[a] PSAL Coefficient estimate	$|t|$
Intercept	151.759	—	1,387.757	—	1,278.606	—
SEX	592.515	4.97	137.280	1.09	7.437	.06
YRS	−20.44	3.56	31.975	5.35	37.854	5.99
SSAL	—	—	—	—	.257	2.44
ED	44.047	2.41	29.156	1.54	19.461	1.03
EX	280.243	2.66	297.989	2.67	247.309	2.23
M	—	—	766.724	12.19	711.494	10.87
(SEX)(YRS)	−43.399	4.24	18.101	1.70	30.299	2.63
(SEX)(EX)	259.439	2.37	60.730	.53	−12.004	.10
(YRS)(EX)	−17.024	1.96	−17.458	1.92	−14.306	1.60
R^2	.765		.815		.826	
Standard error of estimate	258.812		267.241		261.042	

[a]Justification of ordinary least-squares estimation in eq. (3) is based on the argument that the estimates, though inconsistent, may have smaller mean square error. When terms are manipulated such that the structural equation for PSAL is identified, two-stage least-squares (2SLS) estimation leads to inefficient estimates. The reason for this is that $R^2 = .765$ for eq. (1) is not sufficiently high to provide more efficient estimates in eq. (3); see sec. 2.8 of Chap. 14, Methodological Overview.

ED effect on PSAL (in eq. [2] in Table 3.2) is an overall effect (the aggregate of the direct and indirect ED effects on PSAL), the implication is that the overall ED effect on PSAL is largely indirect and through SSAL; that is, ED would have a nonsignificant effect on PSAL if SSAL were included as a predictor—as will be shown in fitting the structural system. Other effects are interactive; for example, the effects of SEX on both SSAL and PSAL are contingent on the value of YRS and, in the case of SSAL, on the value of EX.

Table 3.3 presents results of exercising Table 3.2 equations (1) and (2) to illustrate average differences in monthly salaries between sexes as a function of EX and YRS. Consider individuals with more than 5 years' experience in a related field when hired (EX = 1). A male hired in 1980 (YRS = 3) received a starting salary that averaged $721.76 higher than his female counterpart. In this 3-year period (from 1980 to 1983), the female has made up, on the average, 65% of the initial deficit; that is, ($721.76 − $253.31)/$721.76 = .65. Next, consider those with less than 5 years' experience when hired (EX = 0). For YRS = 3, the average difference in SSAL was $462.32 in favor of the males, while the difference as of 1983 was $191.58. In this case, the females have made up 58.6% of the initial deficit.

TABLE 3.3. Average Differences in Monthly Salaries between Sexes Based on the Equations in Table 3.2

	More than 5 years' related experience when hired		
Years employed	3	5	7
Year employed	1980	1978	1976
(1) SSAL(male) − SSAL(female)	$721.76	$634.96	$548.16
(2) PSAL(male) − PSAL(female)	252.31	288.52	324.72
[(1) − (2)]/(2)	.650	.546	.408
	Less than five years' related experience when hired		
Years employed	3	5	7
Year employed	1980	1978	1976
(1) SSAL(male) − SSAL(female)	$462.32	$375.52	$288.72
(2) PSAL(male) − PSAL(female)	191.58	227.79	263.99
[(1) − (2)]/(2)	.586	.393	.086
	SSAL(male) = SSAL(female) when hired; EX = 0		
Years employed	3	5	7
Year employed	1980	1978	1976
PSAL(male) − PSAL(female)	$98.33	$158.93	$219.53

Questions regarding differences in PSAL, given that starting salaries were the same, are addressed through the structural system estimated by equations (1) and (3) in Table 3.2. In equation (3), the (SEX)(YRS) interaction has a significant direct effect on PSAL, indicating that the overall (SEX)(YRS) effect on PSAL (in eq. [2]) is the aggregate of a positive direct effect (i.e., the coefficient of (SEX)(YRS) in eq. [3] is 30.299) and a negative indirect effect (i.e., the indirect effect is estimated by the product of the coefficient of SSAL in eq. [3] and the coefficient of (SEX)(YRS) in eq. [1]). The direct (SEX)(EX) effect on PSAL is nonsignificant, so that the overall (SEX)(EX) effect on PSAL is simply an indirect effect.

The bottom portion of Table 3.3 presents results of exercising equation (3) under conditions that an average male-female duo was the same in terms of YRS, EX, ED, and SSAL. (For the insignificant (SEX)(EX) term, EX is taken as 0.) If, for example, this duo was hired in 1980, the male averages $98.33 more per month. The earlier the hiring date, the greater the inequity. This exercise is important because it provides evidence against the argument that pay differentials in PSAL were strictly due to differences in SSAL.

3.0 Analysis Interpretations and Ramifications

3.1 Arguments and Counterarguments

In response to Table 3.3 results, bank attorneys presented the following arguments. (1) The finding that men's salaries tend to advance more quickly than women's, given equality of starting salaries, is attributable to the assertion that women are far more likely to interrupt their careers—and for longer periods of time—to care for home and family. (Support for this assertion is given in a U.S. Census Bureau study reported in the *Fresno Bee,* 18 July 1984.) (2) The lower average starting salaries for women are attributable to the method of determining SSAL. Namely, SSAL is partially based on previous earnings, which tend to be higher for men. (3) Even though there are large average differences between starting salaries, the analysis shows that such differences have been considerably reduced, at least for those women hired in recent years. Hence, on a percentage basis, women's salaries are advancing more quickly than men's.

An immediate response to the first argument is that effects of career interruptions should be addressed individually, not collectively. A resolution of this issue would likely have resulted had data been collected on the following variables:

1. Absences: How long has the individual been absent following employment and for what reasons?

2. Educational achievement: What education programs has the individual participated in following employment?

3. Professional achievement: What is the individual's record in performance appraisals?

There is every reason to expect that the above variables affect PSAL and would not only increase the values of R^2 in Table 3.2 but would resolve points of contention.

Results of a recent class-action suit can be used in response to argument (2). The suit, filed in 1977 against Allstate Insurance Company in behalf of all female agents who worked between 1974 and 1984, was settled in midtrial on 6 June 1984. Attorneys for the plaintiffs said the agreement represented a "tremendous victory" for working women across the country. The suit challenged Allstate's practice of basing starting salaries, in part, on previous salaries. U.S. District Judge L. Karlton ruled in 1981 that Allstate's use of prior salaries constituted sex discrimination, but a federal appeals court reversed the decision in 1982 and returned the case to Karlton to decide whether prior salaries were being used as part of a reasonable business practice. Attorneys for the women presented statistical evidence showing no relationship between prior salaries and current productivity. As part of the 1984 agreement, prior salary would not be used in the compensation-setting procedure.

The response to argument (3) seems quite clear. It is irrelevant whether women's salaries are advancing more quickly than men's if, in fact, there was sex discrimination in determining starting salaries.

3.2 Recommendations

The data base in the present study is inadequate; central issues that should have been resolved could not be resolved. Such circumstances can lead to conflicting and, perhaps, misleading depositions. To minimize such pitfalls, the following ground rules are proposed.

1. Both parties should have access to a data base that is sufficiently comprehensive to allow the estimation of all effects required for problem resolution. All efforts should be made to minimize the likelihood that a relevant effect is an alias effect; for example, relevant variables should be chosen such that one cannot reasonably argue that a significant sex effect is an alias for the likelihood that women are more likely to interrupt their careers for home and family. Preliminary hearings may be required if defendant attorneys argue that access to employee data constitutes invasion of privacy while plaintiff attorneys argue that such data are necessary for problem resolution.

2. The relation between past salaries and present performance should be given greater scrutiny on a per case basis. Statistical testimony in the Allstate case, though possibly valid, seems counterintuitive. Is it really true that previous salaries have no effect on subsequent performance? The writer knows of no business executive who would answer this question in the affirmative.

3. A cloistered view is that statistical inferences will not materially differ given a comprehensive data base and competent statisticians. However, the reality of the adversarial contest is that inferences do differ—often diametrically. The problem is not easily rectified, because the judge and jury almost always lack the expertise to properly evaluate statistical testimony. One resolution is to provide the court with an advisory board of impartial statisticians who, at the very least, could quickly discredit testimony such as that given in *People* v. *Collins* and *State* v. *Sneed* (see Chap. 2). Statistical debate is generally worthwhile when judged by qualified individuals. It is often worthless when judged by an unqualified audience. A second resolution runs counter to the Anglo-American judicial system. If statisticians are to present evidence, they should do so, not as adversaries, but as friends of the court. Adversaries are tasked to win. Nonadversaries are tasked to draw existing truths from the data.

Exercise 1

Following the acquisition of bank X by bank Y, a large number of bank X employees were terminated. Terminated employees filed a class-action age discrimination suit against bank Y. You are asked to provide statistical evidence, if any, that age formed a criterion for termination. Define the dependent variable, possible independent variables, the method of analysis, and data requirements.

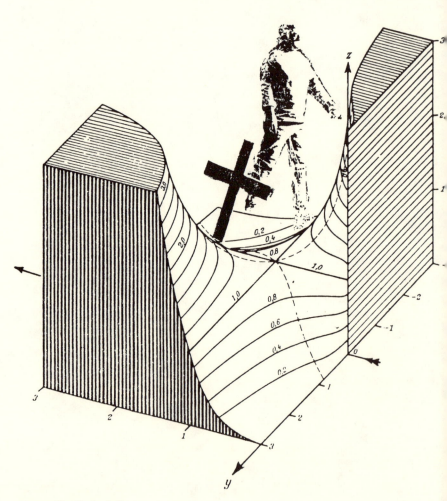

We could sell city hall.

versus the City of Fresno, California

In 1983 the firefighters union sued the city of Fresno, California. The suit claimed damages for loss of overtime opportunities due to the city's unilateral decision to reduce the minimum staffing level for a fire company from four to three. Previously, whenever a member of a four-man company failed to report to work, a replacement had to be brought in and paid at overtime rates. The judge ruled in favor of the union and instructed that compensation be made, not to the union, but to individual union members. To obtain a basis for compensation, the judge directed that mathematical probabilities be developed. Such probabilities would establish the likelihood that a particular firefighter would have capitalized on overtime opportunities during the period in question.

In this study, three major issues are addressed. First, how can these probabilities be developed using an existing data file and possible ad hoc information per firefighter? Second, given that the probabilities are estimated per firefighter, how can their validity be demonstrated as enunciated in the New Mexico case of *State* v. *Sneed* (see Chap. 2)?[1] Finally, given that validity has been demonstrated, what probabilities necessitate payment?

1.0   A Decision in Favor of the Union

1.1   Background

Fresno's firefighting personnel at the rank of captain and below are represented by the International Association of Firefighters, Local No. 753. Their contract officially expired 1 July 1983. However, on 28 June, the Fresno City Council extended their contract with the exception of the minimum staffing levels for fire companies. Effective 1 July, the fire department discontinued maintenance of four-man companies (the minimum number of people allowed per company under the existing contract) and established a three-man minimum. Prior to 1 July, whenever someone was absent from a four-man company (because of, say, illness), a qualified replacement was sent in who was compensated at the appropriate overtime rate. Effective 1 July, augmentations were no longer necessary so long as a three-man minimum was maintained.

The union sued the city, claiming damages for loss of overtime opportunities due to the city's unilateral staffing reduction. In August 1983 the judge (Superior Court of California, County of Fresno) ruled that the city could not unilaterally reduce staffing levels until the negotiation process had been exhausted. By court order, the city was required to maintain the four-man company staffing level in accordance with the expired contract.

1.2   Determining Compensation

Fire department records were subpoenaed to establish the exact number of overtime opportunities lost during the period the three-man minimum was in effect. Knowledge of the number of opportunities by position (given by captain, firefighter specialist, and firefighter) provided an exact dollar figure lost by union members. Plaintiff counsel argued that the union be awarded this sum. Contrary to expectations, the judge ruled that payment be made not to the union, but to individual union members. Payment was to be based on the likelihood that the individual would have capitalized on an overtime opportunity during the period in question. Accordingly, the judge instructed that mathematical probabilities be developed to determine the amount to be paid to each individual.

At this point, the writer was hired by the defendant to develop such probabilities. Central issues to be addressed are as follows. (1) How does one develop such probabilities using an existing data file and possible ad hoc information per firefighter? (2) Given that such probabilities are developed, how can one demonstrate their validity to the court? (3) Given that model validity has been demonstrated, what probabilities necessitate payment?

2.0   Modeling Procedure

2.1   The Variables

The question at hand is not only whether an individual would have worked a 24-hour overtime shift during July and August of 1983, but how many times he would have worked. (The judge did not make this distinction in issuing his directive. The writer, working with defendant counsel, made the distinction in anticipation of possible challenges by the plaintiff.) Previous records indicated that the individual may have worked up to two overtime shifts in a two-month period, but very rarely more.

Because the period of lost overtime opportunities is two months in duration, all variables are aggregated over two-month intervals. Specifically, the variables are aggregated within each value of $t = \ldots, -3, -2, -1, 0$, where $t = 0$ denotes July–August, $t = -1$ denotes May–June, $t = -2$ denotes March–April, etc.

From the personnel files maintained by the fire department, the following variables are defined. Variable $y(i, j, t, u)$ denotes the number of 24-hour overtime shifts the ith individual worked during time interval t in year u. The individual's position is identified by $j = 1$ for captain, $j = 2$ for firefighter specialist, and $j = 3$ for firefighter. Variable $x(h, i, j, t, u)$ denotes the aggregate of the hth variable, where values of h are defined as follows:

$h = 1$: number of opportunities available for working a 24-hour shift;
$h = 2$: number of hours taken for vacation/holiday;
$h = 3$: number of hours taken for sick/military/jury duty/instructional leave;
$h = 4$: number of absence hours taken (which occur when a cohort works in place of the ith individual during a regular 24-hour shift);
$h = 5$: number of absence hours worked (which occur when the ith individual works in place of a cohort during a regular 24-hour shift).

The value of $x(h, i, j, t, u)$ for $h = 6$ is not an aggregate but denotes whether the individual is a paramedic [$x(6, i, j, t, u) = 1$] or a nonparamedic [$x(6, i, j, t, u) = 0$].

2.2 Modeling Strategy

The objective is to estimate the probabilities that $y(i, j, t, u)$ takes the values 0, 1, and 2 conditional on both $x(h, i, j, t \leq 0, u)$ and lags of $y(i, j, t, u)$. Specifically, $p(y|x)$ is to be modeled, where $y = y(i, j, t, u)$ and x denotes a vector of predictors based on $x(h, i, j, t \leq 0, u)$ and $y(i, j, t, < 0, u)$. Bayesian discriminant analysis is an obvious modeling approach because the dependent variable is categorical and ad hoc information per individual can be incorporated in the posterior probabilities through the prior probabilities.

Aggregate variables are determined for comparable periods of 1982 and 1983. Prior to 1982, overtime assignments followed different dictates. The modeling strategy is (1) to model $p(y|x)$ for July and August of 1982 based on the 1982 data, (2) to establish model validity based on observed and predicted values for July and August of 1982, and (3) to estimate $p(y|x)$, per individual for July–August of 1983, based on the 1982 model with predictors evaluated at 1983 levels. Specifically, the probabilities $p[y(i, j, t = 0, 1982)|x(1982)]$ are modeled, where $x(1982)$ is that value of x based on the $x(h, i, j, t \leq 0, 1982)$ and the $y(i, j, t <$ 0, 1982). Model validity is established by showing that the model adequately predicts what actually happened in July and August of 1982. (Given that a model can adequately predict the observed overtime work in July and August of 1982, the inference is that the model could do likewise in the comparable period of 1983.) Finally,

$$p[y(i, j, t = 0, 1983)|x(1983)] \qquad (4.1)$$

is estimated in terms of the 1982 model, which provides the odds of overtime work during July and August of 1983. Table 4.1 illustrates values of probabilities in equation (4.1) for three selected individuals.

2.3   A Revised Discriminant Analysis

To enhance model validity, the three positions are modeled separately. Per analysis, stepwise discriminant analysis (BMDP7M)[2] is utilized in identifying predictors. The predictors are chosen from the $x(h, i, j, t \leq 0, 1982)$, the sum

$$s(82) = s(i, j, 1982) = \sum_{h=3}^{5} x(h, i, j, t = 0, 1982) \qquad (4.2)$$

the ratios

$$r(t, 82) = r(i, j, t, 1982) = y(i, j, t, 1982)/x(1, i, j, t, 1982) \qquad (4.3)$$

TABLE 4.1.   Posterior Probabilities of Overtime (OT) Shifts during July–August 1983 for Three Selected Individuals

Individual	Position	Compensation per 24-hr OT shift	Posterior probabilities		
			No OT shift	One OT shift	Two OT shifts
1	Captain	$436.32	.558	.279	.163
2	Firefighter specialist	$392.76	.044	.614	.342
3	Firefighter	$349.20	.723	.277	.011

for $t < 0$, and selected interactions. Over all analyses, the following variables are particularly significant: $s(82)$ and $r(82)$ for $t = 1, 2, 3$, and the interactions $[r(1, 82)][r(2, 82)]$, $[r(1, 82)][r(2, 82)][r(3, 82)]$, $[x(1, i, j, 0, 1982)][x(6, i, j, 0, 1982)]$, and $[x(3, i, j, 0, 1982)][x(3, i, j, 0, 1982)]$.

Analysis assumptions are that the predictors follow a multivariate normal probability density function (pdf) with constant dispersion matrices between categories. (Tests of significance do not reject the hypothesis of dispersion homogeneity.) Uniform priors are utilized in developing the models. However, once the models are developed, posterior probabilities may be based on non-uniform priors if such priors are justified by ad hoc information; see the discussion in section 2.4.

The customary analysis is altered to further enhance model validity. Let the three categories corresponding to $y(i, j, t = 0, 1982) = 0, 1$, and 2 be denoted by $c(0)$, $c(1)$, and $c(2)$, respectively. In the direct analysis approach, denoted by

$$c(0) \text{ vs. } c(1) \text{ vs. } c(2) \qquad (4.4)$$

we obtain probabilities, say, $p(0|x)$, $p(1|x)$, and $p(2|x)$ that the individual belongs to the three respective categories. We may also obtain these probabilities indirectly through two analyses:

$$c(0) \text{ vs. } c(1 \text{ or } 2) \qquad (4.5)$$

and

$$c(1) \text{ vs. } c(2) \qquad (4.6)$$

From (4.5) we obtain $p(0|x)$ and $1 - p(0|x)$ as the probabilities corresponding to $c(0)$ and $c(1 \text{ or } 2)$, respectively. From (4.6), we obtain $p(1|x, w)$ $1 - p(1|x, w)$ as the probabilities corresponding to $c(1)$ and $c(2)$, respectively, where w denotes the conditional state that the individual worked at least one overtime shift. Using results from (4.5) and (4.6), we find that $p(0|x)$, $p(1|x) = [1 - p(0|x)][p(1|x, w)]$, and $p(2|x) = [1 - p(0|x)][1 - p(1|x, w)]$ are the probabilities corresponding to $c(0)$, $c(1)$, and $c(2)$, respectively.

The rationale for this indirect approach is as follows. Under (4.4) a variable that discriminates well between, say, $c(0)$ and $c(1)$ might discriminate poorly between, say, $c(1)$ and $c(2)$. The result may be that this variable is excluded as a predictor in (4.4) and model validity may, in turn, be reduced. However, in performing separate analyses, as in (4.5) and (4.6), we allow predictors to differ between analyses (or between pairwise categories). The net result is that probabilities obtained through the indirect approach may lead to enhanced model validity relative to the direct approach of (4.4).

2.4   Model Validity

Based on previous court decisions, a demonstration of model validity is imperative. In *State* v. *Sneed*,[1] the New Mexico Supreme Court held that "mathematical odds are not admissible as evidence . . . so long as the odds are based on estimates, the validity of which have not been demonstrated." The California Supreme Court used the New Mexico ruling as precedent in *People* v. *Collins*[3] (see Chap. 2). Although these cases dealt with criminal identification, the implication is that the ruling could apply in general. Unfortunately, the issue is somewhat muddled without a court definition of "demonstrated validity."

An obvious characterization of a valid model is that it provides good predictions during periods when outcomes are known. Two methods of evaluating validity are (1) splitting the data (where some of the data are used to build the model and some are used to evaluate predictive validity) and (2) the jackknife (where observations are deleted one at a time and predicted by the model based on the remaining observations). Results of the jackknife, obtained through BMDP7M, are illustrated in Table 4.2.

TABLE 4.2.   Analysis Results for $c(0)$ versus $c(1$ or $2)$, Position = Firefighter, and Year = 1982

A.   Jackknife classification

Actual category	Classification[a]		Correct classification
	No overtime	overtime	
No overtime	15	4	78.9%
Overtime	3	38	92.7%

B.   The probabilities $p(0|x)$ and $1 - p(0|x)$ and associated Mahalanobis distances (D^2) for six firefighters who worked at least one overtime shift

Firefighter	No overtime		Overtime	
	D^2	$p(0|x)$	D^2	$1 - p(0|x)$
1	32.7	.006	22.4	.994
2 M[b]	21.5	.963	28.0	.037
3	10.4	.175	7.3	.825
4	15.5	.015	7.2	.985
5	6.9	.341	5.6	.659
6	10.9	.042	4.6	.958

[a]An individual is classified into a particular category if his posterior probability of belonging to that category is greater than .50.
[b]M denotes a misclassification.

These results correspond to the analysis of (4.5) based on 60 individuals in the firefighter position. Application of the jackknife shows that of the 19 firefighters who did not work overtime, 78.9% are correctly classified according to the rule that the individual is classified in $c(0)$ if $p(0|x) >$ .50. For those in the category $c(1$ or $2)$, 92.7% are correctly classified. These figures are representative of those for the other analyses in this study.

Results in Table 4.2 are based on uniform priors. Since approximately one-third of the firefighters did not work overtime, an alternative analysis is conducted with the following non-uniform priors: $p(0) = 1/3$ and $p(1$ or $2) = 2/3$. Classification results based on this analysis are inferior to those using uniform priors.

The bottom portion of Table 4.2 presents posterior probabilities and associated Mahalanobis D^2 distances for six firefighters in category $c(0)$. The second firefighter is misclassified with $p(0|x) = .963$. Because past records indicated that this individual rarely worked overtime, reasons were sought for the misclassification. It turned out that this individual experienced a financial setback in the summer of 1982 and sought overtime work at every opportunity. In this situation, a non-uniform prior probability should properly dominate the value of the posterior probability. A repetition of such situations should, however, be carefully scrutinized—especially in adversarial contests. Why? On the one hand, there is no question that the priors can be manipulated to justify any view. On the other hand, there are very few jurists who are sufficiently versed in Bayesian inference and multivariate analysis to detect improper manipulations of prior probabilities. A partial answer to this dilemma is to require that posterior probabilities be presented under both uniform and subjective, non-uniform priors and that explanations be given for each discrepancy. A repetition of major discrepancies between the two may reflect on the validity of the deposition.

3.0   What Probabilities Necessitate Payment?

For ease of presentation, assume that compensation is with reference to $c(1$ or $2)$, not its subdivisions. Estimated values of $1 - p(0|x)$ for July and August of 1983 are summarized, by position, in Table 4.3. It is seen, for example, that 1 captain, 16 firefighter specialists, and 22 firefighters have posterior probabilities greater than .9 of belonging to $c(1$ or $2)$ during the period in question.

As to what values of $P = 1 - p(0|x)$ should necessitate payment, opinions are varied:

TABLE 4.3.   Estimation of 1 − $p(0|x)$ for July–August 1983: Frequencies of Individuals Categorized by Position and Intervals of 1 − $p(0|x)$

Probability of working overtime: 1 − $p(0|x)$	Position		
	Captain	Firefighter specialist	Firefighter
>.9	1	16	22
(.8, .9]	16	16	11
(.7, .8]	7	3	6
(.6, .7]	8	2	6
(.5, .6]	15	2	0
(.4, .5]	8	12	0
(.3, .4]	10	4	1
(.2, .3]	10	16	7
(.1, .2]	11	4	2
≤.1	32	6	4
Total	118	81	59

1. Full payment for any individual with $P > .5$.

2. Payment in proportion to P.

3. Payment in proportion to P given that $p > .5$.

4. Full payment for any individual whose P value is "significantly beyond" .5.

The majority view was that there may be legal precedent for plan 1. Under plan 1, the city would have paid out 47($436.32) + 39($392.76) + 45($349.20) = $51,538.68, where overtime rates (per 24-hour shift, per position) are given in Table 4.1. Discussions became academic when compensation was settled out of court. Settlement may have been influenced by the lack of clear precedent or vagueness regarding the statistical issues.

4.0   Epilogue: Firefighters Challenged

The following text is drawn from an article by Neal Pierce, *Washington Post* correspondent. The column appeared in the *Fresno Bee* on 30 June 1985.

Fire departments are wildly inefficient, politicized, and sanctified. They're the Department of Defense of city government. But politically, you can't touch them. . . . Off the record, mayors candidly admit firefighting has torn a gaping hole in municipal productivity. How could it be otherwise when firefighters work just 11 or 12 [24-hour] days a month [with] most of their "duty" hours spent cooking, watching television, or sleeping. . . .

Henry Gardner, city manager of financially pinched Oakland, is willing to be quoted. He's proposed, seriously, that Oakland's city hall and 21 other buildings be sold to raise cash for annuities to cover the $600 million the city owes in pensions to firefighters and policemen. . . . The city must shell out $790 for every $1000 it pays in firefighter or police salaries. . . . The great firefighter mystique . . . is not altogether false. Firefighters in some tough inner-city areas face double peril when alarms go off. But why shouldn't Oakland, with battalions of poor people, shell out $61,392 in benefits for a fireman with just four years of service? . . . Smaller cities seem especially willing to contract out fire services to private providers. Many are using workers from other departments, released from their regular duties when a fire breaks out, to fight most fires. . . . Let's hope questions . . . and innovations . . . keep coming.

Exercise 1

Define alternative criteria for determining probabilities necessitating payment. How would you use the constraint that a known dollar amount would have been spent in the absence of the city's decision to reduce staffing levels?

References

1. *State* v. *Sneed*, 76 N.M. 349, 414 P. 2d 858 (1966).

2. Dixon, W. J., ed. *BMDP Statistical Software*. Berkeley and Los Angeles: University of California Press, 1985.

3. *People* v. *Collins*, 66 Cal. 497, 438 P. 2d 33 (1969).

5

A Program for Controlling

Commentary on the drug scene.

he Drunk-Driving Epidemic

This study began as an academic exercise: to develop a probabilistic model for identifying likely recidivists among convicted drunk drivers. Based on the model's potential, the idea was expanded and ultimately resulted in the current screening, referral, and tracking program in New Mexico.

The study developed in stages. First, data were collected from an early program wherein convicted drunk drivers responded to a psychological inventory. Recidivist and nonrecidivist samples were then defined, and Bayesian discriminant analysis was performed in obtaining probabilistic profiles of recidivists based on inventory responses. Probabilistic assessments were then contrasted with psychological assessments. The former were always more cost effective and, oftentimes, more accurate. With such a cost effective device, all convicted drunk drivers could be screened efficiently. Those identified as likely recidivists could be channeled into an appropriate treatment program through court-imposed sanctions. In tracking the offenders through treatment, the efficacy of various treatment programs could also be evaluated. All costs would be paid by the offender.

The next step was to convince key jurists of the merits of this plan. After considerable lobbying by the writer and others, a request for proposal was issued by the Metropolitan Court in Albuquerque. Programs were sought that could effectively control the drunk-driving epidemic. The screening, tracking, and referral program formed the basis of the proposal.

1.0   Introduction

1.1   The Problem

This study proposes a program for controlling the epidemic of drunk driving. A premise is that control of the epidemic is not wholly within the domain of the criminal justice system. Many who drink and drive have alcohol-related problems. Given that such problems may be ameliorated through appropriate treatment, all DUI (driving under the influence of intoxicating liquor) offenders should be screened. Those identified as problem drinkers should be referred to appropriate treatment. This is made possible by giving the DUI offender a choice: submit to screening and, if necessary, treatment or incur punitive sanction such as a fine, loss of license, and/or incarceration.

Past means of controlling the epidemic have included media campaigns, police roadblocks, and stiffer punitive sanctions. Results have not been encouraging. Media slogans such as "If you drive, don't drink; if you drink, don't drive" seem to appeal only to those who abstain or who hardly need reminding. The roadblock is anathema to the driving public and promotes schisms in police-public relations. Regarding sanctions, Buikhuisen's study[1] indicates that more severe penalties have little effect on problem drinkers.

Given that the automobile underlies the economy and that drinking is part of the social fabric, drinking and driving will inevitably be mixed under present and anticipated law. Granting DUI offenders one arrest and conviction and successfully treating those found to be likely recidivists— as opposed to preventing individuals from drinking and driving in the first place—is perhaps the most to be hoped for at present.

1.2   Background

In the late 1960s, events began to focus on the drunk driver. Prior to that time, emphasis was on the alcoholic; public opinion held that drunk drivers were merely a random sample from the general population despite studies[2,3] showing the contrary. Recognition of the plight of the alcoholic was highlighted in March of 1966 in the case of *Easter* v. *District of Columbia*.[4] The U.S. Court of Appeals unanimously held that a chronic alcoholic cannot be convicted of public intoxication. The court stated that "the public intoxication of a chronic alcoholic lacks the essential element of criminality." In the same year, a similar decision was reached by the Fourth Circuit Court in the case of *Driver* v. *Hinnant*.[5]

Following the Easter case, it was found that, in the entire history of the District of Columbia courts, the only intoxication case to ever reach the appellate level was the *Easter* case. This is a startling fact because, prior to *Easter,* public intoxication was the basis for approximately 50% of the criminal arrests and 75% of the commitments to prison in the District of Columbia.

The reversal came in 1968 in the case of *Powell* v. *Texas,*[6] where the U.S. Supreme Court, in a 5 to 4 decision, ruled that punishment is barred for being an alcoholic but not for being intoxicated in public. Writing for the majority, Justice Marshall concluded that "faced with the reality that there is no known generally effective method of treatment or adequate facilities or manpower for a full scale attack on the enormous problem of alcoholics, it cannot be asserted that the use of the criminal process to deal with public aspects of problem drinking can never be defended as rational."

In debate during the Fifth International Conference on Alcohol and Road Safety, held in 1969, an underlying theme was that there was too much emphasis on the alcoholic and not enough on the drunk driver. In 1970 the Department of Transportation reported that of 54,000 traffic fatalities, 50% were alcohol related. The emphasis had clearly changed.

2.0 Assessment of the Likelihood of Recidivism

2.1 The Chancellor and the Veteran

The chancellor of a West Coast university pleaded guilty to killing two women in an auto crash. The chancellor's blood alcohol concentration following the accident was .23%, more than twice the legal limit for drunkenness. It was his second drunk-driving conviction. The judge sentenced him to one year in jail but stayed execution of sentence for six months, during which time the chancellor was to lecture on drunk driving. Following that period the judge was to make a determination whether the chancellor made a "meaningful contribution to society."[7] The decision seems to have been influenced by the chancellor's presentencing statement to the judge, which every criminal is entitled to write. In his statement, the chancellor described his worry over the university's $900,000 debt and his inability to reconcile his intellectual goals for the university with the demands of the fundamentalist church that owned the school.

A veteran was convicted of vehicular manslaughter. He had been out of work for nine months. His wife had left him, taking with her their only child, whom he deeply missed. He got drunk and killed an innocent person in an auto crash. Like the chancellor, the veteran composed a written statement to the judge; he wrote that he had been depressed and promised never to do it again. The judge sent him to jail.

What criterion influenced these two sentences? In the first case the judge made a determination that "the chances of his committing another violent crime seem small."[7] The judge in the veteran's case was seemingly unable to convince himself that the defendant was an unlikely recidivist. The key here is the defendant's likelihood of recidivism. Assessment of this likelihood and the risk of an incorrect assessment thus become vital in determining the sentence.

2.2 Probabilistic versus Clinical Assessments

To this point, no distinction has been made between likely recidivists and problem drinkers among DUI offenders. Clearly, a likely recidivist is not necessarily a problem drinker and a problem drinker is not necessarily a likely recidivist. If screening priorities are to be given, screening for likely recidivists comes first and that for problem drinkers second. However, until specifics of the Albuquerque program are discussed, the two are not distinguished unless otherwise noted.

The likelihood of recidivism may be assessed heuristically, clinically, probabilistically, or by a combination of methods. In the chancellor's case, the judge's assessment appeared to be heuristic and based, perhaps, on empathy. A clinical assessment is subjective and based on personal interview and/or evaluation of defendant responses on psychological/alcohol-related inventories. The probabilistic assessment can be objective and quantifies the recidivism likelihood in terms of a probability. The probability is usually derived from mathematical modeling based on known recidivists and nonrecidivists. Discrimination between the two groups is in terms of known characteristics such as defendant demographics and/or responses on inventories.

The clinical assessment is given as expert opinion in the specific case. Probabilistic assessments transcend cases when probabilities are given a frequency interpretation. For example, based on inventory responses, the defendant's chances of repeating the offense are .82. A frequency interpretation of this probability is that if 100 other defendants were to give inventory responses identical to the defendant's, 82 would, on the average, repeat the offense.

Clinical assessments have two drawbacks. They are expensive to obtain and they are often incorrect. (Regarding correctness, recall the expert, clinical testimonies for prosecution and defense in the P. Hearst and J. Hinckley trials.) "Many researchers suggest that if society needs special tools to predict a person's future behavior, it ought to rely on a statistical formula. . . . This statistical approach, while (possibly) impre-

cise, has two advantages over clinical diagnosis: It's generally more accurate and it doesn't pretend to provide 'expert' analysis of an individual case."[8]
In a three-year longitudinal study the "data suggest that the confidence placed in psychiatry's ability to predict the potential of dangerous behavior is unjustified." The study's authors further state that "psychiatry is seen by the public, by the courts and the legal community, and by the legislators as the professional group most rightfully charged with the responsibility to predict the potential danger of individuals. This authority is granted on the basis of the perceived body of expert knowledge available to psychiatrists as a result of their training and experience. The findings presented here seriously question the existence of any such special knowledge."[9]

In what is to follow, probabilistic assessments are developed based on data from the Salinas, California, screening program.

3.0 A Model for Probabilistic Assessment
3.1 Characteristics of the Sample

Data used for model building were drawn from a screening program in the Municipal Court of Salinas, California. Presentence screening of all individuals convicted of DUI is performed by a court alcoholism specialist, who recommends a course of action to the judge. If treatment is recommended and the judge concurs, the individual may choose treatment in lieu of punitive sanction.

Characteristics of the sample are presented in Table 5.1. All individuals in the sample were convicted of DUI between 1972 and 1974; there are 153 first offenders, 98 second offenders, and 75 with three or more convictions. Two criteria were imposed in attempting to ensure that the 153 first offenders were nonrecidivists. First, all were clinically judged to be social drinkers. Second, no first offender was considered for the sample unless a minimum of 28 months had elapsed since the first conviction. (Past studies have shown that 35% to 50% of the first offenders will be reconvicted of the same offense within 28 months.) At best, then, the 153 are nonrecidivists. At worst, there are recidivists among the 153 who have not been caught or who have been caught in another jurisdiction.

In presentence screening, the offender responds to the questionnaire in Table 5.2. The questionnaire is called a "risk of alcoholic profile" (RAP) since the specialist's scoring of the answers provides a rough indication of the extent of the offender's drinking problem. Offender demographics, blood alcohol concentration (BAC) at the time of arrest, and

TABLE 5.1. Characteristics of the Sample by Number of Prior Drunk-driving Offenses

Number of priors:	0	1	2 or more	Percentages for general population of Salinas, Calif.[a]
Sample size:	153	98	75	
	% of 153	% of 98	% of 75	
Sex[b]				
Female	16	04	04	48
Male	84	96	96	52
Age				
18–29	27	27	26	28
30–39	27	30	28	19
40–49	27	27	29	18
50 and older	19	16	17	35
Race				
Hispanic surname (or language)	23	38	35	27
White	66	56	60	66
Black	08	04	05	02
Other[c]	03	02	00	05
Marital status				
Married	54	55	55	
Single	16	15	08	
Separated	09	09	14	
Divorced	16	16	19	
Widowed	05	05	04	
Years of schooling				
0–8	22	24	35	26[e]
9–12	56	64	61	48
More than 12	22	12	04	26
Present income($)				
Less than 3,000	13	12	19	08
3,000–4,999	14	07	16	09
5,000–6,999	15	21	21	10
7,000–9,999	25	25	21	21
10,000–14,999	22	29	20	29
More than 15,000	11	06	03	23
Religion				
None or no answer	13	15	21	
Baptist	08	16	13	
Catholic	43	45	43	
Protestant	34	22	19	
Other	02	02	04	
Occupation[d]				
White collar	13	16	05	
Blue collar	29	46	43	
Service	20	14	16	
Farm	11	09	16	
Military	14	05	04	
Retired	03	02	07	
No established payroll	10	08	09	

[a]Based on the 1970 federal census.

[b]18 years of age and over.

[c]Other includes mostly Polynesian, the remainder Oriental.

[d]Occupation categories include the following professions. *White collar:* professional, technical and kindred workers, sales workers, clerical and kindred workers; *blue collar:*

TABLE 5.2.   Risk of Alcoholic Profile (RAP) Questionnaire

Alcohol-related questions

1. Do discussions about your drinking make you nervous?
2. Are you a shaky, jittery person?
3. Do you have trouble remembering what you did while drinking?
4. Has your drinking caused you legal, family, health, job, or social problems?
5. Do you consume more alcohol than most of your friends?
6. Do you have sensations of numbness or tingling in your fingers or toes?
7. Do you often want more drinks after the party is over?
8. Do you feel guilty about your drinking?
9. Have you ever thought you might have a drinking problem?
10. If so, have you ever sought help?
11. Have you ever had a memory blackout while drinking?
12. When do you drink?

Psychological questions

1. Do you have a strong, clear faith in life?
2. Many times, do you feel uneasy or blue?
3. Is your home life as happy as it should be?
4. Some days, do you feel you are not your real self?
5. Do you feel sorry for yourself and frequently indulge in self-pity?
6. Are you moderate in your habits?
7. Do you often feel guilty or apologetic without knowing why?
8. Are you pretty much like everyone else you know?
9. Do you sometimes go out of your way to avoid people you dislike?
10. Does it seem to you that you are going nowhere in your life?
11. Do you feel there is a barrier between you and the world?
12. Does your interest or enthusiasm fade quickly?
13. Do you keep thinking about things you fear?
14. Are you inclined to be serene and relaxed?
15. Do you feel all alone in the world?
16. Do your moods change rapidly?

RAP responses are factors determining the specialist's clinical recommendation to the judge.

In what is to follow, RAP responses are modeled to provide a probabilistic assessment of an offender's likelihood of recidivism.

3.2   Method of Model Building

Bayesian discriminant analysis is applied in estimating the probabilities that the defendant belongs to each of the following populations: the nonrecidivist population, the recidivist population with one prior conviction, and the recidivist population with two or more priors. Subdivi-

---

craftspeople, semiskilled workers (operatives, including transport), unskilled workers (laborers, except farm); *service:* private household workers, personal service workers (barbers, hairdressers), business and industrial service workers (waiters, waitresses, chefs, bellhops); *farm:* farm laborers and foremen; *no established payroll:* housewives, students.

°25 years of age and over.

sion of the recidivist population is intended to provide levels of degradation.

Principal component analysis (BMDP4M)[10] is applied separately to three sets of questionnaire responses: (1) the alcohol-related responses excepting the response to "When do you drink?" (2) responses to the latter question as categorized in Table 5.3, and (3) the psychological responses. Principal components and selected interactions between components are then scanned for dominant predictors through stepwise discriminant analysis (BMDP7M).[10]

Assumptions underlying the analysis are that predictors follow a multivariate normal probability density function (pdf) and that the prior probabilities are uniform. Through principal component analysis, questionnaire responses are transformed to linear combinations thereof that tend to cluster symmetrically about central values. As such, the normality assumption is reasonable. Between the three populations, the estimated variance/covariance matrices show no significant differences (although selected variances tend to decrease from the nonrecidivist to the recidivist populations).

The use of non-uniform priors based on population frequencies of the recidivist and nonrecidivist categories leads to greater misclassification probabilities than do uniform priors. However, non-uniform priors, determined by supplemental information on a per case basis, should be applied in using the model in screening programs.

3.3 Assessments Based on Alcohol-Related Responses

Two probabilistic assessments are given per defendant, one based on the alcohol-related questions and the other based on the psychological questions. Reasons for two such assessments are that (1) alcohol-related responses supersede psychological responses when the defendant has a drinking problem and responds to the alcohol-related questions nondeceptively (see sec. 3.4), (2) psychological responses tend to act as aliases

TABLE 5.3. Responses of Convicted Drunk Drivers to the Question "When Do You Drink?" in the RAP Questionnaire

1. Seldom
2. Special occasions, holidays, once in a while, once a month
3. Saturday night, once a week, when bowling, at parties, socially, when friends drop by
4. Weekends, twice a week
5. At home, when watching TV, with dinner, evenings
6. When I feel like it, no special time, when in the mood
7. When sad or depressed, when happy
8. All the time

for nondeceptive alcohol-related responses when the alcohol-related questions are answered deceptively, and (3) psychological responses may aid in identifying those with problems that are other than alcohol-related.

Based on the alcohol-related questions, discriminant analysis leads to the probabilistic assessments in Table 5.4. For example, if the defendant's answers are "evenings" to "When do you drink?" and "no" to the other alcohol-related questions, the probability of not repeating the

TABLE 5.4. Model Exercise: Probabilities of Recidivism for Selected Answers to Alcohol-related Questions

	Answers to "When do you drink?"					
	"Evenings"			"Socially"		
Answers[a] to questions in Table 5.2	No. of future DUI convictions			No. of future DUI convictions		
	0	1	2 or more	0	1	2 or more
	Probability					
No to all questions	.94[b]	.05	.01	.98	.02	.00
Yes to 1 (discussions make nervous?)	.92	.07	.01	.96	.03	.01
Yes to 2 (shakey, jittery person?)	.80	.12	.08	.87	.08	.05
Yes to 3 (trouble remembering?)	.64	.32	.04	.82	.16	.02
Yes to 4 (drinking-caused problems?)	.40	.38	.22	.53	.34	.13
Yes to 5 (consume more than friends?)	.90	.08	.02	.95	.04	.01
Yes to 6 (sensations of numbness?)	.93	.06	.01	.97	.02	.01
Yes to 7 (want more after party?)	.39	.59	.02	.54	.44	.02
Yes to 8 (feel guilty?)	.51	.48	.02	.75	.24	.01
Yes to 11 (blackout?)	.70	.28	.02	.81	.18	.01
Yes to 2 and 11	.46	.51	.03	.52	.47	.01
Yes to 3 and 4	.01	.02	.97	.03	.02	.95
Yes to 3, 4, and 8	.01	.01	.98	.01	.03	.96
Yes to 3 and 7	.08	.28	.64	.18	.20	.62
Yes to 3 and 8	.18	.20	.62	.34	.08	.58
Yes to 3 and 9 (problem?)	.42	.04	.54	.58	.02	.40
Yes to 3, 9, and 10 (sought help?)	.35	.11	.54	.50	.10	.40
Yes to 3 and 11	.56	.29	.15	.76	.16	.08
Yes to 4 and 7	.02	.76	.22	.02	.84	.14
Yes to 4 and 8	.03	.82	.15	.04	.82	.14
Yes to 4 and 9	.15	.48	.37	.20	.58	.22
Yes to 4, 9, and 10	.05	.58	.37	.06	.71	.23
Yes to 4 and 11	.08	.87	.05	.10	.89	.01
Yes to 7 and 9	.16	.81	.04	.21	.76	.03
Yes to 8 and 9	.23	.74	.03	.40	.57	.03
Yes to 9, 10, and 11	.23	.75	.02	.24	.75	.01

[a]Accompanying a "yes" answer to the question or questions indicated are "no" answers to the remaining questions.
[b]The probabilities sum to unity across a row for each of the "When do you drink?" answers.

offense is .94. If, however, a different defendant answers identically to the aforementioned defendant with one exception—namely, a "yes" to "Do you want more drinks after the party is over?"—the nonrecidivism probability drops to .39.

Table 5.5 presents the Jellinek[11] model of alcohol addiction. This model conceptualizes alcohol addiction as a disease that progressively worsens with time. The table lists selected recidivism probabilities from Tables 5.4 and 5.7 of characteristics that tend to be associated with the stages of addiction. The probabilities are generally supportive of Jellinek's model in that recidivism probabilities tend to increase for affirmative responses to questions reflecting increasing stages of addiction. An implication is that drunk driving may be symptomatic of the early phases. If so, early detection of problem drinking is expedited through screening of drunk drivers.

Viewed deterministically, Jellinek's model has been criticized because every stage might not occur and/or stages may cluster per individual. If the model is viewed stochastically, one would expect missing stages and/or clustering. Since he was a biometrician, Jellinek probably considered his model to be stochastic, which would nullify these criticisms.

3.4   Assessments Based on Psychological Responses

Thirty percent of the recidivists in the sample claimed to be normal in their use of alcohol by responding negatively to the first 11 alcohol-related questions. By conventional standards, anyone arrested at least twice for DUI and responding in this manner is answering deceptively, whether knowingly or unknowingly. This portion of the sample, termed the denial sample, is excluded from use in developing the model but not from evaluating model validity.

A portion of the denial sample revealed itself through answers to "When do you drink?" as is illustrated in Table 5.6. If, for example, an offender answers "no" to the first 11 alcohol-related questions and "when sad" to question 12, the recidivism probability is .76. Multiple answers to question 12 also increase the likelihood of recidivism. This question thus becomes a means of detecting denial. (Future studies should determine whether the response to a directed question such as "Do you drink when sad?" can distinguish between recidivists and nonrecidivists as well as a volunteered answer of "when sad" to the question "When do you drink?") However, since only 13.3% of the denial sample were revealed in this manner, alternatives to the assessments in Table 5.4 were developed by replacing the first 11 alcohol-related responses with the 16 psy-

TABLE 5.5.   The Jellinek Model for Alcohol Addiction

Phases	Stages per phase	"Yes" answers to the following RAP questions (recidivism probability)
Prealcoholic	Occasional relief drinking	Consume more than friends?
	Increase in alcohol tolerance	(.10)
	Onset of blackouts	Blackouts? (.30)
	Surreptitious drinking	
Prodromal	Guilt feelings about drinking	Feel guilty? (.50)
	Avoids reference to alcohol	
	Increasing blackouts	Blackouts? and Shakey, jittery person? (.54)
	Loss of control	
	Persistent remorse	Drinking-caused problems? (.60)
	Drops friends	
Crucial	Quits job	Indulge in self-pity? (.70)
	Loss of outside interests	
	Marked self-pity	Indulge in self-pity? and Barrier between you and the world? (.83)
Chronic	Regular matutinal drinking	
	Prolonged intoxication	
	Decrease in alcohol tolerance	
	Rationalization system fails	

chological responses and proceeding with the discriminant analysis. Results of this analysis are presented in Table 5.7.

If the offender answers "evenings" to "When do you drink?" and ideally (as defined in Table 5.7) to all psychological questions, the recidivism probability is .18. Changing one response and answering "yes" to "Do you feel sorry for yourself and frequently indulge in self-pity?"—which, according to the Jellinek model, places the individual in the crucial phase (see Table 5.5)—leads to a recidivism probability of .70. The .51 recidivism probability associated with ideal responses excepting a "yes"

TABLE 5.6.   Results of Model Exercise for Selected Answers to the Question "When Do You Drink?"

Answers to "When do you drink?" with all alcohol-related questions in Table 5.2 answered "no"	No. of future DUI convictions		
	0	1	2 or more
Single answers:	Probability		
"When happy"	.60	.39	.01
"When sad"	.24	.54	.22
"Evenings" or "Watching TV"	.94[a]	.05	.01
"Socially" or "Weekends"	.98[a]	.02	.00
Multiple answers:			
"When watching television, when bowling, and with friends"	.37	.52	.11
"Weekends, parties, and holidays"	.61	.32	.07

[a]Taken from Table 5.4.

TABLE 5.7.   Model Exercise: Probabilities of Recidivism for Selected Answers to Psychological Questions

	Answers to "When do you drink?"					
	"Evenings"			"Socially"		
Answers to questions in Table 5.2	No. of future DUI convictions			No. of future DUI convictions		
	0	1	2 or more	0	1	2 or more
	Probability					
All questions answered ideally	.82	.12	.06	.87	.10	.03
No[b] to 1 (strong faith in life?)	.78	.10	.12	.79	.12	.09
Yes to 2 (feel blue?)	.70	.11	.19	.78	.07	.15
No to 3 (home life OK?)	.57	.33	.10	.68	.25	.07
Yes to 4 (not real self?)	.63	.07	.30	.72	.05	.23
Yes to 5 (indulge in self-pity?)	.30	.03	.67	.39	.02	.59
No to 6 (moderate in habits?)	.74	.15	.11	.79	.13	.08
Yes to 7 (feel guilty by nature?)	.62	.30	.08	.73	.20	.07
No to 8 (similar to others?)	.60	.23	.17	.77	.12	.11
Yes to 9 (avoid people you dislike?)	.67	.18	.15	.79	.11	.10
Yes to 10 (going nowhere in life?)	.66	.19	.15	.73	.14	.13
Yes to 11 (barrier between you and world?)	.58	.23	.19	.68	.15	.17
Yes to 12 (interest fades quickly?)	.53	.16	.31	.68	.08	.24
Yes to 13 (fears come to mind?)	.49	.42	.09	.62	.30	.08
No to 14 (serene person?)	.70	.22	.08	.76	.18	.06
Yes to 15 (feel alone in world?)	.45	.52	.03	.58	.39	.03
Yes to 16 (moods change rapidly?)	.57	.28	.15	.71	.17	.12
No to 8, yes to 9	.51	.29	.20	.72	.15	.13
No to 8, 14	.53	.35	.12	.68	.25	.07
Yes to 5, 11	.17	.04	.79	.20	.03	.77
Yes to 5, 10, 11	.12	.04	.84	.13	.03	.84

[a]Ideal answers are "yes" to questions 1, 3, 6, 8, and 14 and "no" to the others.
[b]Accompanying a "no" or "yes" answer to the question or questions indicated are ideal answers to the remaining questions.

to "Do you keep thinking about things you fear?" may support Horton's conjecture that alcohol reduces fear: "The strength of the drinking response in any society tends to vary directly with the level of anxiety in the society."[12]

Aside from the 13.3% of the denial sample that were correctly identified by answers to "When do you drink?" an additional 42.3% were found to be likely or suspected recidivists based on assessments in Table 5.7. (As defined in sec. 3.5, likely or suspected recidivists are those for whom a discrepancy exists between assessments in Tables 5.4 and 5.7.) An implication is that relative to the alcohol-related questions, the psychological questions tend not to challenge the problem drinker's sensitivities and may be answered more truthfully. Given that denial is implicit in at least the prodromal and crucial phases of the Jellinek model, direct alcohol-related questions may tend to be self-defeating.

3.5   On Predictive Validity

Error rates for the RAP probabilistic assessments are based on two samples: the denial sample and the sample on which the model was developed. (For the latter sample, the jackknife technique, as programmed in BMDP7M, is used to estimate probabilities of misclassification.) Define the likely recidivist as one whose recidivism probability is greater than .50 through either the alcohol-related or psychological responses. Define the suspected recidivist as one for whom a discrepancy exists between probabilities. Specifically, a discrepancy is said to occur when the alcohol-related and psychological responses lead to recidivism probabilities of less than .20 and between .40 and .50, respectively. Then for the denial sample, 44% are underdiagnosed (or are designated likely nonrecidivists). For the recidivist sample used in model development, 7% are underdiagnosed. If it is assumed that 30% of the recidivists engage in denial, then 18% of all recidivists are underdiagnosed.

Define the unlikely recidivist as one whose recidivism probabilities are less than .40 for both probabilistic assessments. Then 68% of the sample nonrecidivists are correctly identified and 32% are overdiagnosed. Those overdiagnosed may include offenders who were clinically misclassified and who have not yet been caught a second time. Others may have overresponded to the RAP. This rather large misclassification percentage for the nonrecidivists is a primary reason for structuring the Albuquerque program such that likely or suspected recidivists are further scrutinized in subsequent screening.

3.6   Effects of Demographic Variables

Discussions on the effects of demographic variables and inventory responses on the likelihood of recidivism hinge on an evaluation of two hypotheses.

HYPOTHESIS 1: Demographic variables have no effect on inventory responses.

HYPOTHESIS 2: Given the inventory responses, the demographic variables provide no additional information regarding the likelihood of recidivism.

Rejection of hypothesis 1 implies, for example, that a bracero and a corporate executive are likely to respond differently to certain psychological questions. On the other hand, suppose the bracero and executive respond identically to the inventory. Rejection of hypothesis 2 implies that their recidivism probabilities may differ because of their differing demographics.

There is a connection between hypothesis 2 and Allport's conjecture[13] that background factors never directly cause behavior; they cause attitudes and attitudes in turn determine behavior. If the demographic variables and inventory responses adequately measure background factors and attitudes, respectively, and if behavior is measured in terms of recidivism/nonrecidivism, then nonrejection of hypothesis 2 supports the conjecture.

Through methods described below, hypothesis 1 is rejected while hypothesis 2 is not. Rejection of hypothesis 1 is illustrated through the results in Table 5.8. For example, the white recidivist is more likely to answer "yes" to "Do you keep thinking about things you fear?" than a Hispanic recidivist of the same socioeconomic level. The probabilities of a "yes" answer are .73 for the former and .48 for the latter. Since the current sample cuts across some rather marked sociocultural lines, nonrejection of hypothesis 2 adds to the strength of the model developed herein. Had hypothesis 2 been rejected, application of the model to other localities may have been tenuous.

Let D denote the individual's demographic variables. Individual re-

TABLE 5.8.   Effects of Sociocultural Variables on Respondent Answers: Probability of "yes" Answer by Respondent Profile

	Profile[a]			
	Baptist	Catholic	Protestant	None
Is your home life as happy as it should be?				
Nonrecidivist	.90	.92	.79	.83
Recidivist	.55	.61	.34	.41
Do you consume more alcohol than most of your friends?				
Nonrecidivist	.20	.09	.18	.22
Recidivist	.71	.50	.69	.73

	Profile[b]	
	Hispanic, farm worker, Catholic	White, blue-collar worker, Protestant
Do you keep thinking about things you fear?		
Nonrecidivist	.07	.17
Recidivist	.48	.73
Have you ever thought you may have a drinking problem?		
Nonrecidivist	.04	.12
Recidivist	.62	.86

[a]Other profile characteristics: male, white, 40 years of age, 12 years of schooling, $12,000/year income (in 1970), married, three children.
[b]Other profile characteristics: same as note a except 10 years of schooling and $7,000/year income.

sponses to the psychological and alcohol-related questions are denoted by P and A, respectively. Consider the effects of D, P, and A on B, where B denotes the behavior states of recidivism or nonrecidivism. Based on the identification of direct effects through a path diagram, the diagram $D \rightarrow P \rightarrow A \rightarrow B$ states that the effect of D on B is indirect and through P and A, that the effect of P on B is indirect and through A, and that the effect of A on B is direct. If this diagram is valid, two conclusions follow: (1) given P, D provides no additional information regarding A or B, and (2) given A, P provides no additional information regarding B. Consequently, under $D \rightarrow P \rightarrow A \rightarrow B$, hypothesis 2 cannot be rejected.

Variables forming D include age, sex, race, marital status, number of children, number of siblings, education, income, occupation, and religion. These variables are transformed to linear combinations thereof, say $L(D)$, through principal component analysis. Through separate analyses, the vectors A and P are also converted to principal components as denoted by $L(A)$ and $L(P)$, respectively. Using the transformed variables, the path diagram $D \rightarrow P \rightarrow A \rightarrow B$ is evaluated in terms of $L(D) \rightarrow L(P) \rightarrow L(A) \rightarrow B$ as follows. The variables $L(D)$, $L(P)$, and $L(A)$ are simultaneously scanned through stepwise discriminant analysis to identify dominant predictors for recidivists and nonrecidivists. The result is that only variables from $L(A)$ enter significantly as predictors. The implication is that $L(D)$ and $L(P)$ have no direct effect on B or that, given A, P and D provide no further information regarding B; that is, in the absence of denial, responses to the alcohol-related questions supersede responses to the psychological questions. Otherwise, variables from $L(D)$ and $L(P)$ would have entered significantly as predictors. A second discriminant analysis is performed with all $L(A)$ variables deleted. The result is that only variables from $L(P)$ entered as significant predictors. This supports the hypothesis that, given P, D provides no further information regarding B; that is, $D \rightarrow P \rightarrow B$.

The writer's opinion is that when diagrams such as $D \rightarrow P \rightarrow A \rightarrow B$ are rejected, the error may not be in Allport's conjecture but, rather, in the method of analysis and/or in the adequacy of P and A in measuring attitude. It is archaic, though common, to score inventory responses through factor or principal component analysis and to reduce predictor dimensions without reference to the dependent variable; for example, eigenvectors with eigenroots less than unity are discarded with no consideration given to their effects on dependent variables. This recourse is understandable when computers are not available. In the current day, however, it makes little sense to discard predictors (or to reduce predictor dimensions) without scanning all relevant predictor effects.

3.7   Comments on Other Inventories

Other inventories used in DUI screening include the Michigan Alcohol Screening Test (MAST)[14] and the Mortimer-Filkins (MF) Questionnaire.[15] MAST validity (or the ability of a test to measure what it is supposed to measure) is demonstrated with regard to two groups: hospitalized alcoholics and social drinkers. Test reliability (or the ability of the test to indicate the same score if one were to test and then retest the same person before that person changed) has also been demonstrated by these groups. A problem with MAST is that its questions are alcohol-related, and based on results of the Salinas study, such questions are hardly innocuous to many problem drinkers. This problem was avoided in the MAST study by choosing study groups for whom denial would not be an issue; that is, hospitalized alcoholics are not likely to deny their sickness, and social drinkers, by definition, have no drinking problem. Another problem is that the study groups are very dissimilar, unlike groups in the prealcoholic and prodromal phases of the Jellinek model. Test validity and reliability should be demonstrated with regard to two such close-lying groups. With such a demonstration, predictive validity (or the ability to distinguish between likely recidivists and nonrecidivists) will likely follow.

The MF is used with apparent success in the Denver screening program and is implemented in the Albuquerque program. Its questions are more attuned to the RAP psychological questions; that is, its alcohol-related questions are phrased to be less threatening to the problem drinker. The MF appears to deal effectively with denial because its error rate for underdiagnosis in Denver is reported to be 17% (as compared with 18% for the RAP probabilistic assessment model). A question to be resolved is whether MF, when modeled in the manner of RAP, will lead to lower error rates for over- and underdiagnosis than the RAP model.

4.0   The Albuquerque Program

4.1   Program Overview

The Albuquerque program[a] for screening, referring, and tracking DUI offenders is presented schematically in Figure 5.1. If convicted of DUI, the offender (client) may be allowed to choose between punitive sanctions and entering the program and abiding by its decisions. If the latter choice

---

[a]The Albuquerque program was designed by Dennis Anderson, Laura Bass, and William Mallios.

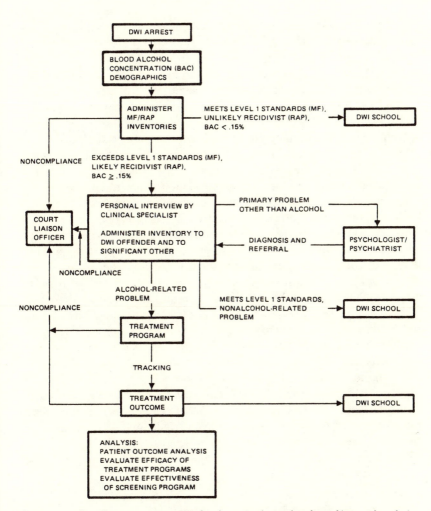

Figure 5.1. The Albuquerque program plan for screening, referral, tracking, and analysis.

is made, the client's demographics and BAC at the time of arrest are forwarded to the screening agency for inclusion in the data base management system. The first step of the program consists of phase 1 screening, where an initial client evaluation is made. The client is referred to DUI school (state law requires DUI school for all first offenders) if each of the following criteria are met: (1) the client is a first offender, (2) BAC <.15% at time of arrest, (3) the RAP probabilistic assessment indicates an unlikely recidivist, and (4) the MF score indicates a social drinker. If any of these criteria are not met, the client is referred to phase 2 for in-depth screening. In phase 2, the client is subject to personal interview by a clinical specialist and is asked to respond to an additional inventory. A "significant other" (a spouse, relative, or close affiliate of the DUI offender) is requested to accompany the client and provide corroborative information. If the clinical specialist judges the client to be a social drinker and a likely nonrecidivist, the client is referred to DUI school and is out of the program. If a primary problem other than alcohol is indicated (such as psychoses or physical disorders), the client is referred to a consultant psychologist or psychiatrist for diagnosis and subsequent referral. This subsequent referral may be a recommendation either for psychiatric or psychological care or for treatment in an alcoholism treatment program. If an alcohol-related problem is indicated, the client is referred to an appropriate education or treatment program and is then tracked through treatment. The client's noncompliance at any point in the program results in referral back to the court liaison officer for appropriate sanctions.

Structuring of the screening program proceeded under the premise that a problem drinker who is sufficiently astute and intent on deception will be able to deceive regardless of the screening devices. The Denver and Salinas programs employ single- rather than two-phase screening. Denver's program attempts to minimize overdiagnosis at the expense of underdiagnosis. Because of the high cost of misclassifying likely recidivists, one may contend that underdiagnosis should be minimized at the expense of overdiagnosis. The Albuquerque program attempts to minimize both errors. Phase 1 criteria are intended to minimize underdiagnosis and isolate social drinkers cost effectively. Individuals falling into the doubtful category in phase 1 are given in-depth scrutiny in phase 2. The second stage of screening is intended to correct overdiagnoses of phase 1 and to minimize underdiagnosis.

4.2 Evaluation of Treatment Programs

Within each of the regimes of inpatient and outpatient treatment, the efficacy of treatment programs is evaluated at year's end with regard to each of the following variables: (1) percentage of clients successfully completing a program (as judged by personnel of the particular program), (2) percentage referred back to court for noncompliance, (3) recidivism rate, and (4) posttest responses. The most powerful comparison of treatment interventions will likely be through pre- and posttest analysis; that is, inventory responses obtained before and after treatment from both client and "significant other" make adjustments possible for pretreatment client differences in evaluating treatment efficacy.

Provisions have been made to include a control program against which outpatient programs can be compared. This aspect was motivated by results of a control versus treatment study[16] in London where individuals in the control were advised that "responsibility for attainment of stated goals lay in their own hands rather than it being anything which could be taken over by others" and that "someone would call [the client] each month and collect news of progress." No significant difference was found between the effectiveness of the control and the treatment programs.

In the Albuquerque program, the screening agency provides the control. Clinical specialists in phase 2 screening are assigned a caseload. A number of clients destined for outpatient treatment are assigned, at random, to the control. The specialist advises the client in the manner of the London study and calls once a month to check on the client's progress.

4.3   Revenues

Funding for the program is entirely through fees paid by the DUI offenders. The screening agency is a consortium of the National Council on Alcoholism as the prime contractor and private industry and the University of New Mexico as subcontractors. Contractor charges are at cost or on a cost-sharing basis.

Variable fee structures had been proposed, with recidivists paying more than first offenders. The reasoning is that, on the average, recidivists will cost the program more than first offenders. A proposal to tie the fee to the BAC at the time of arrest was motivated by a Swedish study[2] wherein a number of individuals involved in traffic accidents were given in-depth interviews and classified according to one of three populations: alcohol addicts/abusers, excessive drinkers, and moderate drinkers/abstainers. BAC was measured at the time of the accident. A discriminant analysis was performed with BAC used to distinguish between the three populations.[b] Results are shown in Table 5.9. For example, given the accident victim has a BAC of .05%, the probabilities of being an alcohol addict/abuser, an excessive drinker, and a moderate drinker/abstainer are, respectively, .49, .19, and .32. Note that under Swedish law, per se evidence of intoxication is that BAC above which the odds tilt in favor of the individual's being an alcohol addict/abuser.

---

[b]To account for curvilinearity with increasing BAC, the following transformations are made in a manner similar to the estimation of curvilinear regression through a series of straight lines (Draper and Smith,[17] p. 140). The variables x_1, x_2, and x_3 are taken as the predictors where $x_1 = x_2 = x_3 = $ BAC. If $x_1 \geq .045$, $x_1 = .045$; if $x_2 \leq .045$, $x_2 = .045$; if $x_2 \geq .115$, $x_2 = .115$; if $x_3 < .115$, $x_3 = .115$.

TABLE 5.9.   Probabilities Relating Blood Alcohol Concentration at the Time of the Traffic Accident to Degrees of Alcohol Addiction

	BAC	Alcohol addicts or alcohol abusers	Excessive drinkers	Moderate drinkers
	Percent	Probability		
	.00	.03	.30	.67
	.01	.06	.30	.64
	.02	.13	.29	.58
	.03	.23	.26	.51
	.04	.39	.21	.40
Per se evidence of intoxication under Swedish law	.05	.49	.19	.32
	.06	.52	.20	.28
	.07	.55	.21	.24
Per se evidence of intoxication under 1976 British Road Safety Act	.08	.57	.22	.21
	.09	.60	.22	.18
Presumed evidence of intoxication under U.S. Uniform Vehicle Code	.10	.62	.23	.15
	.11	.63	.24	.13
	.12	.65	.24	.11
	.13	.66	.24	.10
	.14	.67	.25	.08
	.15	.68	.25	.07
	.20	.72	.25	.03
	.25	.74	.25	.01
	.30	.75	.25	.00

Because the probability of problem drinking increases with increasing BAC (at least regarding accident victims[c]) and because problem drinkers will more heavily tax program resources, tying the client fee to the BAC at time of arrest is a logical recourse. However, once the program was implemented, a flat fee was imposed.

5.0   Epilogue: The California Experience

Following implementation of the Albuquerque program, the writer proposed a similar plan for Fresno, California. California State University was to be a contender for prime contractor. The university was well-qualified for this role because of its varied expertise in social welfare,

---

[c]Data from the Albuquerque program will be used to establish the relation between the probability of problem drinking/recidivism and BAC at time of arrest for non-accident victims.

criminology, computer science, and business. Moreover, the contract would lead to close university-community ties and enhance the university's teaching and research programs in related areas.

For the program to succeed, it is preferable that the cognizant court be the contracting agency and necessary that judges handling DUI cases be fully supportive. This is the case in New Mexico, where judges of the Metropolitan Court (Bernalillo County) make the program possible. Reactions in Fresno were varied. In discussions with the writer, the presiding judge of the Municipal Court (Fresno County) argued that if a first offender is forced into screening and possible treatment (in lieu of court sanctions), then the defendant may demand a court trial, which, in turn, would swamp the court dockets. The Albuquerque experience negates this argument, as the writer pointed out at the time. The judge also opposed proposed increases in the fine in order that defendants pay the costs of the program because the judged believed it would place an undue burden on the first offender. A general response appeared as an editorial in the *Fresno Bee* (Fig. 5.2).

State officials in Sacramento were open to the possibility of supplying money for a feasibility study if requests were made through appropriate channels (even though feasibility had been clearly established through the Albuquerque program). During these discussions, a high-ranking official made the following statement to the writer after being given the assurance of anonymity: "If you solve the drunk-driving problem, where are we going to find revenues to replace those obtained through DUI fines?" Which is cause for greater concern, the drunk-driving epidemic or the loss of revenues generated by drunk driving? In California, revenues from DUI fines exceed $300 million annually. Revenue recipients include the Fish and Game Commission, jailhouse construction, and the police retirement fund. Perhaps the current media campaigns against drunk driving need a different slogan: "Support law enforcement: drink, drive, and get caught."

Exercise 1

Of accused felons who awaited trial in jail (Monterey County, California, 1973), 18% were convicted, 40% were acquitted and thus had been held in jail at a loss of personal freedom and at a cost to the taxpayer, and 42% were convicted of misdemeanor offenses and sent to a minimum-security facility if they were required to serve time at all.

Based on figures such as these, the granting of pretrial parole (pretrial release on bail or on own recognizance) has been reexamined.[18] The problem is one of

The Fresno Bee

Founded 1922
Published every morning

CARLOS McCLATCHY, *editor, 1922-1933*

Monday, December 19, 1983 • Vol. 123, No. 22135

GEORGE F. GRUNER, *executive editor*
DONALD R. SLINKARD, *managing editor*
TOM KIRWAN, *editorial page editor*
GENE GRIGG, *associate editor*
VERNE H. COLE, *associate editor*

JOHN B. RAYTIS, *general manager*

—————————————Editorials—————————

Screening drunken drivers

The drunken driver is often a problem drinker. It's one of the ways an alcoholic goes public.

In that light, one would think that the municipal judges and others in the court system who deal with drunken drivers would be responsive to a new idea for early intervention — for identifying and trying to help the drinker whose problem has been dramatized by a drunken driving arrest.

Yet the judges in Fresno County apparently reacted negatively to a proposal by a Fresno State professor, Dr. William Mallios, for a screening, referral and tracking program for those convicted of drunken driving for the first time.

It's not just another bright untested idea from academia. Mallios' program is being used in Albuquerque, N.M., and preliminary results are encouraging. First offenders who go through the program are much less likely to be arrested again for drunken driving than those who do not go through the program.

The approach is voluntary and self-funding. As a condition of the probation that is offered with first-offense punishment, the offender would have to put up an estimated $85 for screening to determine if he has a drinking problem, and a larger sum — one estimate is $300 — for treatment if the screening indicates treatment is necessary. His progress would be followed to make sure he gets the treatment, and he would be re-tested after completing treatment.

First offenders already face a fine of about $600 and must pay $75 to $100 to attend a few

sessions of a Driving While Intoxicated School — which is not "treatment" in the generally accepted sense of the word. Presiding Municipal Judge James Ardaiz fears that many offenders would balk at having to put up additional funds for a screening/treatment program and would choose jail time instead, rejecting probation.

Ardaiz also believes keeping track of offenders through treatment would strain the caseload of the probation department beyond endurance.

The judge may be right, but should conjecture — even informed conjecture — be the basis for turning away from a promising program?

Who knows, really, at what point conditions of probation would be considered so burdensome that an offender would choose jail time? Our guess is that for most offenders that point would not be reached as soon as Ardaiz thinks.

As for the problem of monitoring offenders to make sure they are getting prescribed treatment, that might well call for additional help in the probation department. It could be a cost-effective investment, considering what's at stake socially and economically in trying to reclaim problem drinkers as soon as they run afoul of the law.

There is a tendency in the justice system to react negatively to ideas that come from outside the circle. Ideas with academic origins might be discounted too quickly for that reason. But we hope that the courthouse people give some more thought to the Mallios proposal.

Figure 5.2. *Fresno Bee* editorial.

identifying accused felons who are likely to jump bail. What variables would aid in this identification? Devise a quantitative method for discriminating between bail-jumpers and non–bail-jumpers. How might the study be funded?

Exercise 2

Shoplifting is estimated to add 10% to consumer costs. To combat this problem, schools for people convicted of petty larceny have been established in certain jurisdictions. These schools are similar in intent to the schools for those convicted of DUI. It has been proposed that those convicted of petty larceny be screened for likely recidivism. What are the various profiles of likely recidivists for this offense? In what ways would a screening, tracking, and referral program be similar or dissimilar to the drunk-driving program? Set up such a program.

References

1. Buikhuisen, W. *Criminological and Psychological Aspects of Drunken Drivers.* Groningen: Criminological Institute, State University of Groningen, Netherlands, 1969.

2. Bjerver, K. B., Goldberg, L., and Linda, P. "Blood Alcohol Levels in Hospitalized Victims of Traffic Accidents." In *Proceedings of the Second International Conference on Alcohol and Road Safety, Toronto, Canada, 1953,* pp. 92–102. Toronto: Brewers' Warehousing Co.

3. Goldberg, L. "Drunken Drivers in Sweden." In ref. 2, pp. 112–27.

4. *Easter* v. *District of Columbia,* 361 F. 2d 50 (1966).

5. *Driver* v. *Hinant,* 356 F. 2d 761 (1966).

6. *Powell* v. *Texas,* 392 U.S. 514, 549–52 (1968).

7. Brycel, B. "A Case of Real, If Unequal, Justice." *Los Angeles Times,* 4 February 1976.

8. Tierney, J. "Doctor, Is This Man Dangerous?" *Science 82* June 1982, 59.

9. Cocozza, J., and Steadman, H. "Prediction in Psychiatry: An Example of Misplaced Confidence in Experts." *Social Problems* 25 (1978): 93.

10. Dixon, W. J., ed. *BMDP Statistical Software.* Berkeley and Los Angeles: University of California Press, 1985.

11. Jellinek, E. M. "Phases of Alcohol Addiction." In *Society, Culture, and Drinking Patterns,* ed. D. J. Pitman and C. R. Snyder, pp. 356–68. New York: Wiley, 1962.

12. Horton, D. "The Function of Alcohol in Primitive Societies." *Quarterly Journal of Studies on Alcohol* 4 (1943): 42.

13. Allport, G. W. "Review of the American Soldier," *Journal of Abnormal and Social Psychology* 45 (1950): 210–18.

14. Selzer, M. L., and Lowenstein, J. "The Michigan Alcohol Screening

Test." In *Proceedings of the Fifth International Conference on Alcohol and Traffic Safety, Freiburg im Breisgau, Federal Republic of Germany, 1969*, pp. 1.1–1.5.

15. Filkins, L. D., Mortimer, R. G., Post, D. V., and Post, M. W. *Field Evaluation of Court Procedures for Identifying Problem Drinkers*. Ann Arbor: Highway Safety Research Institute, University of Michigan, 1973.

16. Edwards, G., Ordord, J., Egert, S., Guthrie, S., Hawker, A., Hensman, C., Mitcheson, M., Oppenheimer, E., and Taylor, C. "Alcoholism: A Controlled Trial of 'Treatment' and 'Advice.'" *Journal of Studies on Alcohol* 38 (1977): 1004–31.

17. Draper, N. R., and Smith, H. *Applied Regression Analysis*. New York: Wiley, 1966.

18. Ares, C., Rankin, A., and Sturz, H. "The Manhattan Bail Project: An Interim Report on the Use of Pre-Trial Parole." *New York University Law Review*, 1963, pp. 67–95.

The first forward pass.

eague Game Outcomes

I n this chapter a forecasting model is developed for National Football League (NFL) games. The focus is on predicting the winning point spread and beating the oddsmaker's line. Predictions are based on (1) long- and short-term aggregates of opposing teams' performance statistics (such as total rushing and passing yardage gained by the offense and allowed by the defense) and (2) lagged shocks. The latter are defined as the difference between actual and expected performance in past games. For example, if the oddsmaker establishes a team as a 7-point favorite and it loses by 10, the game is termed an upset; the shocks for the winning and losing teams are −17 and 17 points, respectively. The upset of a team has a direct effect on its performance the following week. Ad hoc information relating to the forthcoming game is incorporated in the forecasting model—which is based on Bayesian discriminant analysis—through the prior probabilities.

The forecasting model formed the basis for placing bets during the 1974–75 season, when Pittsburgh won its first Super Bowl. For purposes of forecasting, the first week of that season was treated as the last week of the previous season; data from the entire previous season formed the sample. As new data became available each week, the sample was trimmed—in the sense that the most distant week was dropped from the sample as the new week was added—and the model was updated. Moreover, a damping factor was placed on past shocks that were excessive, either positively or negatively. In all games played during the 1974–75 season, the forecasting model beat the oddsmaker's line in 70% of the games.

1.0   Model Utility

In 1982 it was estimated that Americans bet $50 billion on football, which included $7 billion on the Super Bowl alone.

Forget about the winner. How'd you do against the line?

Fifty billion in bounty and the state coffers go wanting. Lotterists versus antilotterists. The antis have it—for the present. One view is that states will eventually sanction football lotteries—lotteries, unlike Delaware's, that offer reasonable odds. The path won't be easy. Aside from special-interest groups, there is the NFL. When Delaware first proposed its lottery, the NFL was in opposition, arguing that lotteries teach more people to gamble and thus increase participation in the gaming process.

Should NFL legal action, if any, fail in its bid to prevent further legalization of football lotteries, the NFL will presumably broaden surveillance in its regulatory practices. As part of surveillance, probabilistic models could be used to scrutinize the likelihood of game outcomes. For example, suppose (1) the Rams are 3-point favorites over the Cowboys and (2) the probability is .01 that the Rams will lose by more than 21 points. The game is played and the Rams lose by 24. An unlikely outcome? Yes. Irregularities? No, unless other circumstances make the game suspect. However, a repetition of unlikely outcomes may signal possible irregularities.

Such modeling has other uses. The model weights aspects of team play that contribute to winning and losing. For coaches and general managers, such information complements subjective judgment and has obvious utility in trades and the player draft. In a similar vein, models could be developed that identify prospective players who are likely to succeed or fail based on personal or physical characteristics and prior performance. Such modeling should be routine in the age of multimillion dollar contracts.

2.0   The Oddsmaker's Model: The Line

In Super Bowl XII, the Denver Broncos were 5-point underdogs to the Dallas Cowboys (final score was Dallas, 27; Denver, 10). The spread was set by Robert Martin, Las Vegas oddsmaker, whose method is to score, on a scale of 1 to 10, various aspects of team play. Table 6.1 illustrates Martin's method. Summing the respective scores over all 10 items leads to a total of 100.5 for Dallas and 95.5 for Denver. The difference, 5 points in favor of Dallas, is the first step in establishing the betting line and is termed the early, or outlaw, line.[1] In the second step, a number of knowledgeable professionals are allowed to bet a limited

TABLE 6.1.   Making the Line for Super Bowl XII: Dallas versus Denver +5
            Points

Attribute	Comments	Dallas score	Denver score
Coaches	Landry is by far the superior coach and his record proves it. Miller (coach of the year by the Associated Press) is an unknown but you can't question the job he did this year.	10	10
Quarterbacks	Staubach is better than Morton and at the top of his game. Morton is underrated and gets the job done.	10	9
Running backs	The Cowboys have excellent backs in Dorsett (offensive rookie of the year), Pearson, and Newhouse. Denver's Armstrong, Lytle, and Keyworth are good.	10	9
Receivers	Both teams match up well regarding both side receivers and tight ends.	10	9.5
Offensive line	Not a household name in the bunch but both lines are effective. Staubach was sacked 37 times and Morton 50. There's a message here somewhere.	10	9
Kicking	Punters White of Dallas and Dilts of Denver are even, but Herrera gets a slight edge over Turner.	10	9.5
Defensive secondary	For Dallas, they're all super. Denver is excellent.	10	9.5
Defensive linemen and linebackers	A four-man front against a three-man front. Denver has better linebackers but Dallas is better up front.	10	10
Special teams	Both are well-coached and do excellent jobs.	10	10
American Football Conference versus National Football Conference	The AFC was 19–9 against the NFC. Denver played a stronger schedule.	8.5	10
Total		98.5	95.5
Other considerations	Dallas is a "public team." They will draw money no matter what line you put up. A tax of 2 points is imposed as an incentive to lure money to the Denver side.	2	0
Grand total		100.5	95.5

Source: Some of the comments have been drawn from "Why Is Dallas Favored?"
Monterey Peninsula Herald, 10 January 1978.

amount on the early line. The oddsmaker then makes an adjustment, if
necessary, such that the professionals' money would have split, approximately, on both sides of the adjusted line. This adjustment leads to the
official line, which is made available to the public. If the public's money
starts to fall heavily on either side of the official line, the oddsmaker

makes further adjustments. The oddsmaker's objective is to choose a line such that the amount bet on both sides is nearly equal; his profits come from a 10% fee imposed per wager. Thus, the line model is nothing more than a sample survey designed to estimate that point spread that will evenly divide the public's money.

Keep in mind that the oddsmaker's line is not the oddsmaker's opinion of the outcome but, rather, his opinion of what the public's opinion will be. Nonetheless, the official line model produces some remarkably good forecasts, possibly because it can readily incorporate ad hoc information. For example, effects of injured players can be subjectively scored, item by item, in Table 6.1. Or, consider the story told the writer by a well-known sportswriter. Several years ago, Miami was heavily favored over Baltimore, whose coach was to be fired if his team lost by the anticipated margin. A number of the Miami players were close friends with the Baltimore coach and played the game, unwittingly, without their usual zeal. The result? Miami was upset and the Baltimore coach kept his job, temporarily. These examples illustrate effects of temporal factors that affect game outcomes. Even though such ad hoc information can be incorporated in a Bayesian model, the oddsmaker's model may do so as effectively and compete with the Bayesian model, at least for more atypical games.

3.0   Predictions for the 1974–75 Playoff Games: A First for Pittsburgh

Based on discriminant analysis, a model was developed and predictions were made for each game of the regular 1974–75 season plus the playoff games. The predictions were more accurate than the betting line in just under 70% of 140 game forecasts.

In 1975 Pittsburgh won its first Super Bowl. They were the titlists who shouldn't have been. Why? According to regular season won-lost records and other measures of performance, Oakland and Miami were the best teams. An archaic playoff system paired the Raiders and Dolphins in the first round, while Pittsburgh met Buffalo, one of the weakest playoff teams. As regards the Oakland-Miami game: "Oakland's Ken Stabler, master of the last-ditch drive, had to go through the same routine twice . . . before upending Miami 28–26 in a game in which the lead changed three times in the last 4.5 minutes. . . . Stabler was hit just as he made the winning touchdown pass to Davis in the last 26 seconds. . . . [It was] one of the all-time great classics of football" (Associated Press, 22 December 1974).

TABLE 6.2.   Results of the 1974–75 NFL Playoff Games

Oak*	28	Oak*	13		
Mia	26				
				Pitt	16
Pitt*	32	Pitt	24		
Buff	14				
Minn*	30	Minn*	14		
StL	14				
				Minn	10
LA*	19	LA	10		
Wash	10				

Note: An asterisk denotes the home team.

Beating Buffalo with ease, Pittsburgh upset the Raiders the following week. For the title, Pittsburgh beat Minnesota, whose appearance in the final game was by virtue of the chill factor, which accompanied the Vikings' late-season home games. Scores of the playoff games are given in Table 6.2.

The Oakland-Miami game was predicted as shown in Table 6.3. The win probabilities can be given a frequency interpretation as follows. Had these teams played repeatedly prior to the actual playoff game, Oakland (Miami) would have won 21% (6%) of the games by more than 12 points, 18% (19%) by 7 to 12 points, and 19% (17%) by 1 to 6 points. If the difference between the Oakland score and the Miami score were averaged over all games, the average—or the expected winning margin (EWM)—is 2.83 points in favor of Oakland. The EWM is found by multiplying the probability associated with a particular point interval by the midpoint of that interval and summing products. For the outer intervals (<12 points), the midpoint was taken as 19 points. However, the sensitivity of the EWM was evaluated by varying the midpoints for the outer intervals. For example, during the regular season, Oakland wins by more than 12 points averaged less than 19 points, while Miami wins by more than 12 points

TABLE 6.3.   Predictions for the Oakland-Miami Game

Winner (by points)	Win probability	Odds to $1
Oak (>12 points)	.21	$3.76
Oak (7–12 points)	.18	4.55
Oak (1–6 points)	.19	4.26
Mia (1–6 points)	.17	4.88
Mia (7–12 points)	.19	4.26
Mia (>12 points)	.06	15.67

Expected winning margin: Oak to win by 2.83 points.
Betting line: Oak to win by 3 points.
Actual winning margin: Oak won by 2 points.

averaged more than 19 points. When the actual averages were taken as the outer interval midpoints, the betting line was not straddled. (Other sensitivity analyses included variations in values of the prior probabilities.) If negative midpoints are assigned to Oakland wins and positive midpoints are assigned to Miami wins, the EWM of 2.83 points in favor of Oakland is calculated as follows: $(-19)(.21) + (-9.5)(.18) + (-3.5)(.19) + (3.5)(.18) + (9.5)(.19) + (19)(.06) = -2.83$. Regarding odds, a wager on Oakland's winning by 1 to 6 points should have returned \$4.26 for each dollar bet; that is, odds $= (1 - p)/p$, where p denotes the win probability.

In terms of the betting line, the options were to pick Oakland minus 3 points or Miami plus 3. The EWM of 2.83 points indicated that one should have chosen Miami plus the points, which would have been a winning bet.

Predictions for the other playoff games are given in Table 6.4. It is seen that only the outcome of the Oakland-Pittsburgh game went against the odds. However, the EWM provided a winning bet not only in the Raider-Steeler game but in five of seven playoff games (which is nearly the same winning percentage for all forecasts during the regular season).

For the 1974–75 season, the home field advantage amounted to 3.16 points. For the championship game, there is presumably no advantage. With Minnesota as the home team, Pittsburgh had an EWM of 1.09 points. With Pittsburgh as the home team, their EWM was 4.25 points. The two EWMs thus straddled the betting line of 3 points. When the prediction was made, an average was taken between the two sets of predictions, which led to a losing bet. In hindsight, the game was a no-bet situation; or, Pittsburgh should have been given the home field advantage, since it was clear, once the game began, that Art Rooney's team was the crowd favorite.

4.0   The Delaware Lottery

Following model development, the writer submitted a proposal to the *New York Times* concerning the provision of weekly forecasts for the 1974–75 season. In response, William Wallace, major sportswriter for the *Times,* stated that "any stress on predicting the outcomes of games would be to encourage an illegal activity" and that such forecasts "are too complex for comprehension by the fan." The state of Delaware apparently thought otherwise. In 1976 Delaware introduced the nation's first state-run football pool. The lottery provided a game in which the type of

TABLE 6.4.   Predictions for the 1974–75 NFL Playoff Games

Winner (by points)	Win probability	Odds to $1	Expected winning margin (EWM) and actual winning margin (AWM)
Minn (>12 points)	.65	.54	EWM: Minn to win by 12.23 points
Minn (7–12 points)	.07	13.29	Betting line: Minn to win by 7 points
Minn (1–6 points)	.11	8.09	AWM: Minn won by 16 points
StL (1 to 6 points)	.09	10.11	
StL (7 to 12 points)	.07	13.29	
StL (>12 points)	.01	99.00	
LA (>12 points)	.03	32.33	EWM: LA to win by 1.10 points
LA (7 to 12 points)	.22	3.55	Betting line: LA to win by 3 points
LA (1 to 6 points)	.37	1.70	AWM: LA won by 9 points
Wash (1 to 6 points)	.22	3.55	
Wash (7 to 12 points)	.08	11.50	
Wash (>12 points)	.08	11.50	
Pitt (>12 points)	.33	2.03	EWM: Pitt to win by 7.34 points
Pitt (7 to 12 points)	.17	4.88	Betting line: Pitt to win by 6 points
Pitt (1 to 6 points)	.22	3.55	AWM: Pitt won by 18 points
Buff (1 to 6 points)	.24	3.17	
Buff (7 to 12 points)	.03	32.33	
Buff (>12 points)	.01	99.00	
Oak (>12 points)	.04	24.00	EWM: Oak to win by 2.71 points
Oak (7 to 12 points)	.39	1.56	Betting line: Oak to win by 6 points
Oak (1 to 6 points)	.13	6.69	AWM: Oak lost by 11 points
Pitt (1 to 6 points)	.36	1.78	
Pitt (7 to 12 points)	.06	15.67	
Pitt (>12 points)	.02	49.00	
Minn (>12 points)	.06	15.67	EWM: Minn to win by 1.94 points
Minn (7 to 12 points)	.24	3.17	Betting line: Minn to win by 5 points
Minn (1 to 6 points)	.34	1.94	AWM: Minn won by 4 points
LA (1 to 6 points)	.14	6.14	
LA (7 to 12 points)	.21	3.76	
LA (>12 points)	.01	99.00	
Pitt (>12 points)	.15	5.67	EWM: Pitt to win by 2.67 points
Pitt (7 to 12 points)	.14	6.14	Betting line: Pitt to win by 3 points
Pitt (1 to 6 points)	.27	2.70	AWM: Pitt won by 6 points
Minn (1 to 6 points)	.25	3.00	
Minn (7 to 12 points)	.14	6.14	
Minn (>12 points)	.05	19.00	

bets made bore a striking resemblance to the predictions in Table 6.4. The game was as follows. If Oakland is favored over Pittsburgh by 6, the player cannot take, say, Pittsburgh and 6. Instead, the player must pick the winner and predict the margin of victory by marking one of three boxes: 0 to 7 points, 8 to 14 points, and 15 points and over. The player loses if he picks a team to win by 0 to 7 and it wins by 10.

This game prompted *Philadelphia Daily News* columnist Stan Hochman to write that "the Delaware football lottery is a scheme concocted by fools to be patronized by idiots. It deserves to fail because it doesn't come within 100 yards of giving the sucker an even break. The sucker is much better off continuing to bet those 'illegal' parlay cards, even if the cards cheat outrageously on the proper odds" (Associated Press, 12 September 1977). The forecasts for the playoff games strengthen Hochman's comments. Suppose the bettor imposes the rule that, to bet on a game under the lottery rules, there must be at least a .50 probability of winning. This rule is met for only one playoff game, the Minnesota–St. Louis game, where the probability of Minnesota winning by more than 12 points was .65. For no other point interval of any other playoff game does the probability exceed even .39. Clearly, if one is asked to play this game, appropriate odds should be given. Thus, if the bettor chose Minnesota to beat St. Louis by more than 12 points, the payoff should have been 54 cents on the dollar. However, if Oakland was picked to beat Miami by 1 to 6 points, the payoff should have been $4.26 for each dollar bet.

The fans' reaction to the Delaware lottery was one of indifference. The betting public realized the lottery was a sham and largely abstained. The *New York Times* writer underestimated the fans, who are able to understand football forecasts, particularly when money is involved.

5.0   Modeling Methods

5.1   Aggregates and Shocks

Let $x(m, i, y, t)$ denote the mth aspect of defensive ($y = d$) or offensive ($y = o$) performance for team i in week t. Values of m are defined below. Other aspects such as third down conversions are excluded from the analysis because they are not given in the sports page coverage of summary statistics per game.

$m =$ 1: number of first downs,
$m =$ 2: number of rushing attempts,
$m =$ 3: net yards rushing,
$m =$ 4: net yards passing,
$m =$ 5: net yards (passing and rushing),
$m =$ 6: number of passing attempts,
$m =$ 7: number of passing completions,
$m =$ 8: number of interceptions,
$m =$ 9: number of touchdown passes,
$m =$ 10: total yards passing (equals net yards passing plus yards lost when the quarterback is sacked),

$m = 11$: number of penalties,
$m = 12$: yards penalized,
$m = 13$: number of punts,
$m = 14$: average distance per punt,
$m = 15$: number of field goals,
$m = 16$: average field goal distance,
$m = 17$: number of fumbles,
$m = 18$: number of fumbles lost.

If, for example, teams i and i^* play in week t, $x(1, i, o, t)$ is the number of first downs by team i's offense and the number of first downs allowed by team i^*'s defense; that is, $x(1, i, o, t) = x(1, i^*, d, t)$. Thus, a team's offensive performance quantifies its opponent's defensive performance and conversely.

The forecast of the i versus i^* outcome in week $t + 1$ utilized both long- and short-term aggregates of the variables

$$x(m, i, y, t) - x(m, i^*, y, t) \qquad (6.1)$$

Short-term aggregates were considered because of the insensitivity of long-term aggregates to short-term changes (e.g., a losing team can become a winner in a matter of weeks).

For the prediction of early and midseason games, data from the previous season were used. For example, in predicting outcomes for the first week of the 1974–75 season, the first week was viewed as the last week of the previous season. Then as the 1974–75 season progressed, the sample was trimmed by deleting earlier weeks of the 1973–74 season. For the playoff games, only games from the 1974–75 season were utilized.

For long-term aggregates, variables in (6.1) were aggregated over the entire sample. Based on trial and error, the most effective short-term aggregates were those for which the variables are summed over the three weeks prior to the game forecast.

Aggregating (6.1), we have

$$\sum_{t^*=t-j}^{t} [x(m, i, y, t^*) - x(m, i^*, y, t^*)] \qquad (6.2)$$

where j takes the values $t - 1$ and 2 for long- and short-term aggregates, respectively. A second class of aggregates is

$$\sum_{t^*=t-j}^{t} \left[\frac{x(m, i, y, t^*)}{x(m^*, i, y, t^*)} - \frac{x(m, i^*, y, t^*)}{x(m^*, i^*, y, t^*)} \right] \qquad (6.3)$$

where values of (m, m^*) included $(3, 2)$, $(5, 3)$, $(7, 6)$, $(9, 6)$, $(9, 4)$, $(8, 6)$, $(5, 6)$, $(10, 4)$, and $(5, 15)$ for each of $y = o$ and $y = d$. A third class of aggregates reflects the strength of the opponent's competition in previous weeks. For example, a strong (weak) performance by team i in each of the three previous weeks may have been due to weak (strong) competition. These variables are measured by

$$\sum_{t^{**}=t-2}^{t} \sum_{t^{*}=1}^{t-1} \{x[m, I(t^{**}), y, t^{*}]\} - \{x[m, I^{*}(t^{**}), y, t^{*}]\} \tag{6.4}$$

where $I(t^{**})$ and $I^{*}(t^{**})$ denote, respectively, the opponents of teams i and i^* in week t^{**}.

Aside from these aggregates, another set of variables was scanned for significant predictors: lagged shocks. The shock for team i in week t is the difference between its actual performance (as measured in terms of winning or losing by a certain number of points) and its expected performance. For example, if a team wins by 10 points and was expected to lose by 3, its shock for that week is $10 - (-3) = 13$ points. One may argue that lagged shocks quantify human factors that affect subsequent games and that are not reflected by the aggregates in (6.2) to (6.4). Shocks for both the home and the away teams in each of the three weeks prior to the game were considered. Also considered was the shock for when the two teams met previously. If they did not meet previously within the sample, this shock was set equal to zero.

If the oddsmaker's spread is used to quantify expected performance (as is the case in this study), the shock is known and need not be estimated. (However, when known, lagged shocks are included as predictors; regression residuals should always be scrutinized for correlations over time.) If no line is available (or if one chooses, unwisely, to ignore it), shocks can be estimated iteratively as in BMDP2T.[2] This study and the modeling of competitive sports in general illustrate situations where lagged shocks are known—so long as a publicized betting line exists. This is in contrast to modeling, say, fluctuations of the British pound, where shocks are unknown and must be estimated. (Converting futures prices of the pound into a betting line has the weakest of analogies with the oddsmaker's spread.)

5.2 Discriminant versus Regression Analysis

In week $t + 1$, $h(i, t + 1)$ and $a(i^*, t + 1)$ denote respective point totals for home team i and away team i^*. Regression analysis provides a direct prediction of

$$h(i, t + 1) - a(i^*, t + 1) = d(i, i^*, t + 1) \qquad (6.5)$$

while discriminant analysis estimates the probability that $d(i, i^*, t + 1)$ belongs to each of the point intervals, say

$$< -12, (-12, -7), (-6, 0), (1, 6), (7, 12), > 12 \qquad (6.6)$$

as used in Table 6.4. Other intervals, say

$$< -10, (-10, -3), (-2, 2), (3, 10), > 10 \qquad (6.7)$$

may also be relevant when probabilities corresponding to the intervals in (6.6) are unreliable.

When there are sufficient observations per interval and modeling assumptions are valid, discriminant analysis can provide more informative predictions for the following reasons. (1) Based on probabilities associated with the point intervals, discriminant analysis provides the EWM indirectly. Sensitivity analysis is straightforward in varying both the outer interval midpoints and the prior probabilities. Regression modeling provides the EWM directly in terms of the estimate of (6.5). However, associated confidence bounds usually straddle the oddsmaker's spread. Moreover, the sensitivity of the EWM to changes in the Bayesian prior probability density functions (pdf) in multiple regression can be "messy." (2) Probabilities derived from discriminant analysis are based on Mahalanobis D^2 distances. If all distances are relatively large for a particular game, the resulting probabilities may be unreliable. However, more reliable probabilities can usually be obtained from alternative point intervals; for example, for a particular game, the intervals in (6.7) may lead to more reliable probabilities than those in (6.6). Such flexibility is usually not possible in regression analysis. (3) Suppose that three different games are predicted as follows:

	$< -1, 0$	$(-10, -3)$	$(-2, 2)$	$(3, 10)$	> 10
Prediction for game 1	.02	.10	.76	.10	.02
Prediction for game 2	.35	.13	.04	.13	.35
Prediction for game 3	.20	.20	.20	.20	.20

Though all three predictions lead to the same EWM, the interpretation of each differs. The first prediction indicates that the game will be very close, the second that either team will win big, and the third that anything can happen. A regression prediction of the EWM would not distinguish between the three except in terms of the width of the confidence bounds.

5.3   Assumptions and Analysis Results

For both the 1974–75 and the 1973–74 seasons, models based on discriminant analysis outperformed those based on regression. Significant predictors for each analysis were obtained through the standard scanning procedures of stepwise regression (BMDP2R)[2] analysis and stepwise discriminant (BMDP7M)[2] analysis. For both analyses, two approaches were used to select predictors. First, lagged shocks, aggregates in (6.2) to (6.4), and numerous two-factor interactions were scanned for significance. The second, more fruitful approach was to group the aggregates into four subsets: long-term offensive aggregates, long-term defensive aggregates, short-term offensive aggregates, and short-term defensive aggregates. A principal component analysis was performed for each subset. The lagged shocks, all principal components, and selected interactions were then scanned for significant predictors. Why is the second approach preferable? In reality, all aggregates have some effect on game outcomes. By replacing individual aggregates with linear combinations thereof, all aggregates are brought into the prediction—even though many of the individual aggregates will have small weights. Relatively few aggregates become predictors when they are scanned individually as in the first approach. Additionally, the linear combinations are more symmetrically distributed than a number of the individual aggregates. This has relevance because predictors obtained through BMDP7M are assumed to follow a multivariate normal pdf.

Variables obtained through the second approach showed no evidence of differences in predictor dispersion matrices between point intervals.

Because the discriminant analysis is given Bayesian formulation, assumptions are required regarding the prior probabilities assigned to the intervals. Prediction results based on uniform priors were compared with those based on non-uniform priors as determined by past frequencies of game outcomes according to the intervals in (6.6). Uniform priors gave better predictions. However, even though uniform priors were utilized in the 1974–75 forecasts, non-uniform priors would be very useful in the utilization of valid, ad hoc information. (As a side study, the writer converted pregame commentaries by several sportswriters into non-uniform priors for a number of key games; forecasts based on uniform priors were clearly superior.)

Regarding their effect on the EWM, whether analyzed through regression or discriminant analysis, each of the opposing teams' shocks for the previous week was highly significant, both individually and when their interaction with principal components reflecting short-term aggregates of offensive and defensive rushing performance was considered.

The meaning of these effects is illustrated as follows. Suppose team i is upset in week t. The coefficient of this shock for team i indicates that team i's chances of winning in week $t + 1$ are enhanced. Suppose, in addition, that team i is a strong team as reflected through aggregates of its rushing game, both offensively and defensively. The coefficients of the interactions between lagged shocks and principal components reflecting rushing performance indicate that team i's chances of winning in week $t + 1$ are particularly enhanced. Put simply, if a good team is upset, it returns to basics and comes on particularly strong the following week.

For games where the shock was excessive, it was found that damped shocks led to better forecasts than raw shocks. In the final model, a team's lagged shock was limited to a maximum absolute value of 14 points.

5.4   Other Modeling Approaches

Other published approaches to modeling NFL game outcomes utilize regression analysis. Goode's approach,[3] also discussed by Marshall,[4] is to apply factor analysis to the correlation matrix of predictor variables and to use the factors as predictors in regression. A drawback of this approach is that predictor dimensions are reduced without having examined effects of discarded dimensions (those with small eigenvalues) on the dependent variable in (6.5).

Harville[5] develops a regression-type model based only on scores. Although Harville's predictions are less accurate than the betting line, Morris[6] commends the model because it is parsimonious (though hardly more parsimonious than the oddsmaker's model). A discipline that emphasizes oversimplification at the expense of solving the problem—beating the oddsmaker's line—seems misdirected.

In an early stage of this study, the writer applied autoregressive, moving-average methodology in modeling $d(i, i^*, t + 1)$ in (6.5). Predictors excluded aggregates of the performance statistics (m) and included lags of observed score differentials. The model was based on a first-order expansion of the function

$$d(i, i^*, t + 1) = f(D, D^*, \mathbf{e}, \mathbf{e}_*, \mathbf{r}, \mathbf{r}_*) \tag{6.8}$$

where

$$D = \sum_{k=0}^{t} d(i, I, t - k) \qquad \text{and} \qquad D^* = \sum_{k=0}^{t} d(i^*, I^*, t - k)$$

where I and I^* are, respectively, the opponents of i and i^* in week $t -$

k; $e(i, I, t - k)$ and $e(i^*, I^*, t - k)$ are typical elements of the vectors **e** and $\mathbf{e}_*$, where $e(i, I, t - k) = d(i, I, t - k) - o(i, I, t - k)$, and $o(i, I, t - k)$ denotes the oddsmaker's line on the team i versus team I encounter in week $t - k$; $r(i, I, t - k^*)$ and $r(i^*, I^*, t - k^*)$ are typical elements of **r** and $\mathbf{r}_*$, where $r(i, I, t - k^*)$ is the difference between $d(i, I, t - k^*)$ and is statistical expectation—as opposed to the oddsmaker's expectation—in week $t - k^*$.

Forecasts based on a first-order expansion of f in (6.8) were inferior to those using aggregates in (6.2) to (6.4). However, a second-order expansion of f was not considered; see the discussion of bilinear models in Chapter 12. Subsequent modeling will evaluate higher-order expansions of f.

6.0 Ratings: A Round-Robin Tournament

A weekly rating of NFL teams could be based on results of a hypothetical round-robin tournament conducted following each week's regularly scheduled games. Tournament results could be determined by the type of model developed herein. In the round-robin, each team would play every other team on a home and away basis. The rating would be based on the won-lost records. In the event of ties, point differentials would be used.

The forecasting model was used to obtain results of a hypothetical round-robin tournament between playoff teams just prior to the playoffs. With Oakland hosting Pittsburgh in the first week of the playoffs, the EWM was 6.34 points in favor of Oakland. (Recall from Table 6.4 that Oakland's EWM over Pittsburgh was 2.71 points in the second week of playoffs.) The round-robin had Pittsburgh losing, both at home and away, to Oakland and Miami. Pittsburgh split with both Los Angeles and Washington, winning at home and losing away, and won all games with Buffalo, Minnesota, and St. Louis. Oakland won the round-robin, losing only at Miami, which placed second. Third place went to Los Angeles, followed by Pittsburgh, Washington, Minnesota, Buffalo, and St. Louis.

Exercise 1

You are asked to model winners and winning point spreads for National Basketball Association games. As with football, the oddsmaker's line is available prior to each game. To what extent are shocks in basketball analogous to shocks in football? Identify all predictors you would scan for significance in your modeling procedure. Would you use stepwise regression, stepwise discriminant analysis, or some other procedure? How would you incorporate supplementary information, when available, in your forecast through a Bayesian regression analysis?

References

1. Merchant, L. *The National Football Lottery*. New York: Holt, Rinehart, and Winston, 1973.

2. Dixon, W. J., ed. *BMDP Statistical Software*. Berkeley and Los Angeles: University of California Press, 1985.

3. Goode, B. "Relevant Variables in Professional Football." *Proceedings of the American Statistical Association, Social Statistics Section*, 1978, 83–86.

4. Marshall, J. "Doing It by the Numbers." *Sports Illustrated* 40 (1974): 40–49.

5. Harville, D. "Predictions for National Football League Games via Linear Model Methodology." *Journal of the American Statistical Association* 75 (1980): 516–24.

6. Morris, C. "Football Ratings and Predictions: Discussion." *Proceedings of the American Statistical Association, Social Statistics Section*, 1978, 87–88.

Predicting the Winner

Together we fall.

n Presidential Campaigns

This study analyzes data on the U.S. presidential elections from 1900 to 1980. Objectives are to estimate the posterior probability that the incumbent party candidate will win the election and to predict the percentage of the two-party, popular vote to be received by the incumbent party candidate. The predictions are based on the change in unemployment over the four-year period prior to the election and the degree to which the incumbent party is unified—as measured by the percentage of votes received by the incumbent candidate on the first ballot at the nominating convention. Variables that are unique to a particular election can be incorporated in the model through the Bayesian prior probabilities.

1.0 Introduction

1.1 Historians and Laws of History

The data for this study, presented in Table 7.1, are based on the U.S. presidential elections from the years 1900 to 1980. The study is designed to estimate the posterior probability that the incumbent party candidate will win the election and to predict the percentage of the two-party (Democrat and Republican), popular vote to be received by the incumbent party candidate.

Two considerations pervade the modeling of historical events: the reliability of the assembled data and the views of historians on modeling. On the subject of historical modeling (which may be described as uncovering "laws of history"), historians tend to fall into two groups: nomothetic and idiographic.[1] Nomothetic historians are those who attempt to

TABLE 7.1 Data and Variable Designation: Presidential Elections from 1900 to 1980

Election year	Incumbent v. opposition candidate (party)[a]	Variables[b]							
		V	U_I	U_o	E	S	H	C	I
1900	McKinley* (R) v. Bryan	.532	1.000	1.000	-.094	.876	-.053	.000	1
1904	T. Roosevelt* (R) v. Parker	.600	1.000	.658	.004	.750	.031	.020	1
1908	Taft* (R) v. Bryan	.545	.716	.887	.026	.726	-.073	.000	0
1912	Taft (R) v. Wilson*	.357	.516	.298	-.034	.486	-.148	.020	1
1916	Wilson* (D) v. Hughes	.517	.999	.257	.005	.483	-.140	.037	0
1920	Cox (D) v. Harding*	.362	.122	.067	.001	.213	-.060	.273	1
1924	Coolidge* (R) v. Davis	.652	.960	.028	-.002	.784	-.176	-.088	1
1928	Hoover* (R) v. Smith	.588	.769	.659	-.008	.539	-.023	-.001	0
1932	Hoover (R) v. F. Roosevelt*	.409	.976	.577	.194	.564	-.122	-.104	1
1936	F. Roosevelt* (D) v. Landon	.625	1.000	.981	-.067	.369	.021	-.006	1
1940	F. Roosevelt* (D) v. Wilkie	.550	.860	.105	-.023	.446	-.162	.005	1
1944	F. Roosevelt* (D) v. Dewey	.538	.923	.997	-.134	.434	-.115	.107	1
1948	Truman* (D) v. Dewey	.523	.750	.397	.026	.563	-.124	.194	1
1952	Stevenson (D) v. Eisenhower*	.446	.222	.493	-.008	.432	-.067	.074	0
1956	Eisenhower* (R) v. Stevenson	.578	1.000	.660	.011	.604	-.042	.019	1
1960	Nixon (R) v. Kennedy*	.499	.992	.530	.014	.508	-.109	.073	0
1964	Johnson* (D) v. Goldwater	.613	1.000	.675	-.003	.353	-.011	.042	1
1968	Humphrey (D) v. Nixon*	.496	.671	.519	-.016	.313	-.113	.113	0
1972	Nixon* (R) v. McGovern	.618	.999	.573	.020	.509	-.028	.211	1
1976	Ford (R) v. Carter*	.490	.525	.744	.021	.495	-.110	.452	1
1980	Carter (D) v. Reagan*	.447	.637	.972	-.006	.502	-.037	.763	1

[a]The winner is designated by an asterisk.

[b] V = proportion of two-party, popular presidential vote received by incumbent party candidate.
U_I = proportion of first ballot vote received by incumbent candidate at nominating convention.
U_o = proportion of first ballot vote received by opposition candidate at nominating convention.
E = proportional change in annual unemployment rate during the four-year period preceding the election.
S = proportion of two-party campaign spending on presidential election by incumbent party.
H = proportional change in House seats for incumbent party due to congressional elections held two years before the presidential election.
C = proportional change in the consumer price index for all items during the four-year period preceding the election.
I = 1 if the incumbent candidate is the president; I = 0 otherwise.

discover and postulate fundamental regularities in the overall pattern of historical events. Idiographic historians doubt the existence of laws; or at the very least, they believe that the discovery or validation of such laws is impossible.

Generally, idiographic opposition to nomothetic views is based on two arguments. First, it is purportedly easy to find historical events that contradict nomothetic conclusions. Second, every historical event is a unique change dominated by unique individuals—individuals such as Alexander the Great, Napoleon Bonaparte, and Adolf Hitler. Indeed, "the facts of history are peculiar . . . individual, concrete, unrepeatable events and entities"[2] and are not subject to unified interpretations. In the same vein, though germane to the presidential sweepstakes, Bean in his book *How to Predict the 1972 Election*[3] emphasizes that each presidential election is influenced by variables unique to that particular (unique) election.

A response to the first idiographic argument is that any stochastic model admits anomalies; the fewer, of course, the better. The second argument seems to be given, possibly, in ignorance of stochastic modeling in general and Bayesian inference in particular. Consider a historical event characterized by appropriate dependent and predictor variables. In terms of their effect on a dependent variable, predictor variables that are unique to a particular event can be quantified in two ways: (1) in terms of variables that not only are non-unique but convey the same meaning between events and/or (2) in terms of Bayesian priors when the non-unique variables do not adequately reflect some of the unique variables. Based on the combination of non-unique predictor variables and Bayesian priors, unique events can be adjusted so that they become, approximately, a series of non-unique events. This adjustment process underlies the stochastic modeling of historical events.

A historian's response to idiographic views is provided by Cheyney, who rejected explanations of historical events that were based on personal factors: "Human history, like the stars, has been controlled by immutable, self-existent laws, by what Mr. Gladstone in his sonorous eloquence once described in Parliament as 'those great social forces which move on in their might and majesty, and which the tumult of our debates does not for a moment impede or disturb.'"[4]

1.2 Allied Studies

The variables under consideration (see Table 7.1) are drawn from a study by Taylor.[5] The dependent variables are defined in terms of the incumbent party candidate versus the opposition party candidate—as opposed to the Democratic candidate versus the Republican candidate. This definition, used by both Taylor and political historian Allen Lichtman, is based on the premise that over the years philosophies of the parties have fluctuated and interchanged (e.g., U.S. Senator Henry Cabot Lodge, a Republican, and his Senate cohorts blocked America's entry into the League of Nations; but Lodge's son, also a Republican, became America's ambassador to the United Nations). Under this definition, two dependent variables of interest are whether the incumbent party candidate wins and the percentage of the two-party, popular vote received by said candidate.

According to Lichtman's model, which uses 13 "keys" (predictors), the incumbent party candidate will win unless more than five of the indicators go against him. David S. Broder, columnist for the *Washington Post,* described Lichtman's predictors in his column early in the 1984 election year.

I called Lichtman and asked him how things were looking for Ronald Reagan. . . . He said that so far only two of the keys have turned against the Republicans. . . . Reagan cannot claim a major success in foreign or military policy. Also the yearly mean per-capita rate of growth in real gross national product has been slightly lower than that of the previous administration. . . . The other keys are all turned in Reagan's favor: Republicans did win 51 percent of the popular vote in the previous election; Reagan is . . . running for re-election; he did initiate major changes in national policy; and he is charismatic; . . . he does not face a serious contest for the nomination; there is not, at this point, what Lichtman regards as major third-party or independent campaign activity; there is no election year recession . . . in the forecasts; there has not been a major social unrest; nor a major scandal; nor a major setback in foreign or military policy; nor will the opposition nominate a charismatic candidate or war hero, if the polls putting Walter F. Mondale in front are right.

Broder points out that in the spring of 1981, Lichtman "sat down with Volodia Keilis-Borok of Moscow's Academy of Sciences, a specialist in earthquake analysis, and together they contrived [the model] . . . which correctly predicted every presidential election in the last 120 years."[6]

Taylor's model uses variables that reflect the degrees to which opposing parties are unified behind their respective candidates. The unification variables are measured in terms of the percentage of votes received by each of the opposing presidential candidates on the first ballot at their respective nominating conventions. The implication is that the unification variables are a partial reflection of Lichtman's predictors. A reanalysis of Taylor's data is presented in the following section.

2.0 Modeling: Procedures and Results

2.1 The Variables

Of the variables listed in Table 7.1, data for U_I and U_O are obtained from the *Congressional Quarterly*.[7] Three variables are given in terms of proportional change: in the annual employment rate and consumer price index (each over the four-year period preceding the election) and in the number of House seats won or lost by the incumbent party in the congressional elections preceding the presidential election. The reason changes are utilized as opposed to absolute figures is that over longer periods of time changes tend to have more stable interpretations than absolute figures.

The variables' lack of stability can be a major problem in historical modeling. A variable may change in interpretation and/or in assessment over time (such as the roles of blacks, Hispanics, and women and the perceived accomplishments and personal characteristics of the candidates). New variables may become important (such as televised debates and public opinion polls), and other variables, once significant in their effect, may become obsolete (such as the "Solid South" and the Anti-Saloon League of America). These difficulties become more pronounced as the time span under study increases. This is one reason elections prior to 1900 were not included in the data base.

Transformed variables are included in the data base. The variable $W = 1$ if the incumbent candidate wins the election and $W = 0$ otherwise. The variable ET, a transform of E, is defined as follows: $ET = -2$ if $E < -.10$; $ET = -1$ if $-.10 \leq E \leq -.05$; $ET = 0$ if $-.05 \leq E \leq .05$; $ET = 1$ if $.05 \leq E \leq .10$; $ET = 2$ if $E > .10$. The ET transform is intended to dampen two extreme values of E: those for the 1932 and 1944 elections. Without these extreme values, E would have little, if any, effect on the selected dependent variables. Simple correlations between all the variables are presented in Table 7.2.

2.2 Results of Discriminant Analysis

With W as the categorical dependent variable, the conventional discriminant analysis is applied to the data in Table 7.1. As determined through the scanning procedure in BMDP7M,[8] the variables U_I and ET enter as significant predictors. Under uniform priors, the posterior probability that the incumbent party candidate wins is estimated by

$$P(W \mid U_I, \ ET) = [1 + \exp(7.043 - 9.291 U_I + 1.985 ET)]^{-1} \quad \textbf{(7.1)}$$

TABLE 7.2. Matrix of Simple Correlations between Variables in Table 7.1

	V	U_I	U_O	E	S	H	C	I	ET	W
V	(.084)									
U_I	.693	(.264)								
U_O	.204	.269	(.303)							
E	−.239	.003	−.267	(.067)						
S	.357	.447	.203	.054	(.161)					
H	.331	.109	.572	−.128	−.010	(.059)				
C	−.311	−.414	.230	−.061	−.283	.137	(.196)			
I	.261	.516	.105	−.053	.267	−.056	.055	(.463)		
ET	−.315	−.084	−.393	.955	.026	−.169	−.079	−.088	(.700)	
W	.816	.638	.133	−.322	.412	.227	−.420	.372	−.396	(.498)

Note: Standard deviations (in parentheses) are given as diagonal elements.

(see Eq. [14.9] in Chap. 14). Based on model (7.1), the estimated posterior probabilities for each of the 21 elections are given in Table 7.3 under the headings Conventional Discriminant Analysis and No JK (i.e., "no jackknife" means that the model is based on the full sample). Jackknifed probabilities are presented alongside the full-sample probabilities. Using the classification rule that the incumbent candidate is the predicted winner if $P(W \mid U_I, ET) > .50$, we see that jackknifed and full-sample results are the same with the exception of the 1932 election. This discrepancy is a result of the single, extreme, positive change in unemployment due to the depression. The discrepancy illustrates how a single extreme value can influence the resulting model.

Recall that the conventional analysis is based on the assumption that the variance-covariance matrix of (U_I, ET) is the same between winning and losing incumbents. Examination of the following estimates shows this assumption to be invalid.

Estimates of—	Winning population	Losing population
Variance U_I	.01192	.09758
Variance ET	.39720	.4954
Correlation (U_I, ET)	−.19506	.50882
Sample size	13	8

Application of standard, univariate tests shows that only variance ET conforms to the assumption. For U_I, the variance of the losing population is larger than that of the winning population. The simple correlations differ between populations. For the winning population, party unity is marginally related to the change in unemployment. Unfortunately, the positive correlation for the losing population is due largely to the 1932 election.

To account for the differences, we perform a quadratic discriminant analysis using uniform priors, U_I and ET as predictors, and a pooled vari-

TABLE 7.3. Posterior Probability of the Incumbent Candidate Winning (PPIW) Conditional on U_I, CT, and Uniform Priors

Election year	Incumbent v. opposition candidate (party)	PPIW — Conventional discriminant analysis JK	PPIW — Conventional discriminant analysis No JK	PPIW — Quadratic discriminant analysis, no JK	V — Regression analysis Obs.	V — Regression analysis Pre.
1900	McKinley* (R) v. Bryan	.985	.986	.985	.532	.595
1904	T. Roosevelt* (R) v. Parker	.892	.904	.892	.600	.564
1908	Taft* (R) v. Bryan	.368 M	.403 M	.390 M	.545	.504
1912	Taft* (R) v. Wilson*	.109	.095	.002	.357	.461
1916	Wilson* (D) v. Hughes	.891	.904	.909	.517	.564
1920	Cox (D) v. Harding*	.001	.003	.000	.362	.378
1924	Coolidge* (R) v. Davis	.853	.867	.925	.652	.556
1928	Hoover* (R) v. Smith	.504	.525	.700	.588	.515
1932	Hoover (R) v. F. Roosevelt*	.729 M	.125	.000	.409	.497
1936	F. Roosevelt* (D) v. Landon	.985	.986	.985	.625	.595
1940	F. Roosevelt* (D) v. Wilkie	.706	.720	.910	.550	.534
1944	F. Roosevelt* (D) v. Dewey	.999	.996	.985	.538	.610
1948	Truman* (D) v. Dewey	.456 M	.481 M	.530	.523	.511
1952	Stevenson (D) v. Eisenhower*	.006	.007	.000	.446	.399
1956	Eisenhower* (R) v. Stevenson	.892	.904	.891	.578	.564
1960	Nixon (R) v. Kennedy*	.979 M	.898 M	.882 M	.499	.562 M
1964	Johnson* (D) v. Goldwater	.892	.904	.928	.613	.564
1968	Humphrey (D) v. Nixon*	.327	.308	.240	.496	.494
1972	Nixon* (R) v. McGovern	.891	.904	.857	.618	.564
1976	Ford (R) v. Carter*	.117	.103	.005	.490	.463
1980	Carter (D) v. Reagan*	.261	.245	.116	.447	.487

Note: Probabilities are based on the jackknife technique (JK) and/or on the full sample (no JK). Per analysis, results include observed and predicted values—conditional on U_I and CT—of the two-party, popular vote received by the incumbent candidate.
M indicates a misclassification in that a winning candidate is projected to lose or a losing candidate is projected to win.

ance estimate for variance ET (see model [14.14] in Chap. 14). Results of this analysis are presented in Table 7.3.

In terms of the simple classification rule used for the conventional analysis, there is an improvement for one event: the 1948 election. Overall, however, the posterior probabilities are quite similar between the conventional and quadratic analyses with no jackknife. This result is supportive of Monte Carlo studies that indicate that the conventional analysis is robust under moderate heteroscedasticity.

2.3   Results of Regression Analysis

Stepwise regression analysis (BMDP2R)[8] is applied in modeling V. With $\hat{V}$ denoting the predicted value of V, the resulting prediction equation is

$$\hat{V} = .3516 + .2121U_I - .03091ET \qquad (7.2)$$
$$\phantom{\hat{V} = .3516 + }(.0504) \quad\ (.0190)$$

where $R^2 = .55$ and standard errors are in parentheses. Observed and predicted values of V are given in Table 7.3. Under the rule that the incumbent candidate is the projected winner if $V > .50$, we see that only the Nixon-Kennedy election is misclassified. Results of regression are superior to those of discriminant analysis (assuming uniform priors in the latter analysis and diffuse priors[9] for the coefficients and error variance in the regression analysis).

Because U_I is the dominant predictor in both models, it is of interest to establish which of the other variables U_I reflects. Accordingly, a stepwise regression analysis (BMDP2R) was performed with U_I as the dependent variable. With $\hat{U}_I$ denoting the predicted value of U_I, the resulting prediction equation is

$$\hat{V}_I = .4908 + .2918U_O + .2905I - .6992C \qquad (7.3)$$
$$\phantom{\hat{V}_I = .4908 + }(.1433) \quad\ (.0915) \quad (.2211)$$

where $R^2 = .57$ and standard errors are in parentheses. Thus, the incumbent party tends to be more unified if the president is up for reelection, if the consumer price index has decreased during his administration, and if the opposition party is unified.

2.4   Discussion of Analysis Results

In both the regression and the discriminant analyses, U_I is the dominant predictor. Its effect is illustrated as follows. For the conventional

TABLE 7.4. Posterior Probability of Incumbent Winning

ET	U_I			
	.7	.8	.9	1.0
−1	.809	.915	.995	.986
0	.368	.596	.789	.904
1	.074	.169	.339	.565

analysis (with uniform priors), Table 7.4 shows an exercise of model (7.1). Thus, for the typical situation of $CT = 0$, the performance of incumbent party candidate on the first ballot has a pronounced effect on his chances of winning the election.

For the 1984 election—which was excluded from model building— Ronald Reagan, the president and incumbent party candidate, received 2,233 of 2,235 votes on the first ballot at the Republican nominating convention. Based on model (7.2), Reagan's percentage of the two-party, popular vote was projected as $.3516 + .2121(2233/2235) - .0391(0) = 56.35\%$. He received 59.17% of the vote.

Based on the predictions in Table 7.3, the Nixon-Kennedy election was consistently misclassified. It has been conjectured that several unique variables affected the outcome—variables that were not reflected by either U_I or CT. These variables include the role of television in general and the televised debates in particular and Nixon's allocation of campaign resources. Regarding the last variable, Nixon kept his promise of visiting all 50 states during the campaign. This, according to Brams,[10] was ill-advised because the seven most populous states (with 39% of the vote in the electoral college) should have received 57% of a candidate's time and resources.

In the 1960 election, relevant unique variables were obviously not adequately reflected by U_I and CT. Accordingly, their effect could have been incorporated in the model through the Bayesian prior probability. Given that the unique variables were to Nixon's detriment, what prior probability (of Nixon's winning the election) would have reduced Nixon's posterior probability of winning to .50? Based on the conventional analysis (using model [14.3] in Chap. 14), a prior probability of .102 would have made the election result a toss-up. A smaller prior would have tilted the odds in favor of Kennedy.

Exercise 1

Develop an aggregate model predicting changes in party proportions after the congressional elections for the U.S. Senate and House of Representatives.

Define appropriate dependent and independent variables that should be considered. Identify methods of analysis.

References

1. Naroll, R., Bullough, V. L., and Naroll, F. *Military Deterrence History*. Albany: State University of New York Press, 1974.

2. Meyerhoff, H., ed. *The Philosophy of History in Our Time*. New York: Doubleday, 1959. (Quotation, p. 162.)

3. Bean, L. *How to Predict the 1972 Election*. New York: Quadrangle Books, 1972.

4. Ausubel, H. *Historians and Their Craft*. New York: Columbia University Press, 1950. (Quotation, p. 76.)

5. Taylor, B. "Predicting Outcomes of United States Presidential Elections," Master's thesis, California State University, Fresno, 1987.

6. Broder, D. S. "Indicators Favor Reagan." *Fresno Bee,* 2 January 1984, B11.

7. "National Party Conventions 1831–1976." *Congressional Quarterly* 35 (1979).

8. Dixon, W. J., ed. *BMDP Statistical Software*. Berkeley and Los Angeles: University of California Press, 1985.

9. Zellner, A. *An Introduction to Bayesian Inference in Econometrics*. New York: Wiley, 1971.

10. Brams, S. J. *The Presidential Election Game*. New Haven: Yale University Press, 1978.

8

A Marketing Mode

Synergism.

A marketing model is developed here for estimating the odds of winning a contract under a system of closed bidding. Consider the situation where a company submits a proposal in response to a request for proposal (RFP) by a government agency. Throughout the marketing effort, the company schedules periodic, internal reviews of its chances of winning the contract. These reviews are important because the win probability affects forecasts of future revenues and personnel requirements, hiring schedules, marketing strategies and the allocation of marketing monies, and the "best and final bid," when the agency selects finalists among the bidders.

The model is based on assessments by cognizant marketing personnel. Assessments are standardized in terms of answers to a marketing questionnaire. Questionnaire responses and the nature of the competition are used as predictors in a Bayesian discriminant analysis. The dependent variable is binary: winning or not winning the contract. Ad hoc information, such as insider information, is quantified in terms of the prior probability.

The fitted marketing model is applicable only to a specific company and reflects the abilities of the marketing personnel to properly assess the potential of each proposal. If a viable model cannot be developed through this approach, one must question the competence of the company's marketing organization.

1.0 Competitive Bidding

Consider the situation where a government agency solicits bids for a contract to render a service. Opposing bidders compete for such opportunities under rules established by the agency. The bidding is assumed closed (as opposed to the open bidding of an auction), and generally, the competition is relatively pure, at least with respect to a subset of the bidders (e.g., unqualified bidders may be disqualified through an initial screening of the proposals).

A company—whom we shall call M Corporation—responds to the RFP by submitting a proposal. What are its chances of winning? The question is relevant for several reasons. First, the win probability affects hiring schedules and forecasts of future revenues and personnel requirements. Second, the chances of success for proposals in new marketing areas affect future allocations of marketing monies. Low or high probabilities may indicate the need for revised strategies in these areas. Third, there may be an opportunity to revise the proposal before the final award; the contracting agency may select finalists among the bidders and request a best and final bid. A finalist with knowledge of its chances of winning prior to this final bid is in an enhanced position.

2.0   Models Based on the Lowest Bid

In responding to an RFP, bidders may have differing objectives in mind. A bidder may seek to maximize expected profits, to minimize expected losses, to regain a certain percentage of an investment, to minimize competitors' profits, or to gain a foothold with the contracting agency through lowballing (attempting to obtain the contract at a loss). The contracting agency's objectives are reflected by the criteria used to select the winning proposal. General criteria include (1) the company's qualifications, (2) its approach to the problem defined in the RFP, and (3) the dollar bid.

Churchman et al.[1] present a model for estimating win probabilities based on the premise that the lowest bidder wins. This premise may or may not be realistic, depending on the bidders' objectives and the contracting agency's weighting of the selection criteria. Churchman et al.'s approach is as follows. Let c and κ denote, respectively, the M Corporation estimate and the true cost of fulfilling the contract, and set $r = c/\kappa$. Let $h(r)$, b, and $P(b)$ denote, respectively, the probability density function (pdf) of r, the amount bid for the contract, and the probability that a bid b will be the lowest (winning) bid.

If the bid b wins, the ultimate profit will be $\pi = b - (rc) = b - \kappa$. The expected profit for a bid b is

$$E(\pi) = \int_0^\infty P(b)[b - (rc)]h(r)\,dr$$

Churchman et al. make the simplifying assumption that $P(b)$ and r are independent, whereupon

$$E(\pi) = P(b)(b - c^*) \quad \text{where} \quad c^* = c \int_0^\infty rh(r)\,dr = cE(r)$$

is the estimated cost corrected for bias. In order to choose b such that $E(\pi)$ is maximized, $P(b)$ must first be specified. Churchman et al. determine $P(b)$ as follows. Let R_i denote the ratio of the ith competitor's bid to the M Corporation cost estimate, c. If $g(R_i)$ denotes the pdf of R_i, then

$$\int_{b/c}^\infty g(R_i)\,dR_i = \pi_i$$

is the probability that M Corporation's bid is lower than the ith competitor's bid. If, say, n competitors are known exactly, the probability that the M Corporation bid is lower than all n bids is

$$P(b) = \pi_i \ldots \pi_i \ldots \pi_n$$

For the case where some of the competitors are unknown, Churchman et al. use the concept of an "average" bidder, where R_a replaces R_i as the value for the average bidder and $g(R_a)$ is the pdf of R_a. The probability that the M Corporation bid is lower than that of one average bidder is

$$\int_{b/c}^\infty g(R_a)\,dR_a = \pi_a$$

and the probability that the M Corporation bid is lower than those of n average bidders is $(\pi_a)^n$. Let $h(n)$ denote the pdf of n so that

$$P(b) = \sum_{n=0}^\infty h(n)(\pi_a)^n$$

Churchman et al. choose $h(n)$ as a Poisson pdf,

$$h(n) = \exp(-\lambda)\lambda^n/n!$$

and $g(R_a)$ as a gamma pdf,

$$g(R_a) = (\alpha^{\beta+1}/\beta!)(R_a)^{\beta} \exp(-\alpha R_a)$$

so that $P(b)$ becomes the cumulative of a Poisson pdf:

$$P(b) = \exp\left[-\lambda\{1 - \exp(-\alpha R_a)\sum_{i=0}^{\beta} (\alpha R_a)^i/i!\}\right]$$

Data from past bids can be used to test the adequacy of the pdf's chosen for $h(n)$ and $g(R_a)$.

3.0   Models Based on Marketing Assessments

3.1   A Marketing Questionnaire

Most contractors adhere to the marketing fundamentals contained in the following path diagram:

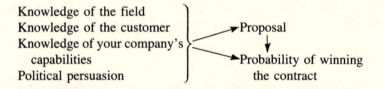

The proposal should reflect the factors on the left-hand side of the diagram. These factors and the dollar bid may affect the probability of winning the contract both directly and indirectly. Through the factor of political persuasion, the bidder seeks to establish that it can make the most constructive contribution to the customer's needs.

Factors on the left-hand side of the diagram can be partially quantified in terms of answers to the marketing questionnaire in Table 8.1. These responses, plus the nature of the competition, are used as predictors in estimating win probabilities.

3.2   The Competition

Since the nature of the competition is paramount in modeling win probabilities, each of M Corporation's competitors is grouped into one of five mutually exclusive categories per proposal: a frequent competitor (competing with M Corporation at least 10 times over the past two years), a relatively frequent competitor (competing from 5 to 9 times), a relatively infrequent competitor (competing from 2 to 4 times), an infrequent

TABLE 8.1. M Corporation Marketing Questionnaire

Contracting agency: Internal Revenue Service
Title: Assess existing designs for computer security systems
Date:
Rated by:

	Yes	No
1. Did we know any of the details of the RFP before we received it?		×
2. Do we know the technical people?	×	
3. Were we invited to bid?		×
4. Have we marketed the agency in depth?		×
5. Are our experience and reputation really credible?	×	
6. Did we know the funding level?		×
7. Did we have to bid it in any case?		×
8. What is the major competition? Booz Allen, General Electric, Research Triangle Institute, TRW		

Comments by rater:
The contract requirements coupled with no designated level of effort will result in a broad range of responses in terms of scope and price. The critical question is how thorough a job IRS wants. Our proposal gives IRS the needed answers. However, the danger lies in their willingness to accept less. The four competitors listed above appeared to be the most viable at the pre-bid conference.

competitor (competing at most 1 time), and unknown. Clearly, a competitor's designation is subject to change, especially when M Corporation enters and establishes a foothold in new marketing areas.

M Corporation's frequent competitors include Boeing, GE, SRI, GRC, SAI, CSC, and TRW. Relatively frequent competitors include ADL, Booz Allen, EGG, PRC, and SDC. Proposals under discussion are in response to RFPs issued by agencies of the Department of Defense and the National Regulatory Commission.

3.3 Modeling Procedure

The data under study include 46 winning bids and 115 losing bids during the two-year period 1980–81. For each proposal at least one and usually not more than four cognizant marketing team members responded to the questionnaire in Table 8.1. When responses to a question differed, the modal response was taken. This response provides better predictions than either the average response or the response of the individual in charge of the proposal effort.

Bayesian discriminant analysis is applied in modeling the binary dependent variable: M Corporation either wins or does not win the contract. Because questionnaire responses are used as predictors and because a multivariate normal pdf is assumed for the predictors, the marketing re-

sponses are converted to principal components. (The principal components are symmetrically distributed, which tends to support the normality
assumption.) Results of the principal component analysis are given in
Table 8.2, which contains eigenroots and eigenvectors of the 7×7 correlation matrix corresponding to the first seven questions in Table 8.1.
(The responses are quantified as follows: yes $= 1$, no $= -1$, and no
response $= 0$.)

Another set of predictors is based on the competition, which is quantified as follows:

$c(1)$ = percentage of the competition that is frequent,
$c(2)$ = percentage of the competition that is relatively frequent,
$c(3)$ = percentage of the competition that is relatively infrequent,
$c(4)$ = percentage of the competition that is infrequent,
$c(5)$ = percentage of the competition that is unknown.

The competition was completely unknown in 16% of the bids.

First- and second-order terms are scanned for significance through
stepwise discriminant analysis (BMDP7M).[2] The first-order terms include
the principal components and the c variables. Second-order terms include
all two-factor interactions between first-order terms. Sample covariance
matrices (for predictors) between winning and losing proposals are pooled
since a test of dispersion homogeneity is not rejected. Moreover, uniform
prior probabilities are utilized in selecting predictors. (Uniform priors lead
to better predictions than non-uniform priors according to past frequencies
of winning and losing proposals.) Non-uniform priors are utilized in M

TABLE 8.2. Principal Component Analysis of the First Seven Questions in Table 8.1

Question	Eigenvectors						
	1	2	3	4	5	6	7
1	−.4686	.0142	−.1807	.2053	−.5508	−.0893	−.6277
2	−.4340	.2618	.0022	−.5166	.2211	−.6511	.0589
3	−.4609	−.2275	−.0112	.4256	−.2241	−.1351	.6972
4	−.4144	.1210	.4425	−.4354	−.1713	.6230	.1040
5	.0459	.6914	.5210	.4802	.0478	−.1190	−.0366
6	−.2854	.4332	−.6340	.1507	.3968	.3822	.0521
7	−.3527	−.4463	.3129	.2587	.6391	.0396	−.3187
Eigenroots	2.4159	1.1197	.9744	.8050	.6766	.5159	.4926
Percentage of original variation explained	34.5	50.5	64.4	75.9	85.6	93.0	100.0

Corporation's periodic, internal reviews of proposals outstanding, where new information (leaks, insider information, etc.) is quantified in terms of non-uniform prior probabilities. The issue is the extent to which the new information changes the posterior probability based on uniform priors.

3.4 Analysis Results

Among dominant predictors, certain interactions are particularly significant. Specifically, the effect (on winning) of positive responses to questions 1 through 7 differs depending on the nature of the competition. Positive responses in the presence of frequent competition indicate a high probability of winning. The win probability decreases as the competition becomes less frequent. Another significant interaction indicates that the effect (on winning) of knowing the agency's technical personnel (question 2) differs depending on the perceived credibility of M Corporation (question 5).

Regarding model validity, the jackknifed classification is given in Table 8.3 along with the jackknifed predictions for the 46 winning bids. For each jackknifed prediction, the Mahalanobis D^2 distance is given alongside the posterior probability (based on uniform priors). Probabilities based on relatively large D^2 values are used with caution.

According to the classification rule used in BMDP7M, a bid is classified as a win if its win probability is greater than its lose probability. Based on this rule, the model correctly predicts the outcome of approximately 75% of the proposals. However, the M Corporation classification rule is variable and based on circumstances accompanying the particular proposal (such as the size of the bid and the importance of the contract). Moreover, the posterior probabilities change as new information is introduced in the form of non-uniform priors.

3.5 Model Exercise

The model is exercised to illustrate effects of changes in selected questionnaire responses. Results are presented in Table 8.4. If questions 1 through 7 are answered yes, the win probability ranges from .81 when the competition is primarily frequent (defined as 75% frequent competitors and 25% relatively frequent competitors) to .21 when the competition is primarily infrequent (defined as 25% relatively infrequent competitors and 75% infrequent competitors). These results indicate that M Corporation does well when it competes in its fields of specialization against frequent competitors. When the competition is infrequent, an implication is that M Corporation is competing in an area in which it is not established or has insufficient expertise.

TABLE 8.3. Jackknife Classification and Posterior Probabilities for Winning Proposals

A. Jackknife classification			
	Number of proposals classified into—		Correct classification
Population	Win population	Lose population	
Winning proposals	34	12	73.9%
Losing proposals	28	87	75.7%

B. Winning proposals									
Proposal	D^2	Win prob.	D^2	Lose prob.	Proposal	D^2	Win prob.	D^2	Lose prob.
1	1.1	.865	4.8	.135	24*	10.6	.055	4.9	.945
2*	4.5	.499	4.5	.501	25	24.0	.530	24.3	.470
3	8.8	.954	14.9	.046	26	4.3	.827	7.5	.173
4	4.8	.844	8.2	.156	27	.8	.841	4.2	.153
5	2.0	.561	2.5	.439	28	67.5	.771	69.9	.229
6	3.4	.681	4.9	.319	29*	2.3	.327	.8	.673
7	1.7	.607	2.6	.393	30*	2.0	.424	1.4	.576
8*	5.6	.386	4.7	.614	31	.4	.805	3.2	.195
9	1.4	.677	2.8	.323	32	14.0	.950	19.9	.050
10	10.4	.950	16.3	.050	33	1.9	.845	5.2	.155
11	.9	.566	1.4	.434	34*	5.1	.175	2.0	.825
12*	5.6	.437	5.1	.563	35	1.9	.834	5.1	.166
13	14.7	.719	16.6	.281	36*	4.5	.365	3.4	.635
14	1.0	.766	3.4	.234	37*	3.1	.441	2.6	.559
15	1.0	.732	3.0	.268	38	1.4	.597	2.1	.403
16	2.2	.712	4.0	.288	39	2.6	.531	2.8	.469
17*	5.3	.220	2.8	.780	40	2.7	.837	6.0	.163
18	6.4	.703	8.2	.297	41	3.9	.614	4.9	.386
19*	13.0	.387	12.0	.613	42	8.5	.940	14.0	.060
20	25.7	.912	30.4	.088	43	8.5	.940	14.0	.060
21	53.8	.996	65.1	.004	44	45.5	.992	55.0	.008
22*	62.6	.298	60.9	.702	45	8.7	.545	9.0	.455
23	5.0	.776	7.4	.224	46	1.1	.587	1.8	.413

Note: An asterisk indicates an incorrect classification.

When the competition is unknown, the win probability drops to .13 even though questions 1 through 7 are answered positively. This may indicate situations where the marketing staff have not researched the matter adequately, which usually results in a losing bid. Or, perhaps the agency has the contract reserved for a competitor who remains anonymous.

The negative response to question 7 (and positive responses to the others), accompanied by primarily frequent competition, yields a higher win probability, .91, than when all questions are answered positively. This peculiarity is explained by situations where M Corporation's reputation is so well established with a particular agency that they do not have to bid on each of the agency's RFPs. Usually, M Corporation will bid on each of an agency's RFPs when it is striving to maintain or strengthen its position.

TABLE 8.4. Model Exercise

Win probability	Competition (%)			
	Freq.	Rel. freq.	Rel. infreq.	Infreq.
Yes to Q 1–Q 7:				
.81	75	25	0	0
.65	25	25	25	25
.21	0	0	25	75
.13		Unknown		
No to Q 7, yes to others:				
.91	75	25	0	0
No to Q 3, yes to others:				
.23	75	25	0	0

Note: Questions from Table 8.1:
Q 1: Know details before?   Q 5: Experience credible?
Q 2: Know technical people?   Q 6: Know funding level?
Q 3: Invited to bid?   Q 7: Have to bid it?
Q 4: Marketed agency in depth?

The .23 win probability resulting from a negative response to question 3 (and positive responses to the others) illustrates the importance of being asked to bid. This result supports the adage that "if you learn about the RFP for the first time in the *Commerce Business Daily,* it's too late."

3.6   Remarks

Though our modeling approach has general application, the fitted model is applicable only to M Corporation. The main reason is that model validity is a reflection of the marketing staff's competence—which varies between companies. Indeed, if a viable model cannot be developed through this approach, fault lies with the marketing organization.

The model should be updated periodically with new data replacing older data to accommodate (1) turnover in marketing personnel, (2) changing roles of competitors regarding the frequency with which they are encountered in the bidding process, and (3) possible changes in M Corporation marketing policies.

In reviewing the status of proposals outstanding, one should anticipate and incorporate ad hoc information in the prior probabilities. The sensitivity of the posterior probability to varying priors can thus be evaluated.

The model can be improved by considering additional factors as predictors: (1) What are the buying patterns of the contracting agency? (2) What are the competition's traits; for example, do they lowball? (3) What are the agency's procurement rules and evaluation criteria? (4) Is the current proposal one of several bids to the same agency? (5) Will there be a best and final bid?

Exercise 1

You are personnel director for a large corporation whose business is based on government and commercial contracts. In making a decision to hire experienced individuals applying for marketing positions, you would like a model that forecasts each applicant's future professional success, if hired. Define possible dependent variables, independent variables, method of analysis, and data requirements.

References

1. Churchman, C. W., Ackoff, R. L., and Arnoff, E. L. *Introduction to Operations Research*. New York: Wiley, 1975.

2. Dixon, W. J., ed. *BMDP Statistical Software*. Los Angeles: University of California Press, 1985.

9

Smiles and profiles in bankruptcy.

ofiles in Bankruptcy

An individual applies for a loan from a financial institution. What are the odds the individual will eventually default and file for bankruptcy under Chapter 7 or 13? This study develops a model profiling bankruptcy. The model is based on Bayesian discriminant analysis and includes age, debt ratio, length of time in the current job, and credit rating as dominant predictors. The chances of default are shown to decrease with increased age, lower debt ratios, and higher credit ratings. On a per case basis, supplementary information, if any, is incorporated in the posterior probability of default through the Bayesian prior probability; uniform priors are utilized in the absence of supplementary information.

1.0   Introduction

1.1   The Bankruptcy Reform Act of 1979

In attempting to provide a workable system of debt relief, Congress enacted the Bankruptcy Reform Act of 1979. The Bankruptcy Code,[1] contained in the first title of the act, contains eight chapters. Chapters 1, 3, and 5 contain general provisions applying to all bankruptcy cases. For most debtors, the choice is among Chapters 7, 11, and 13. Chapter 7 provides that a debtor's nonexempt assets are liquidated and the proceeds divided among the creditors. Chapter 11 concerns business organizations and is an appropriate recourse when a business is having temporary difficulties due to a business cycle. Chapter 13 allows debtors to develop a plan to pay off debts over a period of time, now five years. Because Chapter 13 is usually voluntary, it is termed the "gentleman's bankruptcy."

Since the act makes it easier for an individual to file for bankruptcy and retain assets, bankruptcy seems to have become an acceptable business practice for many debtors. The act has been faulted, along with inflation, unemployment, and high levels of real interest rates, for the record number of bankruptcies. It has also been noted that bankruptcies "became the domain of a new generation of imaginative deal makers. . . . [S]ome of the nation's most expensive lawyers . . . discovered . . . profitable enterprise."[2]

1.2 The Current Study

This study focuses on individuals obtaining small loans from financial institutions and subsequently filing for bankruptcy under Chapter 7 or 13. The decision to grant or refuse credit is based on the creditor's guidelines. Most financial institutions use 1.5 to 2 years on the job, a satisfactory credit rating, a debt ratio of 50% or less, and sufficient collateral, per dollars borrowed, as minimum guidelines. Based on these and other variables, the objective is to establish, at the time of loan application, the odds that the applicant will eventually default. Concomitants in such predictions establish profiles in bankruptcy.

1.3 Remarks on Allied Studies

A number of previous studies deal with predicting corporate bankruptcy.[3,4,5] More recently, Ohlson[6] bases bankruptcy forecasts on a logistic regression model[7] using company size and measures of financial structure, performance, and current liquidity as predictors. Ohlson emphasizes that earlier studies employ predictors derived from statements issued after the date of bankruptcy and that such predictors may exaggerate the predictive power of resulting models.

Ohlson is critical of discriminant analysis as a method of modeling because "the variance-covariance matrices of predictors should be the same for both groups (failed and non-failed firms); moreover, a requirement of normally distributed predictors certainly mitigates against the use of dummy independent variables." Responses to these criticisms are as follows.

1. With large sample sizes (Ohlson uses observations from 105 bankrupt firms and 2,058 nonbankrupt firms), one may disregard discrepancies between sample and population dispersion matrices and proceed with quadratic discriminant analysis[8] (which is based on unequal dispersion matrices between groups). In fact, heterogeneity of dispersion matrices in discriminant analysis is as common as heterogeneous variance in

regression—which causes no problems if it is recognized and handled properly. Moreover, it is known[8] that misclassification probabilities in linear discriminant analysis (which assumes equal dispersion matrices) are rather insensitive to moderate dispersion heterogeneity.

2. Since it is common in practice that predictors are both continuous and categorical, one may readily transform to principal components and use the components as predictors.[9] In addition to resolving problems of multicollinearity, the components tend to cluster about central values, which supports the normality assumption. Also, with large sample sizes, one need not be concerned with the variability of the sample eigenvectors that define the components.

3. If prior probabilities are assumed to be uniform in Bayesian linear discriminant analysis, the resulting model for the posterior probability is identical to the logistic regression model—given a common set of predictors. Thus, when stepwise estimation procedures (as implemented in BMDP7M[9] software in the case of discriminant analysis and BMDPLR[9] in the case of logistic regression) are used to scan variables and identify significant predictors, the fitted models often lead to comparable predictions, as in the present application. In such instances, Bayesian discriminant analysis is preferable since per case, supplemental information (i.e., information apart from that provided by the predictor variables) can be incorporated in the model through the prior probabilities.

4. Finally, if the focus is on prediction and the predictive validity of discriminant analysis is clearly established through, say, the jackknife technique, then it makes little practical difference whether underlying assumptions have been violated.

2.0   Modeling Procedures and Results

2.1   The Data and the Variables

The data were made available by a financial institution in Fresno, California. The sample includes 213 customers who filed under Chapter 7 or 13 and 98 customers who paid their loans as agreed. The bankruptcy cases were filed under the provisions of the 1979 act and were under the jurisdiction of the Federal Bankruptcy Court in Fresno.

Data for the following variables are available per customer:

NI: net income per month,
HR: homeowner or renter,
MS: marital status,
A: age,

D: number of dependents,
DR: debt ratio (total installment debt divided by NI),
CR: credit rating (1 = highest to 5 = lowest),
M: monthly rent or home payment,
L: length of time on current job (in months),
R: reason for bankruptcy (for bankruptcy cases).

2.2 Modeling Approach

The dependent variable is categorical and binary, with each case belonging to either the bankruptcy (B) or the nonbankruptcy (NB) samples. Since several possible predictors are categorical, both stepwise logistic regression (BMDPLR) and stepwise discriminant analysis (BMDP7M) are applied. Excluding R, all the variables listed above and their squares and cross products are scanned for significant predictors. Predictions (based on uniform priors for BMDP7M) are nearly the same between the fitted models. Consequently, BMDP7M results are presented. Quadratic discriminant analysis is not necessary since the hypothesized equality of predictor dispersion matrices between the B and NB populations is tested[10] and not rejected.

2.3 The Model

Let $P(B|x)$ denote the posterior probability that a customer will file for bankruptcy, where x denotes the vector of predictors. In scanning variables for significant predictors, uniform prior probabilities are assumed. In the resulting model,

$$P(B|x) = \{1 + [p(B)]^{-1}[1 - p(B)]$$
$$\times \exp(-.0973 + .0591*A - 2.8163*DR$$
$$+ .0259*L - .5698*CR - .0004*A*L)\}^{-1} \qquad (9.1)$$

where the prior probability of declaring bankruptcy is denoted by $p(B)$. When there is no supplemental information, $p(B) = 1/2$.

By varying values of the predictors and observing their effects on $P(B|x)$, we obtain profiles in bankruptcy. Table 9.1 presents results of exercising model (9.1) with $p(B) = 1/2$. Higher values of $P(B|x)$ are clearly associated with younger individuals who have lower credit ratings, higher debt ratios, and fewer years in their current job.

2.4 Misclassification Probabilities

The predictive validity of model (9.1) is quantified in terms of misclassification probabilities. Suppose we impose the simple statistical de-

TABLE 9.1.   Posterior Probabilities of Bankruptcy—$P(B \mid x)$—Based on
Uniform Prior Probabilities in Model (9.1)

Years on job	Credit rating			Credit rating		
	1	2	3	1	2	3
	Age = 30, debt ratio = .3			Age = 45, debt ratio = .3		
4	.491	.630	.751	.349	.487	.626
6	.411	.552	.686	.311	.444	.585
8	.336	.472	.612	.275	.402	.543
	Age = 30, debt ratio = .4			Age = 45, debt ratio = .4		
4	.629	.750	.841	.485	.625	.747
6	.551	.684	.793	.442	.584	.712
8	.470	.611	.735	.400	.541	.676

cision rule that an individual is classified into the B population if $P(B \mid x)$
> .50 and into the NB population otherwise. Based on this rule, mis-
classification probabilities—the probability of assigning the individual to
the B (NB) population when, in fact, he belongs to the NB (B) population—are estimated by the jackknife technique. (In BMDP7M, the jackknife is applied by deleting each case, one at a time, building the model
on the other cases, and then predicting the outcome of the deleted case.)
The upper portion of Table 9.2 contains results of the jackknife classification. It is seen that the two misclassification probabilities are nearly

TABLE 9.2.   Analysis Results

A. Classification results based on the jackknife technique			
Actual category	Jackknife classification		Correct classification
	B	NB	
B	146	67	68.5%
NB	31	67	68.4%

B. Posterior probability of bankruptcy for representative individuals			
B sample case	$P(B \mid x)$	NB sample case	$P(NB \mid x)$
1	.866	1	.860
2	.762	2	.723
3	.653	3	.898
4	.533	4	.948
5 M[a]	.377	5	.795
6 M	.499	6	.597
7	.572	7 M	.372
8	.771	8 M	.490
9 M	.034	9	.640
10	.801	10	.628
11	.691	11	.901

[a]M denotes a misclassification according to the following rule: an individual is classified into the B population if his value of $P(B \mid x)$ exceeds .50 and into the NB population
otherwise.

equal; that is, misclassification percentages are 100% − 68.5% = 31.5% for bankruptcy cases and 31.6% for nonbankruptcy cases.

It should be noted that the credit manager's decision rule—as opposed to the simple statistical decision rule—is obviously more flexible and could take the following forms. (1) Utilize a complex statistical decision rule[10] that incorporates the dollar figure risks of misclassifying the applicant into the B (NB) population when, in fact, he belongs to the NB (B) population. (2) Utilize $P(B|x)$ (based on uniform priors) as a guide and scrutinize the applicant further if $P(B|x)$ is thought to be excessive. (3) Expand (2) by quantifying supplemental information gained from the scrutiny in terms of the prior probabilities. Rule (3) is illustrated in the next section.

2.5 Model Enhancement

In discussing methods of model enhancement, we first consider reasons given for bankruptcy, as listed in Table 9.3 for the individuals in the B sample. Note that these reasons may inadequately reflect more basic causes of bankruptcy. For example, a credit manager advised the writer that "very few people understand credit and their rights and obligations concerning credit debt. Whether this can be attributed to lack of intellect, ignorance, or any number of sociological/psychological factors is unknown since data haven't been collected and analyzed."

The lower portion of Table 9.2 presents $P(B|x)$ for 11 representative individuals from the B sample and $1 − P(B|x) = P(NB|x)$ for 11 representative individuals from the NB sample. Based on the simple decision rule, the fifth, sixth, and ninth individuals in the B group are misclassified. The fifth and ninth individuals gave, respectively, divorce and a heart attack as the reasons for bankruptcy. Could indications of these factors have been uncovered during loan application and, if so, how might this supplemental information have been utilized in estimating $P(B|x)$?

One might subject the individual to a human behavior inventory to

TABLE 9.3. Reasons for Bankruptcy

Reason	Relative frequencies
Loss of job	26%
Medical	11
Business failure (all proprietorships)	36
Heavy debt load	7
Divorce	8
No answer	12
Total	100%

measure psychological factors.[11] Even though the overall score on a particular inventory may not reflect the individual's propensity to default, the answers to the inventory questions, when added to the variables listed above as possible predictors, may lead to better discrimination between B and NB populations.

If, however, the use of inventories is not feasible, one may obtain supplemental information on an ad hoc basis, usually through interviews. How might one utilize such information (whose validity is largely dependent on the interviewer's capabilities)? Consider, for example, case 5 of the B sample in Table 9.2. Assume that there was prior knowledge of the individual's marital problems (which, unbeknownst to the credit manager, would ultimately lead to divorce and subsequent loan default) and that this information was to be quantified in terms of $p(B)$, the prior probability of default. In order to have increased this individual's $P(B|x)$ value from .377 to at least .5, the value of $p(B)$ should have been chosen, a priori, in excess of .623. In general, to increase the value of $P(B|x)$ to at least P_0, the value of $p(B)$ should be chosen, a priori, in excess of $P_0[1 - P(B|x)]/[P(B|x) + P_0 - 2P_0P(B|x)]$. Similarly, suppose there was prior knowledge of heart disease for case 9 of the B sample in Table 9.2. Increasing this individual's $P(B|x)$ from .034 to at least .50 would have required the a priori selection of $p(B)$ to exceed .966. Had the latter prior been so chosen, we would have an example of the prior judgment overriding information provided by the variables listed above. Such situations merit particular scrutiny, especially when low misclassification probabilities are associated with the uniform prior model.

Exercise 1

A model is to be developed for determining the cost of automobile insurance per driver. Define appropriate dependent variables. Why are demographics usually poor predictors in this type of modeling? What alternative predictors would you propose? Develop a detailed data acquisition plan for all variables under consideration.

References

1. Herzog, R. *Bankruptcy*. New York: Acro, 1983.

2. Dimancescu, D. *Deferred Future*. Cambridge: Ballanger, 1983. (Quotation, p. 15.)

3. Altman, E., Haldeman, R., and Narayanan, P. "ZETA Analysis: A New

Model to Identify Bankruptcy Risk of Corporations." *Journal of Bankruptcy and Finance,* June 1977, pp. 232–49.

4. Beaver, W. "Market Prices, Financial Ratios, and the Prediction of Failure." *Journal of Accounting Research,* Autumn 1968, pp. 305–10.

5. Moyer, R. "Forecasting Financial Failure: A Re-Examination." *Financial Management,* Spring 1977, pp. 91–111.

6. Ohlson, J. "Financial Ratios and the Probabilistic Prediction of Bankruptcy." *Journal of Accounting Research,* Spring 1980, pp. 109–31. (Quotation, p. 112.)

7. Cox, D. R. *The Analysis of Binary Data.* London: Methuen, 1970.

8. Lachenbruch, P. A. *Discriminant Analysis.* New York: Hafner, 1975.

9. Dixon, W. J., ed. *BMDP Statistical Software.* Berkeley and Los Angeles: University of California Press, 1985.

10. Anderson, T. W. *An Introduction to Multivariate Statistical Analysis.* New York: Wiley, 1958.

11. Pfeiffer, J., Heslin, R., and Jones, J. *Instrumentation in Human Relations Training.* 2d ed. La Jolla, Calif.: University Associates, 1976.

Identify: Friend or Foe

M ilitary exercises were conducted to determine the effectiveness of sensors in detecting and identifying approaching aircraft as either friend or foe. Situated within a defense perimeter, the sensors are designed to activate prior to the aircraft's entry into a prescribed airspace. Given that friend and foe utilize different devices to mask their approach, the focus was on the number of sensors activated by each type of aircraft. Within each field trial, a friendly aircraft and one simulating the foe approached a designated area in random sequence. Observed data include the number of sensors activated by each aircraft per trial. The analysis shows that, on the average, fewer sensors are activated for foe than for friend. Bayesian discriminant analysis is applied in estimating the posterior probability that the approaching aircraft is a foe. An alternative form of discriminant analysis is applied in the sense that the probability density function for the observed data within each of the friend and foe populations is not normal but rather, binomial-beta. Per trial, ad hoc information can be incorporated in the model in terms of the Bayesian prior probability.

1.0   Statement of the Problem

1.1   Friend or Foe?

As part of an early warning system, sensors located within a defense perimeter are used to detect and identify approaching aircraft as either friend or foe. The objective is to detect and correctly identify the approaching aircraft at a point well beyond the defense perimeter.

121

At an early date, it was known that friend and foe employed different masking devices to avoid detection by sensors. However, whether these differences were reflected in the performance of the sensors was unknown. An experiment was conducted to determine whether sensors responded differently to approaches of friend and foe and, if so, to discriminate between friend and foe in terms of the number of activated sensors. The discrimination would be in terms of conditional probabilities of friend and foe.

1.2 Design of the Field Trials

Twenty-one sensors were located within a prescribed defense perimeter. Within each of 60 trials, a friend and a simulated foe approached the perimeter in a sequence determined randomly. For each aircraft, the number of activated sensors was recorded per trial; that is, each sensor either activated or did not activate prior to the aircraft's entry into a prescribed airspace. Table 10.1 presents the observed frequencies of activated sensors over the 60 trials for friend and foe. For example, for the friendly aircraft, all 21 sensors were activated in 15 of the 60 trials; for the foe, all 21 sensors were activated in only 8 of the trials.

The approach direction was chosen at random for each trial. Since a large defense perimeter was chosen for these trials, the random approach tended to introduce an environmental source of variation. Moreover, trials were conducted over a period of weeks, which may have introduced a meteorological source of variation due to changing weather conditions. The analysis is presented here makes no attempt to adjust for environmental or meteorological differences through, say, a covariance analysis. Rather, their effect, when known, was incorporated in the model through the Bayesian prior probability.

2.0 Analysis Results

2.1 The Binomial versus the Binomial-Beta Probability Density Function

Because of the variations in the trial conditions, the application of a binomial probability density function (pdf) for y, the number of activated sensors in a particular trial, is inappropriate; with N denoting the number of sensors utilized per trial and π the probability that a sensor activates, the binomial pdf,

$$f(y \mid N, \pi) = \binom{N}{y} \pi^y (1 - \pi)^{N-y}$$

TABLE 10.1   Observed and Expected Frequencies of Sensors Activating

y (no. of sensors activating)	Observed frequency		Expected frequencies			
			Binomial pdf		Binomial-beta pdf	
	Friend	Foe	Friend	Foe	Friend	Foe
0	7	12	0.000	0.003	4.824	18.322
1	1	10	0.000	0.038	2.251	4.506
2	1	4	0.000	0.232	1.697	2.878
3	2	3	0.000	0.883	1.446	2.218
4	0	0	0.000	2.390	1.304	1.858
5	2	5	0.002	4.884	1.216	1.633
6	2	0	0.012	7.828	1.162	1.482
7	1	3	0.055	10.082	1.130	1.376
8	1	1	0.204	10.604	1.115	1.301
9	0	0	0.629	9.205	1.114	1.249
10	0	2	1.606	6.639	1.127	1.215
11	1	0	3.416	3.990	1.153	1.196
12	0	0	6.055	1.998	1.194	1.192
13	1	0	8.914	0.831	1.254	1.203
14	1	2	10.832	0.285	1.336	1.230
15	2	1	10.750	0.080	1.451	1.278
16	3	2	8.572	0.018	1.613	1.353
17	2	3	5.361	0.003	1.853	1.469
18	4	0	2.533	0.000	2.237	1.657
19	6	2	0.850	0.000	2.948	1.990
20	8	2	0.180	0.000	4.784	2.740
21	15	8	0.018	0.000	21.832	6.644
Total	60	60	59.999	59.999	59.999	60.000

Summary

y	Observed frequency		Expected frequencies			
			Binomial pdf		Binomial-beta pdf	
	Friend	Foe	Friend	Foe	Friend	Foe
0–1	8	22	0.00	0.04	7.07	22.83
2–5	5	12	0.00	8.39	5.67	7.59
6–14	7	8	31.73	51.46	10.59	11.44
15–16	5	3	19.32	0.11	3.06	2.63
17–19	12	5	8.75	0.00	7.04	6.13
20–21	23	10	0.20	0.00	26.57	9.38
χ^2 (df)					6.62 (3)	3.92 (3)

fails to describe the variation in y since π will be shown to vary between trials.

To account for this variation in π, we apply the binomial-beta pdf,

$$g(y \mid N, \alpha_1, \alpha_2) = \binom{N}{y} \beta(\alpha_1 + y, \alpha_2 + N - y)/\beta(\alpha_1, \alpha_2) \qquad (10.1)$$

where α_1 and α_2 are parameters of the pdf and the beta function

$$\beta(U, V) = \Gamma(U)\Gamma(V)/\Gamma(U + V)$$
$$E(y) = N\alpha_1/(\alpha_1 + \alpha_2)$$

That is, based on the discussion of model (14.18) in Chapter 14, Methodological Overview, (10.1) is obtained by (1) assuming a beta pdf for π, (2) compounding the binomial and beta pdf's, and (3) integrating out π over the interval (0, 1).

In the iterative process of obtaining the maximum-likelihood estimate of (α_1, α_2), Skellam[1] finds initial values as follows. Since the jth factorial moment about the origin for the binomial pdf is

$$m_{(j)} = N^{(j)}\pi^j$$

the corresponding moment for the beta-binomial pdf is

$$M_{(j)} = \int_0^1 N^{(j)}\pi^j \, \pi^{\alpha_1-1} (1 - \pi)^{\alpha_2-1}/\beta(\alpha_1, \alpha_2) \, d\pi$$
$$= N^{(j)}\beta(j + \alpha_1, \alpha_2)/\beta(\alpha_1, \alpha_2)$$

where $N^{(j)} = N(N - 1) \ldots (N - j + 1)$. Letting

$$R_j = \frac{M_{(j)}}{M_{(j-1)}} = \frac{(N - j + 1)(j + \alpha_1 - 1)}{j + \alpha_1 + \alpha_2 - 1} \tag{10.2}$$

we find expressions for R_1 and R_2, solve for α_1 and α_2, and obtain

$$\alpha_1 = \frac{R_1R_2 - (N - 1)R_1}{(N - 1)R_1 - NR_2} \quad \text{and} \quad \alpha_2 = \alpha_1\left(\frac{N}{R_1} - 1\right)$$

Initial values for α_1 and α_2 are obtained by substituting sample values for R_1 and R_2.

The binomial-beta pdf is fitted to each set of observed frequencies in Table 10.1 through maximum-likelihood estimation. Estimates of (α_1, α_2) are as follows: (.483, .269) for friend and (.297, .434) for foe. For each data set, expected frequencies are given under both the binomial and the binomial-beta pdf's. The summary in the lower portion of Table 10.1 illustrates the poor fit of the binomial pdf. The χ^2 goodness of fit statistic for the binomial-beta pdf, when calculated for the six categories in the table summary, is 6.62 for friend and 3.92 for foe. At the .05 level of significance, the critical value is 7.81. (Note that each test is based on 6 − 1 − 2 = 3 degrees of freedom since two parameters are estimated.) These results indicate that (1) the binomial-beta pdf accounts for the variation in y between trials, (2) on the average, fewer sensors activate for foe than for friend [i.e., since $E(y) = N\alpha_1/(\alpha_1 + \alpha_2)$, an average of

21(.483)/(.483 + .269) = 13.49 sensors activate for friend, and an average of 21(.297)/(.297 + .434) = 8.53 activate for foe], and (3) estimates of (α_1, α_2) are very nearly transposed between friend and foe.

2.2   The Posterior Probability of a Foe

Because more sensors tend to activate with an approaching friend, Bayesian discriminant analysis is applied in estimating the probability of a friend conditional on the number of activated sensors. Bayes's theorem is applied directly by substituting the fitted binomial-beta pdf's for the $P(\mathbf{y})|G_j)$ in (14.1) of Chapter 14; that is, there are two populations, with G_1 denoting the friend population and G_2 the foe population; $y = \mathbf{y}$ denotes the number of sensors activating. Table 10.2 presents the posterior probability of a friend for each of the following prior probabilities: $P(G_1)$ = .25, .50, and .75. It is seen that the posterior probability of a friend increases as the number of activated sensors increases. Ad hoc information may be incorporated in the model in terms of the prior probability.

For uniform priors, $P(G_1)$ = .50, the posterior probability of a friend is compared with the corresponding, observed percentage—as given in the last column of Table 10.2. For example, given that at most one sensor activates, the posterior probability of a friend is .237 and the observed value is .267; that is, in the 30 trials in which at most one sensor activated, 8 were friendly approaches.

2.3   Model Enhancement through the Multinomial-Multivariate Beta Probability Density Function

Suppose we designate a reference coordinate, say, at the center of the defense perimeter, and measure the distance from the approaching aircraft to this coordinate at the instant the sensor activates. A "detection distance" would thus be recorded per sensor per trial for both friend and foe. Used as predictors, these distances, along with measures of envi-

TABLE 10.2.   Posterior Probability of a Friend Given the Prior Probability of a Friend and the Number of Sensors Activating (y)

y	Prior probability			Observed percentage
	.25	.50	.75	
0–1	.108	.237	.465	8/30 = .267
2–5	.180	.397	.665	5/17 = .294
6–14	.236	.480	.735	7/15 = .467
15–16	.280	.538	.778	5/8 = .625
17–19	.314	.579	.805	12/17 = .705
20–21	.486	.739	.895	23/37 = .697

ronmental and meteorological conditions, would very likely improve the discrimination between friend and foe.

A side study was conducted wherein 15 sensors were utilized in each of 13 trials. The study focused only on the detection distances for friendly aircraft. Since the experimental technique caused considerable error in measuring the detection distances, the distances were categorized for each trial into four groups labeled C_1 through C_4; C_1 brackets detection distances in the airspace closest to the reference point, and C_4 brackets those in the most distant airspace. The data are recorded in Table 10.3. In the first trial, all but one sensor remained inactive until the aircraft entered the airspace closest to the reference point.

Let the ith element of $\mathbf{y}$ be denoted by y_i, the number of sensors activating for the first time for a detection distance in category C_i, where $i = 1, 2, 3, 4$; $\Sigma_{i=1} y_i = 15$. Choice of a multinomial pdf for $\mathbf{y}$ is in-

TABLE 10.3. Fitting the Multinomial-Multivariate Beta (MMB) Probability Density Function to Categorized Detection Distances

Trial	No. of activated sensors per category				No. of activated sensors
	C_1	C_2	C_3	C_4	
1	14	1	0	0	15
2	2	4	4	5	15
3	1	7	3	4	15
4	6	8	1	0	15
5	14	1	0	0	15
6	8	7	0	0	15
7	9	5	1	0	15
8	4	11	0	0	15
9	1	6	5	3	15
10	14	1	0	0	15
11	2	8	4	1	15
12	15	0	0	0	15
13	3	4	5	3	15
Total	93	63	23	16	195

MMB parameter estimates				
	Parameter			
	α_1	α_2	α_3	α_4
Initial value:	1.7836	1.2278	.4514	.3118
	1.3268	1.0158	.3897	.2587
	1.3379	1.0237	.3923	.2581
	1.3367	1.0228	.3920	.2581
	1.3369	1.0230	.3921	.2581
Maximum-likelihood estimate:	1.3370	1.0231	.3921	.2581

Estimate of $E(y_i/N)$				
pdf	C_1	C_2	C_3	C_4
Multinomial	.444	.340	.130	.086
MMB	.447	.323	.112	.082

appropriate because the multinomial probabilities vary between trials. To account for this variation, we apply the multinomial-multivariate beta (MMB) pdf

$$h(\mathbf{y}\,|\,N,\,\alpha_1,\,\ldots,\,\alpha_4) = N!\,\frac{\beta(\alpha_1 + y_1,\,\ldots,\alpha_4 + y_4)}{\beta(\alpha_1,\,\ldots,\,\alpha_4)}\prod_{i=1}^{4} y_i! \qquad \textbf{(10.3)}$$

That is, as discussed in the formulation of (14.18) in Chapter 14, model (10.3) is obtained by (1) assuming a multivariate beta pdf for the multinomial probabilities, (2) compounding the multinomial and multivariate beta pdf's, and (3) integrating out the multinomial probabilities.

Model (10.3) is fitted to the data in Table 10.3 through maximum-likelihood estimation. Initial values of the α_i used in the iterative process are obtained as follows. From (14.19) of Chapter 14, we have

$$R_{1ii*} = E(y_i)/E(y_{i*}) = \alpha_i/\alpha_{i*}$$

and

$$R_{2ii*} = \frac{E(y_i^2) - E(y_i)}{E(y_{i*}^2) - E(y_{i*})} = \frac{\alpha_i^2 + \alpha_i}{\alpha_{i*}^2 + \alpha_{i*}}$$

These two relations can be used to identify four equations in the four unknown α_i after sample values are substituted for R_{1ii*} and R_{2ii*}. Initial values and the maximum-likelihood estimates are presented in the lower portion of Table 10.3.

Goodness of fit of the MMB pdf is illustrated in terms of the pdf of $z_i = \sum_{i*\neq i} y_{i*}$. Under the assumption of an MMB pdf for $\mathbf{y}$, the pdf of z_i is

$$h(z_i\,|\,N,\,\alpha_1,\,\ldots,\,\alpha_4) = N!\,\frac{\beta\left[\sum_{i*\neq i}(\alpha_{i*} + Z_{i*}),\,N - \alpha_i - z_i\right]}{z_i!(N - z_i)!\,\beta\left(\sum_{i*\neq i}\alpha_{i*},\,\alpha_i\right)}$$

Table 10.4 presents groupings of the data in Table 10.3. Per grouping, expected values are given for both the multinomial and MMB pdf's. Goodness-of-fit tests are not presented since the degrees of freedom are insufficient. It is clear, however, that, overall, the MMB pdf provides a better fit than the multinomial pdf.

TABLE 10.4. **Observed and Expected Frequencies for the Multinomial (M) and Multinomial-Multivariate Beta (MMB) Probability Density Functions**

z (no. of sensors activating)	Frequency			Frequency		
	Observed	Expected M	Expected MMB	Observed	Expected M	Expected MMB
	C_1			C_2		
0–1	2	0.01	1.52	4	0.03	2.85
2–4	5	7.43	6.03	6	11.73	6.61
8–15	6	5.56	5.45	3	0.97	3.54
Total	13	13.00	13.00	13	13.00	13.00
	C_3			C_4		
0	6	1.98	5.92	8	3.60	7.80
1–2	2	7.68	3.40	1	7.84	2.81
3–15	5	3.34	3.68	4	1.56	2.39
Total	13	13.00	13.00	13	13.00	13.00

An implication of these results is that discrimination between friend and foe would likely be improved if the MMB pdf, when fitted to detection distances for each of friend and foe, is substituted for $P(\mathbf{y}\,|\,G_k)$ in a Bayesian discriminant analysis. When the number of trials is large, we may approximate the MMB pdf by a multivariate normal pdf and perform a nonlinear discriminant analysis. In this approach, the parameters of the multivariate normal pdf would be replaced by estimates of corresponding parameters of the MMB pdf.

3.0   A Related Illustration in Military Operations Research: On Suppressing the Enemy

This study has roots in the Vietnam conflict. Events of that time are described by David Halberstam in his book *The Best and the Brightest*. In the epilogue, Halberstam describes the battle of Ia Drang Valley, where regiments of the North Vietnamese army "stumbled into units of the elite First Cav (the new heliborne division)" in November of 1965. The result of the battle—1,200 enemy killed versus 200 American losses—convinced General William Westmoreland, commander of the American forces, and his influential deputy, General William Depuy, "that the aggressive use of American force and strike power against the enemy in his distant base-camps could eventually destroy his forces and will." Depuy emphasized "the threshold of pain. It was something he believed in, that the enemy had a threshold, and that if we hit him hard enough he would cry out." However, "at this very point, in fact, the North Vietnamese were testing our threshold of pain. They would find that ours was a good deal lower than theirs, that we could not accept heavy casualities as they could."

In the 1970s, we find General Depuy commanding the U.S. Army Training and Doctrine Center and reiterating his views on "thresholds of pain." A means to such pain was through suppressive fire. The dominant view was unequivocal: the larger the caliber of the weapon, the greater the suppressive effect. To prove his point, Depuy tasked an army experimentation agency to conduct experiments to classify various caliber weapons with respect to their suppressive effects.

One such experiment provided measures of suppression by determining the effects of live fire (under fail-safe conditions) on task performance. Ten defenders were individually deployed in dugouts equally spaced along a defense line 100 meters in length. Each defender controlled a periscope device that could be maneuvered up to track an oncoming threat vehicle or down to avoid support fire from a fixed threat. A silhouette situated atop each periscope represented the defender. The silhouette was exposed to threat fire when tracking the vehicle and was concealed when the defender chose a suppressed position in the dugout (Fig. 10.1).

Each defender's objective was to track the oncoming threat vehicle as long as possible without having his silhouette shot by threat cover fire. Thus, as threat fire sprayed defender positions during each trial, the defenders maneuvered their periscopes up and down according to their best instincts. (Rewards were to be given to defenders who tracked the most and got their silhouette shot the least.) Trials were conducted under a balanced experimental design intended to evaluate effects on suppression of different caliber weapons. Throughout each trial, each defender was monitored (on a real-time basis) regarding times spent in tracking and suppressed positions. If a defender's silhouette was shot, that defender was disqualified from participation for the remainder of the trial. Defenders participated in a sufficient number of preliminary trials to mitigate the effects of unfamiliarity with the experimental technique.

A time line for each defender for each trial was constructed from the data. For example, an individual time line may be expressed by a numerical sequence such as T6, S5, T9, S2, ..., which means that, as the threat vehicle became visible to the defender, he tracked the vehicle for the first 6 seconds, was suppressed for the next 5 seconds, tracked for the next 9 seconds, etc. For purposes of analysis, the data were categorized as follows: suppressed for more than 4 seconds, suppressed from 1 to 4 seconds, tracking from 1 to 4 seconds, and tracking for more than 4 seconds. The categories were based on military considerations. For ex-

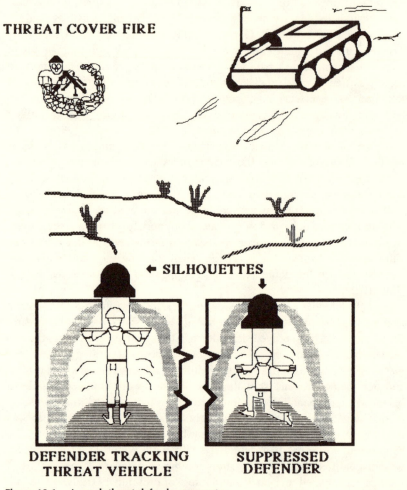

Figure 10.1. A mock threat-defender encounter.

ample, if the defender were to fire on the threat vehicle, he would require more than 4 seconds of tracking, on the average, to have a high kill probability; less than 4 seconds of tracking results in a low kill probability. Suppression times greater than 4 seconds tend to indicate loss of the defensive line.

With the categorical dependent variable defined according to these four categories, the following independent variables were scanned for significance through BMDP7M[3]: lateral miss distance (or the distance on the defensive line between the point at which the threat fire is directed and the particular defender's dugout during the last second of that defender's tracking or suppressed position), lags of the miss distances (indicating whether threat fire is moving toward or away from the particular defender's dugout), the type of weapon (the lower-caliber M60 machine gun versus the higher-caliber Browning M2 machine gun), the rate of fire (sustained versus rapid versus cyclic), the class of fire (which included traverse—or threat fire spraying the defensive line systematically with one burst per dugout—versus fixed—where the spraying is conducted with six bursts per dugout), human factor variables (based on a psychological inventory) measuring each defender's willingness to participate in the experiment, and all two-factor interactions.

Based on the analysis results, there were anomalies—the higher-caliber M2 was not clearly more suppressive than the M60. An exercise of the resulting model, with uniform priors and other predictors held at nominal values, is presented in Table 10.5. Focusing on the M2 versus M60 comparison for the "tracking greater than 4 seconds" category, we see that for miss distances up to 20 meters, the M2 is slightly more suppressive. However, for miss distances greater than 20 meters, the M60 is more suppressive. How can this be explained? Based on postexperiment defender interviews, it developed that the M2 is, indeed, more suppressive when it is fired at or near the defender. However, for larger miss distances, the M2 firing signature is sufficiently pronounced that it provides information to the defender that he is not being shot at—and that he may track safely. The M60 signature is not so pronounced, so that for comparable miss distances, the defender is not as sure where threat fire is directed. These findings were supported by subsequent interviews with Vietnam combat veterans.

To quantify the overall suppressive effect of each weapon, we (1) find the probability of each lateral miss distance (given in Table 10.5 for the traverse class of fire) and (2) sum the products of the probability of tracking for more than 4 seconds at a particular miss distance by the probability of that miss distance. For the M60 and M2, the sums are .349 and .383, respectively; that is, defenders track for more than 4 seconds, on the average, 34.9% of the time when threat fire utilizes the M60 and 38.3% of the time when the M2 is utilized. If we assume uniform probabilities for each miss distance, the comparable figures are .487 for the M60 and .583 for the M2. For Vietnam-type tactical encounters, the pdf for miss distances would likely vary between those considered above.

TABLE 10.5. A Model Exercise Comparing the M60 and M2 Machine Guns (for the Traverse Loss of Fire)

Lateral (miss) distance (m)	M60 machine gun: probability of—				Distribution of lateral distance	Browning M2 machine gun: probability of—				Lateral distance (m)
	Sup >4 sec	Sup (0, 4) sec	Tr (0, 4) sec	Tr >4 sec		Sup >4 sec	Sup (0, 4) sec	Tr (0, 4) sec	Tr >4 sec	
0	.44	.27	.25	.04	.10	.56	.27	.16	.01	0
10	.28	.29	.35	.08	.18	.39	.32	.25	.04	10
20	.17	.27	.40	.16	.16	.22	.35	.29	.14	20
30	.08	.23	.41	.28	.14	.08	.16	.45	.31	30
40	.04	.17	.37	.42	.12	.03	.15	.33	.49	40
50	.02	.11	.30	.57	.10	.01	.06	.24	.69	50
60	.01	.07	.22	.70	.08	.00	.04	.10	.86	60
70	.00	.04	.15	.81	.06	.00	.01	.07	.92	70
80	.00	.02	.10	.88	.04	.00	.01	.04	.95	80
90	.00	.01	.06	.93	.02	.00	.00	.03	.97	90

Note: Sup = suppression; Tr = tracking.

Exercise 1

In identifying an oncoming aircraft, a classification of "neutral" may be necessary. This situation is illustrated by a passenger jet flying over a war zone. How would you alter the design of field trials and analysis procedures to accommodate "Identify: friend, foe, or neutral?"

References

1. Skellam, J. G. "A Probability Distribution Derived from the Binomial Distribution by Regarding the Probability of Success as Variable between Sets of Trials." *Journal of the Royal Statistical Society*, series B, 10 (1948): 257–61.

2. Halberstam, D. *The Best and the Brightest*. New York: Fawcett Crest, 1969. (Quotation, p. 744).

3. Dixon, W. J., ed. *BMDP Statistical Software*. Berkeley and Los Angeles: University of California Press, 1985.

Mock Terrorist Attacks: Design

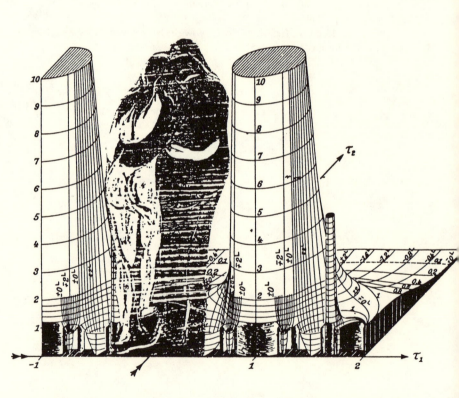

Ben Sabbah's garden.

nd Modeling Considerations

I n this study, the focus is on modeling portions of the following scenario. Terrorists break into a military storage facility to steal small nuclear weapons. The weapons are to be used for political extortion. The objective of the facility guards is to prevent the theft or to hold off the terrorists long enough for reinforcements to arrive.

To evaluate methods of deterrence once the break-in begins, mock terrorist attacks were conducted. The trials took place in a simulated nuclear facility and used real-time casualty assessment (RTCA); that is, harmless laser beams replaced live ammunition, and target attrition occurred in real time. Participants in the trials included actual guards of storage facilities and hired mercenaries.

The experiment had several objectives: (1) to determine the types of guard weapons and protective cover (pillboxes versus guard towers) that decrease chances of terrorist success and (2) to test the validity of existing simulation models of force-on-force encounters. Should existing models prove inadequate, the experimental data can be used to develop a data-based model.

1.0 Introduction

1.1 The Central Park Caper

The place is New York City and the year is 1977, shortly after the Israeli raid on Entebbe. The mayor reads a personal message just handed to him: "Nuclear weapons are emplaced in Central Park. The area will be contaminated unless payment of $50 million is made within 24 hours. Further instructions will follow." Law enforcement officials enter the scene.

MAYOR: A hoax? Terrorists? Where'd they get the bomb?
ANSWER: Several were recently stolen from an upstate arsenal.
MAYOR: Would they detonate the bombs?
ANSWER: Probably not. It's not in their interests to alienate potential sym-
         pathizers by killing a lot of people.
MAYOR: Then how are they going to contaminate the area?
ANSWER: It's not too hard. A B-52 crashed near Palomares, Spain, in
         1966. Plutonium was dispersed over a wide agricultural area
         when TNT detonated in two of the plane's nuclear bombs. The
         cleanup operation cost the United States more than $50 million.

The Central Park caper is fictitious but serves to emphasize a con-
sequence of stolen nuclear material. Was the scenario credible? In the
summer of 1980, a bomb was placed in a casino on the south shore of
Lake Tahoe. Payment of $3 million was demanded. The arrival of per-
sonnel from the Lawrence Livermore National Laboratory indicated concern that the bomb may have contained nuclear material. Demands of the
perpetrators were rejected, possibly because the device (which was discovered before the end of negotiations) was found to contain only conventional high explosives. However, multimillion dollar damage resulted
when the bomb was inadvertently detonated in the removal process. Had
the bomb been constructed with nuclear material, the Central Park caper
may have become the Lake Tahoe caper.

1.2   To Steal a Bomb

Whether the terrorist needs funds or publicity or is bent on mass
destruction, certain ingredients are necessary: a bomb, preferably a small
nuclear weapon, or, if a bomb is to be built, plutonium or enriched uranium. (In 1975 a Princeton University undergraduate designed a crude
but viable 125-pound bomb with about one-third the yield of those dropped
on Japan. Only 7 kilograms of plutonium would have been required to
activate it.) There are arguments for not building one. Joseph Rotblat,
who withdrew from the Manhattan Project on moral grounds before the
bombing of Japan, testified in 1977 at the British Windscale Inquiry: "It
would take a very brave and skilled terrorist to make a bomb from stolen
plutonium. The chances that he would survive to explode the bomb, when
and where he wanted, would be about fifty percent. If a terrorist really
wanted a nuclear bomb, he would be better advised to steal a ready made
one."[1]

O'Ballance suggests that "nuclear weapons would be at their most
vulnerable while being transported from one place to another."[1] The 18

May 1977 edition of the *London Daily Express* suggested an ideal site for seizing nuclear material: ". . . a deserted road between Iverness and Thurso in Scotland, two miles from the nearest village and only ten miles from a small, little used harbor. Nuclear material might be seized in transit to and from the Scottish fast-breeder reactor at Doureay." In the United States, methods of transporting nuclear material are chosen at random to help preserve secrecy, at least until shipment. Therefore, the terrorist may choose to focus on arsenals storing nuclear weapons, which brings us to our central topic: terrorist countermeasures at storage sites.

Security measures in U.S. arsenals are non-uniform. Their effectiveness is still unknown, either because they have been tested only on a superficial basis[a] or because it is unknown whether security has been breached.[b] Since opinions regarding the effectiveness of security measures are varied, objective evaluations should be employed. One means of evaluation is by exercising existing simulation models under scenarios of interest. A second means is through mock terrorist attacks. The latter course is considered herein.

2.0   Force-on-Force Experiments

2.1   Experiments with Real-Time Casualty Assessment

Hoping to add a touch of battlefield realism to its peacetime training exercises, the Army is developing a complex laser beam system that permits two forces to shoot at . . . each other without hurting anyone. . . . When the system goes into operation . . . it will for the first time advance score-keeping in war games significantly beyond the level of children shouting "Bang, bang, you're dead." (*Los Angeles Times*, 23 August 1976)

In force-on-force experimentation, the trend is toward RTCA. Opposing forces use weapons equipped with low-intensity laser guns, laser-sensitive devices (sensors), and automatic telemetric links to and from a computer. When a combatant detects a target and engages it, he fires a blank cartridge in his weapon, which activates the laser gun. If he is on

---

[a]In 1971 the Baader-Meinhof Gang stole conventional weapons from the outer perimeter of a U.S. Army depot in West Germany. Nuclear weapons were stored in the inner perimeter. Theft of nuclear weapons was not attempted, either because this was not their objective or because security measures were tighter in the inner perimeter.

[b]O'Ballance states that "it is not possible to measure the exact amounts of plutonium or uranium held in a nuclear establishment, as the measuring instruments in use have an error between 2 and 4 percent. This means that there can be no way of knowing for certain at any given moment whether or not any is missing."[1]

target, that target's sensors are activated. The physical parameters of the engagement (weapon type, target type, target exposure, range, etc.) are automatically transmitted to the computer, which records the data, assesses the results, and, if a casualty is indicated, transmits that information to the target (in which case, the target's weapon is inactivated). If a casualty is not indicated, the target is informed that he was a near-miss (by means of a two-second tone in his ear), in which case he presumably takes some positive action, such as relocating. Additionally, if a combatant runs out of blanks (ammunition), his laser cannot fire since it can be activated only by firing a blank cartridge.

RTCA, as an Army training device, allows soldiers to know when they make a mistake that would have cost them their lives in actual combat. Such training has an obvious impact on survival, since it is known that if a soldier survives his first two weeks in actual combat, he has a 95% chance of surviving to return home. Aside from training, RTCA has an added advantage. All combatants' actions are recorded almost continuously during the encounter. Thus, all data—measures of both investigational and many extraneous variables—are available on file for future analysis (investigational variables are those under study, and extraneous variables are those not under study.

2.2 Why an Experiment?

Given the plethora of models[2] amenable to scenarios of terrorist attacks, mock encounters are a natural next step. Why? Because all models should be subject to experimental scrutiny. If the models prove inadequate, the RTCA staging of mock encounters provides sufficient data for the building of new models.

In his discourse of models, data, and war, Stockfish[3] states that a coherent and economical experiment can proceed only from the foundation of a well-structured model. However, even the best models become quickly obsolete with changes in politics and advances in weaponry. Under such circumstances, it is appropriate to ask, "Which comes first, the experiment or the model?" (For uncontrolled experiments, it is often the case that the experiment is premised on an ill-structured model and that a better-structural model is conceived through the data analysis.)

3.0 The Experiment

3.1 The Scenario and Objectives

The scene of the nuclear storage site is described as follows. The outer perimeter of the site is a flat area cleared of all vegetation. The inner perimeter is fenced and lighted during nondaylight hours. A building located at the center of the perimeter houses a vault containing mock nuclear material (MNM). Cover for the onsite defense force is located at the corners of this building; the cover may include guard towers or pillboxes. Adjacent to the vault building is a structure housing security operations for the site (all aspects of command, control, and communications for operation of the facility). The mission of the adversary (terrorist) force is to steal MNM from the vault. The mission of the onsite defense force is to prevent such theft by either defeating the adversaries or delaying them long enough for reinforcements to arrive.

The encounter begins once the adversary force is detected as they break through the inner perimeter. Once inside the inner perimeter, adversaries advance to the vault building and place a simulated high explosive (HE) on the building wall. After a delay to allow the HE to "explode," the adversaries enter the building and open the vault by means of a second simulated HE. Following the removal of the MNM (approximately 20 pounds) from the vault, the adversary force attempts to escape with the material.

Primary experimental objectives are to evaluate cover and weapon types for onsite defenders, to evaluate adversary and defender tactics, and to determine the importance of human factors on outcomes. Secondary objectives range from testing the validity of existing combat models to building data-based simulation models if existing models prove inadequate.

3.2   Treatments and Ground Rules

The key to successful mock encounters is simplicity in both treatments and ground rules. Cover and weapon types for onsite defenders are called treatments, as is the time of day of the encounter. Eight treatment combinations are defined by taking all combinations of three factors each at two levels; that is, the comparison of levels for weapons, cover, and time of day are, respectively, small arms and shotguns versus small arms and M16s, towers versus pillboxes, and day versus night. A number of encounters are to be conducted per treatment combination.

Variables quantifying tactics may be difficult to define and successfully control, especially for the adversary force. Consequently, the choice of tactics is left as a free-play variable. Measures of human factors may shed light on the choice of tactics.

Rules for ending an encounter are as follows. A combatant is neutralized if he becomes a casualty or surrenders. Hostages such as human shields captured by adversaries will not be allowed. Simulated combat ends when either force is neutralized, when the encounter exceeds 30 minutes (by that time, defender reinforcements would have arrived), when the adversaries deplete their ammunition (the adversaries will carry a limited ammunition supply, while the defenders will have an unlimited supply), or when the adversary force achieves its mission.

Depending on availability, a number of adversary and defender teams will participate. The adversary teams will be represented by hired mercenaries and the defenders by guards employed in nuclear weapon storage facilities. Force size is a free-play variable under the constraint that it not exceed 12 members. The adversary force has free choice of weapons, including grenades, but no area fire weapons (such as mortars). The adversary force is not permitted land vehicles and aircraft for mobility during the encounter nor mobile, hardened fighting positions (such as tanks). The experiment will not consider hand-to-hand combat (a combatant will be neutralized before such an event), insider-assisted attacks, or female combatants (women were excluded because we were unable to locate female mercenaries).

4.0   A Modeling Approach

4.1   The Data Base and the Variables

Through RTCA staging, the data base will include a time line per participant per trial. Throughout each trial, the time lines record all the participants' actions and locations every 10th of a second. Let the vector y_t, with typical element y_{ht}, denote all relevant variables for all participants measured at time t after the encounter begins; for example, y_t includes each participant's location at time t, whether they fired a particular weapon or were fired upon, whether they were suppressed or neutralized, etc. Let $y_{h,t+dt}$, a typical element of the vector y_{t+dt}, denote the aggregate or average of the variable y_{ht} from t to $t + dt$. The objective is to model y_{t+dt} (or aggregates of subsets of y_{t+dt}) over the course of the encounter.

The proposed modeling of y_{t+dt} is patterned after a model developed for an analogous RTCA experiment wherein a tank force crosses a minefield and is ambushed by a defensive force.[4] In that study, y_{t+dt} contained over 200 variables, while dt was chosen as 30 seconds (a value that is likely too large for the current study).

4.2   Simultaneous Time Series Equations

The modeling procedure is defined in terms of the lagged effects of y_{t+dt} and its lagged shocks on y_{t+dt} as the threat force progresses through the inner perimeter to the building housing the MNM and the return trip (with the MNM) to the outermost perimeter. The encounter may, of course, terminate within any interval $(t, t + dt)$.

Effects on $\mathbf{y}_{t+dt}$ are estimated within each of five time segments associated with the attack. These segments are random in length and defined by the times between six major events. Event 1: The first adversary crosses the inner perimeter. Event 2: The adversary force is detected. Event 3: An adversary enters the building housing the MNM. Event 4: The MNM is removed from the building in which it is housed. Event 5: The MNM is transported across the inner perimeter. Event 6: The MNM is transported across the outer perimeter.

A tentative model for $y_{h,t+dt}$ is given as follows:

$$
\begin{aligned}
y_{h,t+dt} = & \sum_{H} \sum_{i} \alpha_{gHi} y_{H,t+dt-i} + \sum_{j} \beta_{ghj} x_{j} \\
& + \sum_{H} \sum_{k} \gamma_{gHk} \delta_{H,t+dt-k} + \delta_{h,t+dt}
\end{aligned}
\tag{11.1}
$$

where the subscripts h and $H = 1, \ldots, p$ identify the elements of $\mathbf{y}_{t+dt}$ and the subscript $g = 1, \ldots, 5$ identifies the time segments between the six major events; α_{gHi} and γ_{gHk} are, respectively, the effects (either direct or overall) on $y_{h,t+dt}$ of the ith lag of $y_{H,t+dt}$ and the kth lagged shock corresponding to $y_{H,t+dt}$ (i.e., the lagged shock $\delta_{H,t+dt-k}$ is defined as the difference between the observed and expected values of $y_{H,t+dt-k}$); β_{ghj} is the effect (either direct or overall) of x_j on $y_{h,t+dt}$, where the x_j include all exogenous variables (such as treatments and variables quantifying participants' personality traits), which may vary between but not within trials; $\delta_{h,t+dt}$ is the model error (or current shock) for the hth equation.

The model developed for the ambush of the tank force[4] (as described in sec. 4.1) is simpler than model (11.1) in that lagged shocks were excluded from consideration. Current consensus is that lagged shocks are critical to modeling force-on-force encounters; that is, deviations from expectations during encounters often affect outcomes. In the tank ambush model, tactics were partially quantified in terms of the average clustering of the threat force in the interval $(t, t + dt)$. The same approach might be appropriate in the current study. Estimation in model (11.1) follows that discussed in Chapter 12. After model (11.1) is fitted, it may then be exercised to simulate conditions not considered in the trials. In such exercises, one should consider mixtures of probability density functions (pdf) for elements of $\mathbf{y}_{t+dt}$; for example, certain elements of $\mathbf{y}_{t+dt}$ will follow continuous pdf's and others will follow discrete pdf's.

The data-based modeling of RTCA experiments using model (11.1) is no easy task. Accordingly, such modeling should be undertaken only under the following conditions. (1) Existing models should be shown to be inadequate. (2) Sufficient time and qualified analysts should be made available. (3) The experiment should be a "reasonable" imitation of reality. The data-based model is a mathematical model of an experiment that, in itself, if a model of reality, thus, if the experiment is far removed from reality, the data-based model is even farther removed. Mock encounters, therefore, require meticulous planning.

Exercise 1

Suppose the mock trials show an overwhelming success rate for the terrorists—which suggests the need for alternative countermeasures. What are such countermeasures and how would these be implemented in the conduct of subsequent trials? Propose alternative modeling procedures.

References

1. O'Ballance, E. *Language of Violence*. San Rafael: Presidio Press, 1979. (Quotations, pp. 314 and 315).

2. Studies, Analysis, and Gaming Agency, Organization of the Joint Chiefs of Staff. *Catalogue of War Gaming and Military Simulation*. 6th ed., SA6A-236-7S. June 1975.

3. Stockfish, J. A. "Models, Data, and War: A Critique of the Study of Conventional Forces." Report prepared for the U.S. Air Force Project RAND, R-1526-PR. 1975.

4. Mallios, W. S., Batesole, R., Leal, D., and Tran, T. "The Impact of Laser Beam War Games on Modelling: A Model for Mounted Combat." *Proceedings of the 24th Conference on the Design of Experiments in Army research, Development, and Testing*. Durham, N.C.: U.S. Army Research Office, 1978.

12

A Nonrandom Walk throug

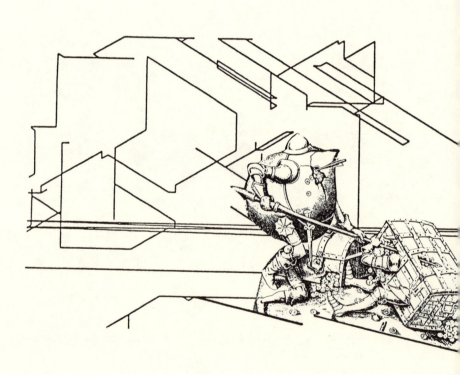

Haven't you heard of Bachelier?

utures Prices of the British Pound

During 1984–86, foreign currencies reached record lows against the dollar and then recovered erratically. The period was characterized by high volatility and enormous losses. In such periods, currency modeling—for purposes of short-term forecasting—would seem a natural recourse. However, results of such modeling appear infrequently in the literature. Possible reasons are that (1) random walk theory prevails (in reality or as a result of inadequate modeling) or (2) viable models are not publicized. Autoregressive, integrated, moving-average (ARIMA) modeling, when applied to forecasting a particular currency without regard to relevant, contemporaneous variables, tends to support random walk theory. Such results are, however, misleading because of interrelations between leading currencies, precious metals, and their respective open interest.

To allow for such interrelations, a reduced system of equations is applied. Each dependent variable may be affected by its own lags and lagged shocks and/or those of other dependent variables, in terms of either first-order or higher-order modeling. Higher-order terms include interactions between lagged variables. Analysis results for the British pound reject the random walk model and support the notion of second-order modeling. Utilization of prior information in updating the model is presented in terms of empirical Bayesian estimation.

1.0 Introduction

1.1 A Period of Volatility

In 1864 during Sherman's march through Georgia, the British pound hit record high of $9.92 and then began its downward trek. With the

145

bombing of Hiroshima, the pound stood at $4.02. During this period, Lord Keynes advised Prime Minister Attlee—during deliberations on development of independent nuclear weaponry—that "hopes for the economic betterment of the [British] people are non-existent."[1] Attlee opted for the bomb.

In early 1985 foreign currencies reached record lows against the dollar. When the pound dropped to $1.05, the unthinkable—a dollar for a pound—became thinkable. However, in subsequent months the dollar weakened somewhat, and by early 1986 the pound traded for $1.43.

The price volatility of the 1984–86 period roiled the currency exchange markets, where it is estimated that $150 billion a day changes hands. (This figure is roughly 40 times the dollar value of turnover on the New York Stock Exchange.) The period was marked by enormous losses. As reported in the *Wall Street Journal* (30 July 1985), Fuji Bank of Japan lost $47.7 million in 1984 when its chief exchange dealer bet, incorrectly, that the yen would strengthen against the dollar. Rupert Murdoch's Australian holding company, News Corporations Ltd., said in its annual report that it realized losses equivalent to $102.9 million "due to a serious misjudgement of the international money markets."

1.2   The Dollar and Precious Metals

During the dollar's surge, the price movements of precious metals were viewed by some analysts as possible indicators of short-term dollar corrections. Usually gold drops in price as the dollar increases. However, when the dollar was approaching its record high, gold shifted and increased in value. Two explanations were given for this peculiarity. (1) Oil prices firmed, which tends to increase the price of gold (gold is a hedge against inflation, which is spurred by increased oil prices). (2) A precious-metal analyst stated that "when gold doesn't react to dollar strength in the way that it should, it suggests that the strength of the dollar is overdone and that a correction is imminent" (*Wall Street Journal*, 12 February 1985).

The second explanation leads to some interesting conjectures evaluated in this study. The first conjecture is that short-term currency fluctuations do not follow a random walk. The second is that the movement of precious metals may foretell the short-term direction of currencies.

1.3   The Random Walk Model

In a Ph.D. thesis written at the University of Paris in 1900, Louis Bachelier was the first to state that stock market prices follow a random walk model. Largely ignored for a number of years, Bachelier's work is said to have influenced Einstein in his 1905 work on Brownian motion—though Einstein makes no such acknowledgment in his book on the topic. An English translation of Bachelier's thesis was published in 1964.[2]

The random walk model is limited to short-term price fluctuations and assumes that the current price of an issue reflects all the information that can be obtained from the past. Thus, under this model, all forms of price information leading up to today's known price are irrelevant in predicting tomorrow's price. Random walk forms the basis for the efficient-market theory.[3] In the most popular version of this theory, which lends itself to the marketing practiced by security analysts, prices adjust as all publicly available information reaches investors. Since security analysts and other "insiders" are usually the first to obtain relevant information and the retail investors are usually the last to be informed, the inference is that the security analysts can benefit retail investors by acting on information not yet reflected in the issue's price.

For stock market studies, the dominant opinion is that the random walk model applies to stock prices. Granger and Morgenstern state their belief in terms of a law: "The price-determining mechanism described as the random walk model is the only mechanism which is consistent with the unrestrained pursuit of the profit motive by participants in markets of this type."[4] Whether the security analyst benefits the retail investor is, however, a different matter. In a 1933 study, Cowles[5] showed that performances by selected security analysts were no different, on the average, than that of a broadly based stock index. A recent study by Morishita[6] comes to the same conclusion.

Studies of commodity prices tend to reject the random walk model. However, criticisms have been leveled at methodological assumptions in some of these studies.[7] Regarding currency modeling, there appears to be a dearth of publications. Redmon and Stronge[8] reject random walk in their analysis of the Mexican peso. They investigate the argument that futures prices represent people's expectations of future spot prices and that such expectations are rational.[9] Through the use of cross spectral analysis[7] of spot and futures prices, they provide supporting arguments that futures prices have an effect on future spot prices.

2.0   Modeling: Procedures and Results

2.1   The Variables and the Data

The data base consists of six related time series, each measured daily from 1 November 1985 to 25 September 1986:

Y_{1t} = the closing spot price of the British pound (in pounds per dollar),
Y_{2t} = the closing spot price of the Japanese yen (in yen per dollar),
Y_{3t} = the Chicago Mercantile Exchange closing price of the gold future (in ounces per dollar) with the highest open interest,
U_{1t} = the open interest for all pound futures,
U_{2t} = the open interest for all yen futures,
U_{3t} = the open interest corresponding to Y_{3t};

where $t = 1, \ldots, 204$. Regarding open interest, preliminary analyses indicate that changes in the natural logarithm between series—as opposed to changes within series—are more meaningful in their effects on Y_{1t}, Y_{2t}, and Y_{3t}. Thus,

$$Y_{4t} = \ln(U_{1t}) - \ln(U_{2t}) \qquad Y_{5t} = \ln(U_{1t}) - \ln(U_{3t}) \qquad \text{and}$$
$$Y_{6t} = \ln(U_{2t}) - \ln(U_{3t}) \tag{12.1}$$

will replace U_{1t}, U_{2t}, and U_{3t}.

Figure 12.1 presents plots of Y_{1t}, Y_{2t}, and $(Y_{3t})^{-1}$ versus t. The 30- and 90-day futures prices for both the pound and the yen were originally included in the data base and subsequently excluded because in all cases, simple correlations between the spot and futures prices exceed .995.

2.2 Autoregressive, Integrated, Moving-Average (ARIMA) Models

All the series depicted in Figure 12.1, as well as those for Y_{4t} through Y_{6t}, are nonstationary. In modeling the Y_{ht}—ignoring, for the present, interrelations between series—each series is first converted to a stationary series through first differences:[10]

$$y_{ht} = Y_{ht} - Y_{h,t-1} \tag{12.2}$$

where $h = 1, \ldots, m = 6$. Table 12.1 presents the sample autocorrelation function (ACF) and the sample partial autocorrelation function (PACF) for y_{1t}, y_{2t}, and y_{3t}. (Calculations are through BMDP2T[11] software.) The ACF and PACF are used to tentatively specify values of p_h and q_h in the equations

$$y_{ht} = \sum_i {}_*\alpha_{hi} y_{h,t-i} + \sum_j {}_*\gamma_{hj} \delta_{h,t-j} + \delta_{ht} \tag{12.3}$$

where ${}_*\alpha_{hi}$ is the effect on y_{ht} of its ith lag, $y_{h,t-i}$, $i = 1, \ldots, p_h$; ${}_*\gamma_{hj}$ is the effect on y_{ht} of its jth lagged shock, $\delta_{h,t-j}$, $j = 1, \ldots, q_h$; δ_{ht} is the

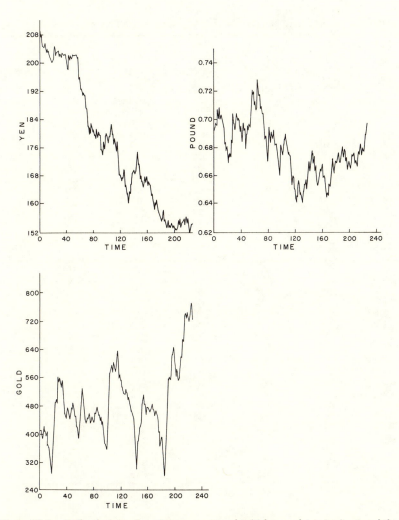

Figure 12.1.   Daily closing prices: Japanese yen and British pound (spot prices) and the most active gold future, November 1985 to September 1986.

error term (or current shock) for the hth equation. Equation (12.3) is an ARIMA model of order p_h in autoregressive (AR) terms and of order r_h in moving-average (MA), or shock, terms. The jth lagged shock, $\delta_{h,t-j}$, is defined as the difference between the observed and expected values of $y_{h,t-j}$. The model descriptor "integrated" refers to differencing required to achieve stationarity.

Box and Jenkins[10] suggest the following guidelines for selecting p_h and q_h. When the model is strictly AR of order p_h, the ACF tails off; the PACF has spikes at lags 1 through p_h and then cuts off. When the model

TABLE 12.1. ACF and Sample PACF for y_{ht} and Its lth Lag, $y_{h,t-l}$; $l = 1, \ldots, 36$

Lag	y_1 ACF[a]	y_1 PACF[b]	y_2 ACF[a]	y_2 PACF[c]	y_3 ACF[d]	y_3 PACF[b]
1	.002	.002	−.097	−.097	.007	.007
2	−.079	−.079	.025	.015	−.122	−.122
3	−.029	−.029	.054	.058	.023	.025
4	−.052	−.059	−.047	−.037	−.065	−.082
5	.083	.079	.046	.036	−.054	−.048
6	.034	.024	−.064	−.058	−.062	−.082
7	.030	.040	−.008	−.017	.082	.076
8	−.059	−.054	−.026	−.032	.086	.065
9	−.021	−.005	.057	.063	−.086	−.074
10	−.012	−.024	.089	.098	.101	.110
11	−.082	−.089	−.050	−.030	.011	−.011
12	.046	.031	.040	.017	−.124	−.083
13	−.007	−.017	−.027	−.027	−.062	−.061
14	−.160	−.160	.028	.026	−.030	−.044
15	.080	.083	−.103	−.107	.111	.095
16	−.034	−.047	−.048	−.049	.049	.046
17	.017	.021	−.024	−.035	.030	.039
18	.068	.057	.106	.128	.071	.035
19	−.092	−.077	−.142	−.149	−.064	−.027
20	.000	.008	.067	.051	−.040	−.004
21	−.023	−.023	−.006	−.015	−.058	−.060
22	.045	.016	.030	.052	.058	.083
23	−.099	−.115	−.075	−.120	.024	−.003
24	.040	.048	−.057	−.037	−.045	−.027
25	−.019	−.067	−.019	−.022	.045	−.003
26	−.084	−.044	−.091	−.069	.003	−.026
27	.091	.062	−.062	−.107	−.007	.032
28	−.021	−.041	−.021	−.027	.035	.049
29	−.108	−.085	−.085	−.054	−.009	.023
30	.059	.044	.025	−.031	.004	.003
31	.064	.069	.024	.023	−.016	−.004
32	−.038	−.043	−.035	−.059	−.029	−.049
33	−.003	−.025	−.062	−.028	.043	.004
34	.055	.071	.058	.047	.074	.102
35	.067	.065	.016	.047	.029	.038
36	.017	.013	−.035	−.045	−.034	−.012

[a]The standard error (s.e.) of the correlation is .07 for the first 18 lags and .08 for the remainder.
[b]The s.e. is .07 for all correlations.
[c]The s.e. is .07 for the first 19 lags and .08 for the remainder.
[d]The s.e. is .07 for the first 12 lags and .08 for the remainder.

is strictly MA of order q_h, the PACF tails off; the ACF has spikes at lags 1 through q_h. For the mixed model in (12.3), both ACF and PACF tail off. The ACF is a mixture of exponentials and damped sine waves after the first $q_h - p_h$ lags. Conversely, the PACF is dominated by a mixture of exponentials and damped sine waves after the first $p_h - q_h$ lags. Application of these guidelines to results in Table 12.1 seems to indicate that each of the three series follows a random walk model, $Y_{ht} = Y_{ht-1} +$

δ_{ht}, assuming one ignores the significant correlations of the 14th lag for the pound and the 19th lag for the yen. Subsequent analysis will reject random walk, which suggests that the selection guidelines may be insufficient for more complex processes and/or that model (12.3) is inadequate. In a related application, Zellner and Palm[12] reach similar conclusions.

2.3 Reduced Equations: Definitions and Assumptions

When contemporaneous time series have possible effects on one another, model (12.3) has restrictive assumptions. For example, in modeling y_{1t} through (12.3), the assumptions are that there exist no direct lagged effects of y_{Ht} and δ_{Ht} (H $\neq$ 1) on y_{1t} and/or that their effects on y_{1t}, if any, are indirect and totally reflected by the lagged, overall effects of y_{1t} and δ_{1t} on y_{1t}. Such prior assumptions may be questionable, especially in exploratory modeling.

To allow for the possibility of direct and/or overall lagged effects of all y_{Ht} and δ_{Ht} on y_{ht}, we consider the following reduced regression system:[12,13]

$$y_{ht} = \sum_H \sum_i \alpha_{Hi} y_{H,t-i} + \sum_H \sum_j \gamma_{Hj} \delta_{H,t-j} + \delta_{ht} \tag{12.4}$$

where α_{Hi} and γ_{Hj} are, respectively, the effects of $y_{H,t-i}$ and $\delta_{H,t-j}$ on y_{ht}; $h, H = 1, \ldots, m = 6$; $i = 1, \ldots, p$; $j = 1, \ldots, q$; and δ_{ht} is the model error for the hth equation.

In matrix notation, (12.4) is rewritten as

$$\mathbf{y}_t = \sum_i A_i \mathbf{y}_{t-1} + \sum_j \Gamma_j \delta_{t-j} + \delta_t \tag{12.5}$$

or

$$A_p(B)\mathbf{y}_t = \Gamma_q(B)\delta_t \tag{12.6}$$

where y_{ht} is a typical element of the $m \times 1$ vector $\mathbf{y}_t$; α_{Hi} is a typical element of the $m \times m$ matrix A_i; γ_{Hj} is a typical element of the $m \times m$ matrix Γ_j; δ_{ht} is a typical element of the $m \times 1$ vector δ_t; $A_p(B) = I - A_1 B - \ldots - A_p B^p$; $\Gamma_q(B) = I - \Gamma_1 B - \ldots - \Gamma_q B^q$; and B is a backshift operator (i.e., $B^k \mathbf{w}_t = \mathbf{w}_{t-k}$). All series are assumed stationary and invertible; that is, the series $\mathbf{y}_t$ is stationary when zeros of $|A_p(B)|$ are outside the unit circle and is invertible when those of $|C_q(B)|$ are all outside the unit circle.[13] Regarding the model error, the assumptions are that the δ_t are normally and independently distributed with expectation $\mathbf{0}$ and variance $\Sigma = (\sigma_{hH})$.

2.4 Reduced Equations: Selection and Estimation

In modeling related time series, model selection is the most troublesome aspect of the selection, estimation, and diagnostic checking stages of model building. Since the number of coefficients increases by $(2m - 1)(p^* + q^*)$ with each added time series, model selection focuses on reducing the number of unknown parameters.

Regarding applications, the literature deals mainly with models containing a small number of related time series (e.g., see Granger and Newbold, pp. 245–48).[13] As the number of related series increases—which Jenkins and Alavi[14] describe as "the curse of higher dimensionality"— model simplification is sought. Considerable simplification occurs when lagged shocks are excluded; that is, model (12.5) becomes purely AR:

$$\mathbf{y}_t = \sum_i A_i \mathbf{y}_{t-i} + \boldsymbol{\delta}_t \qquad\qquad (12.7)$$

To further reduce the number of parameters in (12.7), reduced-rank models[15,16] have been proposed where $A_i = GT_i$. When $\mathbf{y}_t$ is an $m \times 1$ vector, G and T_i are, respectively, $m \times r$ and $r \times m$ matrices; rank (A_i) $= r \le m$. Restrictions are then imposed on G in order that G and T_i are identified. Velu et al.[16] discuss the correspondence between reduced-rank regression and the Box and Tiao[17] canonical analysis of (12.7).

The modeling of currencies differs from those applications referenced above in that (1) the number of related series is relatively large and (2) modeling is not limited, a priori, to the purely AR models. Model selection is based on a stepwise selection of relevant predictors per equation. This could be readily accomplished through conventional stepwise regression (using, for example, BMDP2R[11]) if it were not for the $\delta_{H,t-k}$, which are unknown and estimated iteratively. The stepwise selection (using, per step, the estimation, filter, and cross correlation paragraphs in BMDP2T[11]) is outlined as follows. First, six sets of residuals are calculated, those corrresponding to each of the six ARIMA equations in (12.3). These ARIMA equations should include appropriate predictors as identified by the ACF and PACF. Second, lagged cross correlations are calculated between all pairs of residual sets. Third, significant, lagged cross correlations are scanned to determine the single most significant predictor, if any, per equation. The predictor is then entered in the appropriate equation and all equations are refitted. Based on the residual sets from the new equations, lagged cross correlations are once more calculated and scanned for significant predictors. In this stepwise procedure, predictors that are included or excluded at one step may be excluded or included in a subsequent step. This process is continued until no residual cross correlations are significant. Per step and per equation, estimation is through backcasting;[10] in the iterative process, initial estimates are obtained from the solution to conditional least-squares estimation.[10]

The above approach is applied in selecting and fitting a reduced equation for y_{1t}. For simplicity, the variables $\delta_{H,t-j}$, for $H \neq 1$, have been excluded as possible predictors. Results, as presented in Table 12.2, clearly reject the random walk model for the British pound. At first glance, modeling results appear counterintuitive in two respects. (1) Neither $y_{1,t-1}$ nor $\delta_{1,t-1}$ enters as a predictor, while logic suggests that information on the most recent, known price changes should affect $y_{1,t}$, and (2) there is an excess of significant predictors for y_{1t}. A possible answer to (1) is that $\delta_{1,t-1}$ and/or $y_{1,t-1}$ do affect $y_{1,t}$ but in a second-order model—possibly a bilinear model—as discussed in section 3.2. In general, higher-order models should be considered when logical predictors are not significant in a first-order model. An explanation for (2) may be that both predictors and their corresponding coefficients change as the model is updated; because of these changes, more significant predictors may result. The question of Bayesian estimation in model updates is considered in section 3.4.

One general interpretation of the coefficients in Table 12.2 is that the process seeks equilibrium. For example, the positive effect of the two-day yen lag, $y_{2,t-2}$, is counterbalanced by the negative effect of the two-day pound shock, $\delta_{2,t-2}$. Put simply, higher yen values tend to lead to higher pound values unless the pound is overvalued (in the sense that the $y_{2,t-2}$ is in excess of its expectation). The predictors $\delta_{1,t-29}$ and $y_{2,t-24}$ cor-

TABLE 12.2. Reduced Equation Results for y_{1t} (First Differences, British Pound Spot Price, Pounds/Dollars)

Predictor	Coefficient estimate	Standard error	t
1. $\delta_{1,t-2}$	−.2767	.0505	−5.48
2. $\delta_{1,t-8}$	−.0874	.0508	−1.72
3. $\delta_{1,t-29}$	−.6167	.0448	−13.78
4. $y_{2,t-2}$	.0008	.0002	4.86
5. $y_{2,t-24}$	−.0007	.0002	−4.23
6. $y_{3,t-9}$	−23.59	8.108	−2.91
7. $y_{4,t-1}$	.0107	.0031	3.52
8. $y_{5,t-10}$	−.0084	.0023	−3.59

respond roughly to lagged, one-month futures. Their coefficients indicate that if either is in positive (negative) excess of its expectation, $y_{1,t}$ will tend to decrease (increase). The implication is that stabilizing corrections tend to occur for an under- or overvalued pound during the lifetime of a 30-day futures contract. The effect of the gold lag, $y_{3,t-9}$, is counterintuitive in that its coefficient was expected to be negative instead of positive and that a more recent differenced lag of gold was expected to affect y_{1t}. The following explanations are offered. First, the effect of $y_{3,t-9}$ may be spurious. Second, $y_{3,t-9}$ may be an alias for some other variable. Third, the effect of $y_{3,t-9}$ counterbalances a neglected interaction term that includes $y_{3,t-9}$. Finally, the effect of a more recent differenced lag of gold might appear in second-order modeling. Effects of gold on the pound are thus inconclusive.

The correlation matrix of the coefficient estimates, given in Table 12.3, indicates no apparent problems of multicollinearity.

3.0   Model Enhancement

3.1   Higher-Order Models

When effects of $\delta_{H,t-j}$ on h_{ht} are ignored for $H \neq 1$, critical predictors may be overlooked. For example, abnormal shocks in the daily open interest—reflecting, say, insider trading—may directly affect a price change in the near future. Here, the important question regarding its effects on y_{1t}, y_{2t}, or y_{3t} may not be whether the lagged open interest (in terms of the U_t variables or the V_t variables [12.1]) has shown a large increase or decrease, but whether it has shown a large increase or decrease relative to expectation.

Second-order modeling has intuitive appeal in time series modeling. For example, if the effect of $y_{1,t-1}$ on y_{1t} varies, depending on whether the corresponding price of gold increases or decreases, then y_{1t} is affected by the interaction between $y_{1,t-1}$ and $y_{3,t-1}$. Or, if a lagged shock has a negative effect on y_{1t} when accompanied by a decreased open interest and

TABLE 12.3.   Correlations between Coefficient Estimates in Table 12.2

	2.	3.	4.	5.	6.	7.	8.
1.	−.282	−.540	.238	−.117	−.060	−.111	.055
2.	1.000	−.204	−.059	−.041	.096	.024	−.019
3.		1.000	−.095	.057	−.067	.043	−.063
4.			1.000	−.320	.174	−.064	−.021
5.				1.000	−.169	−.039	−.077
6.					1.000	−.046	−.072
7.						1.000	.033

a positive effect when accompanied by an increased open interest, a significant interaction is again indicated. Bilinear models include two-factor interactions between $y_{h,t-i}$ and $\delta_{h,t-k}$. Such second-order models have been studied[18,19,20] for cases of single time series. In the case of multiple time series, a general second-order model is written as

$$
\begin{aligned}
y_{ht} = &\sum_{H} \sum_{i} (_1\alpha_{Hi})(y_{H,t-i}) \\
&+ \sum_{H,H^*} \sum_{i,i^*} (_2\alpha_{HH^*ii^*})(y_{H,t-i}y_{H^*,t-i^*}) \\
&+ \sum_{H} \sum_{j} (_1\gamma_{Hj})(\delta_{H,t-j}) \\
&+ \sum_{H,H^*} \sum_{j,j^*} (_2\gamma_{HH^*jj^*})(\delta_{H,t-j}\delta_{H^*,t-j^*}) + \delta_{ht}
\end{aligned}
\qquad (12.8)
$$

As the number of time series increases, three-factor interactions may also become relevant. However, stationarity and invertibility conditions have yet to be established for general cases of higher-order models.

3.2   Selecting a Second-Order Model

The following technique is used as a rough guide to selecting second-order predictors for y_{1t}. Let $y_{1t} = \hat{y}_{1t} + e_{1t}$, where $\hat{y}_{1t}$ is the predicted value of y_{1t} based on the equation in Table 12.2 and the e_{1t} denote residuals. In conventional stepwise regression (BMDP2R)[11] with y_{1t} as the dependent variable, scan the following independent variables for significance: y_{1t}, lags of the y_{Ht} and the e_{Ht}, and cross products between lags of y_{ht} and y_{Ht} and between lags of the y_{Ht} and e_{Ht}. This procedure is illustrated by scanning only a few of the most recent lags and associated cross products; lagged shocks are limited to those for e_{1t} but include the differences $d_{1,t-1} = e_{1,t-1} - e_{1,t-2}$. Results of stepwise regression are as follows:

$$
\hat{y}_{1t} = -.0003 + \underset{(.0975)}{.8622y_{1t}} + \underset{(.0711)}{.1886d_{1,t-1}} + \underset{(.2004)}{.3991d_{1,t-1}y_{4,t-1}}
\qquad (12.9)
$$

where $\hat{y}_{1t}$ denotes the stepwise regression prediction of y_{1t}, standard errors are in parentheses, and $R^2 = .3701$. The coefficients of $d_{1,t-1}$ and $d_{1,t-1}y_{4,t-1}$ indicate that when the shocks go from negative to positive in the two most recent days, y_{1t} tends to increase; this increase becomes more pronounced as the corresponding open interest in the pound increases relative to the yen.

One should, of course, scan more interactions, especially those associated with predictors in the model given in Table 12.2. Following selection of a second-order model, the Gauss-Newton method can be applied in estimating model parameters.

3.3 Model Formulation in Terms of Discriminant Analysis

The investor's questions may focus more on categorical predictions such as What are the chances of tomorrow's spot price increasing, decreasing, or remaining about the same? To illustrate such predictions, discriminant analysis is applied after categorizing the y_{1t} according to the following five categories: $y_{1t} < -.006$, $-.006 \leq y_{1t} \leq -.002$, $-.002 < y_{1t} < .002$, $.002 \leq y_{1t} \leq .006$, and $y_{1t} > .006$. The conventional analysis is performed based on the predictors in model (12.9). (In the discriminant analysis of categorized time series responses, it is convenient to utilize predictors selected for reduced regression. Note, however, that lagged shock predictors should be drawn from the final estimate of the reduced model, not from the selection procedure of the previous section.) Based on the discriminant analysis, classification results are presented in Table 12.4. For simplicity, y_{1t} is classified into the category with the largest probability.

Suppose the investment rule is as follows: go long on the pound for either of the first two categories and go short on the pound for either of the last two categories; for the middle category, maintain your current position. Based on this rule, the model seems adequate except for the middle category, the equilibrium state, in which case y_{1t} is not predictable. There is an analogy here with the card game of blackjack. Equilibrium is defined by a full deck—in which case predictions are inaccurate. Nonequilibrium is defined by the deck after the first hand has been dealt and there is either an excess or paucity of tens remaining—in which case predictions are more accurate.

3.4 Use of Prior Information in Model Updates

As new data are collected, the sample is trimmed (in the sense that the most distant observations are deleted from the sample) and the model updated for more accurate forecasts. Frequent updating and trimming allow a quicker detection of changes in the process—since predictors and/ or their coefficients may change over time. (In both the initial fitting and the model update, it may also be appropriate to truncate excessive values of lagged shocks.)

It should be recognized that past model updates provide informative prior information on parameters to be estimated in current model updates.

TABLE 12.4.   Classification of Observations: Bayesian Discriminant Analysis
with Uniform Priors

Observed categories for y_{1t}	Classification categories for y_{1t}				
	$<-.006$	$[-.006, -.002]$	$(-.002, .002)$	$[.002, .006]$	$>.006$
$<-.006$	13	5	2	1	2
$[-.006, -.002]$	8	10	5	4	3
$(-.002, .002)$	10	16	11	14	13
$[.002, .006]$	3	2	4	17	8
$>.006$	2	1	2	1	12

Such prior information can be expressed in terms of prior probability density functions, whose parameters can be estimated empirically from estimates obtained in earlier model updates. The general formulas for model updates that incorporate such prior information are presented in section 2.9 of Chapter 14.

Exercise 1

In modeling fluctuations of the price of the British pound, the dependent variable is defined in terms of daily changes. Discuss modeling approaches when the dependent variable is defined in terms of weekly or monthly changes. What are the advantages and disadvantages of choosing the dependent variable as an index—say, a linear combination[17] of changes of several major currencies such as the pound, yen, and mark?

References

1. Stevenson, W. *Intrepid's Last Case*. New York: Ballantine, 1988. (Quotation, p. 122).

2. Bachelier, L. "Theory of Speculation." In *The Random Character of Stock Market Prices*, ed. P. H. Cootner, pp. 17–78. Cambridge: MIT Press, 1964.

3. Francis, J. *Investment Analysis and Management*. New York: McGraw Hill, 1967.

4. Granger, C. W. J., and Morgenstern, O. *Predictability of Stock Market Prices*. Lexington, Mass.: Heath Lexington, 1970. (Quotation, p. 282).

5. Cowles, A. "Can Stock Market Forecasters Forecast?" *Econometrica* 1 (1933): 309–24.

6. Morishita, G. "An Analysis of the Ability of Account Executives at Full Service Stock Brokerage Firms to Create Managed Common Stock Portfolios That Yield Above Average Capital Gains for Small Investors." M.S. thesis, California State University, Fresno, 1985.

7. Labys, W. C., and Granger, C. W. J. *Speculation, Hedging and Commodity Price Forecast.* Lexington, Mass.: Heath Lexington, 1970.

8. Redmon, M. B., and Stronge, W. B. "The Case of the Mexican Peso." *Review of Business and Economic Research* 16 (Winter 1980–81): 89–97.

9. Muth, J. F. "Rational Expectations and the Theory of Price Movements." *Econometrica* 29 (1961): 315–35.

10. Box, G. E. P., and Jenkins, G. M. *Time Series Analysis: Forecasting and Control.* San Francisco: Holden-Day, 1970.

11. Dixon, W. J., ed. *BMDP Statistical Software.* Berkeley and Los Angeles: University of California Press, 1985.

12. Zellner, A., and Palm, F. "Time Series Analysis and Simultaneous Equation Econometric Models." *Journal of Econometrics* 2 (1974): 17–54.

13. Granger, C. W. J., and Newbold, P. *Forecasting Economic Time Series.* 2d ed. New York: Academic Press, 1986.

14. Jenkins, G. G., and Alavi, A. S. "Some Aspects of Modeling and Forecasting Multivariate Time Series." *Journal of Time Series Analysis* 2 (1981): 1–47.

15. Reinsel, G. C. "Some Results on Multivariate Autoregressive Index Models." *Biometrika* 70 (1983): 145–56.

16. Velu, R. P., Reinsel, G. C., and Wichern, D. W. "Reduced Rank Models for Multiple Time Series." *Biometrika* 73 (1986): 105–18.

17. Box, G. E. P., and Tiao, G. C. "A Canonical Analysis of Multiple Time Series Analysis." *Biometrika* 64 (1977): 355–65.

18. Granger, C. W. J., and Andersen, A. P. *An Introduction to Bilinear Time Series Models.* Göttingen: Vanderhock and Ruprecht, 1978.

19. Subba Rao, T. "On the Theory of Bilinear Time Series." *Journal of the Royal Statistical Society,* series B, 43 (1981): 244–55.

20. Liu, S. I., and Liu, L. "Theory of Bilinear Time Series Models." *Communications in Statistics A,* 1985.

Polio, Pollution, and Profits

Silent night, virulent night.

Modeling Seasonal Time Series

M odels of seasonal time series are developed for purposes of fore-casting, evaluating effects of interventions, and examining historical trends. Interventions are planned or unplanned occurrences that intentionally or unintentionally affect events, either immediately or subsequently.[1,2] A modified Fourier analysis is used to evaluate the effects on air pollution of an intervention, the opening of a new freeway. The freeway was constructed on the premise that pollution would decrease because of the reduction in stop-and-go traffic. Similar modeling is used to track the monthly trend of poliomyelitis in the United States before the vaccine intervention. The focus is on whether epidemics of that period could have been predicted months in advance and whether analogies hold with regard to current influenza outbreaks. In the third study, a variant model is developed to forecast short-term cash flow for a chain of specialty stores and to evaluate effects of advertising interventions on sales.

In modified Fourier modeling, predictors include both harmonics and lagged shocks. Each fitted harmonic should have physical as well as statistical interpretation; otherwise, the model may have limited practical utility. In the absence of physical interpretations, autoregressive, integrated shock modeling is a common recourse (as illustrated in the advertising study). For this class of models, the data are first transformed to a stationary series through appropriate differencing. The dependent variable is then predicted in terms of its lags, lagged shocks, and/or intervention variables.

Modeling results are as follows. (1) The channeling of traffic through freeway corridors, as opposed to the use of city streets, has a negligible effect on improving air quality. (2) Major poliomyelitis outbreaks of the

1950s could have been anticipated two or three months in advance. (3) Effects of advertising monies on sales are contingent on the previous month's sales.

1.0   Historical Trends, Interventions, and Forecasts

This chapter develops models for the following seasonal time series:

1. The monthly mean of the daily maximum ozone level in Fresno, California, from January 1979 to March 1983.
2. The monthly log-incidence of poliomyelitis (per 1 million population) in the United States from April 1949 to March 1957.
3. The monthly sales and advertising outlays for a chain of specialty stores from February 1981 to September 1986.

The data are depicted in Figure 13.1.

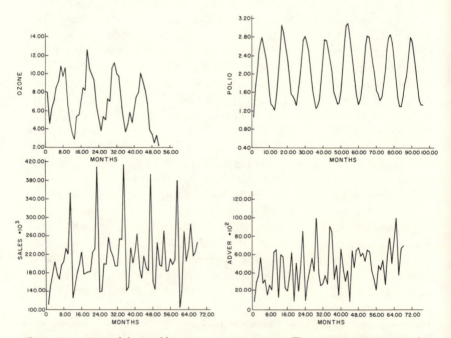

Figure 13.1.   *Upper left:* monthly ozone means (parts per million), January 1979 to March 1983; *upper right:* monthly log-incidence of poliomyelitis (per million population); *lower left and right:* monthly sales (in $1000) and advertising outlays, February 1981 to September 1986.

The purpose of seasonal modeling is to evaluate historical trends and interventions and to provide forecasts in support of decision systems. The study of historical trends is particularly instructive if one acknowledges that history repeats itself.

Periodic regression (Fourier analysis) will be termed the classical analysis, where, typically, the model includes a trend component, a seasonal component, and a random error component.[3] The first two components are usually fitted by polynomial and harmonic terms, respectively. However, it is often the case that the classical model is ill-suited for forecasting even though it may adequately fit the data. This deficiency may result when higher harmonics cannot be given physical interpretation and/or when no consideration is given to effects of lagged shocks. The latter are defined as deviations from expectations in the past, and their effects reflect the influence of past irregularities on subsequent events. Shocks may act as aliases for tangible or intangible variables that affect subsequent events, and they are excluded as predictors.

In the first two applications, periodic regression is modified to include lagged shocks. In the third application, higher harmonics have no physical interpretation, and so we apply a multiplicative, autoregressive, integrated, moving-average (ARIMA) model.[4] The ARIMA model differs from the modified, periodic regression model in that the dependent variable is differenced to achieve stationarity and lags of the differenced dependent variable replace the harmonics as predictors.

2.0 A Modification of the Classical Model: Periodic Regression with Lagged Shocks

A periodic regression model with no interactions is given by

$$Y_t = \alpha_0 + \sum_{h=1} \alpha_h \cos(hct - \theta_h) + \sum_{i=1} \lambda_i t^i + \epsilon_t \qquad (13.1)$$

where Y_t is the response of the dependent variable at time t; α_0 is the intercept; $\Sigma_h \alpha_h \cos(hct - \theta_h)$ is the sum of p sine curves and quantifies the seasonal component; $\Sigma_i \lambda_i t^i$ quantifies the trend component. For ϵ_t (the random error term) the assumption under the classical model is that

$$\epsilon_t : \text{i.i.d.}(0, \sigma_\epsilon^2) \qquad (13.2)$$

For the hth harmonic, α_h is the semiamplitude, θ_h is the phase angle (or the time in angular measure of the maximum for the particular harmonic), and $c = 2\pi/k$ converts the k units of time in a single seasonal cycle to angular measure in radians.

Only Y_t and t are assumed known, so that model (13.1) is nonlinear. However, (13.1) may be linearized by applying the trigonometric identity $\cos(U - V) = \cos(U)\cos(V) + \sin(U)\sin(V)$ as follows:

$$
\begin{aligned}
Y_t &= \alpha_0 + \sum_h \alpha_h[\cos(hct)\cos(\theta_h) + \sin(hct)\sin(\theta_h)] \\
&\quad + \sum_i \lambda_i t^i + \epsilon_t \\
&= \alpha_0 + \sum_h \beta_{1h}x_{1h} + \sum_h \beta_{2h}x_{2h} \\
&\quad + \sum_i \lambda_i t^i + \epsilon_t
\end{aligned}
\tag{13.3}
$$

where

$$
\beta_{1h} = \alpha_h\cos(\theta_h) \quad \text{and} \quad \beta_{2h} = \alpha_h\sin(\theta_h)
\tag{13.4}
$$

$x_{1h} = \cos(hct)$ and $x_{2h} = \sin(hct)$. Let b_{1h} and b_{2h} denote estimates (usually the least-squares estimates) of β_{1h} and β_{2h}, respectively. Then α_h is estimated by

$$
a_h = (b_{1h}^2 + b_{2h}^2)^{1/2}
\tag{13.5}
$$

The estimate of θ_h is based on the signs of b_{1h} and b_{2h}. Letting $\theta_h^* = \tan^{-1}(|b_{2h}/b_{1h}|)$, we estimate θ_h by θ_h^* if both b_{1h} and b_{2h} are positive, by $2\pi - \theta_h^*$ if b_{1h} is positive and b_{2h} is negative, by $\pi + \theta_h^*$ if both b_{1h} and b_{2h} are negative, and by $\pi - \theta_h^*$ if b_{1h} is negative and b_{2h} is positive.

Model (13.1) is modified by writing the error term as

$$
\epsilon_t = \delta_t + \sum_{k=1} \gamma_k \delta_{t-k}
\tag{13.6}
$$

under the assumption that

$$
\delta_t : \text{i.i.d.}(0, \sigma^2)
\tag{13.7}
$$

The regression coefficient γ_k is the effect on Y_t of the kth lagged shock, $\delta_{t-k} = Y_{t-k} - E(Y_{t-k})$. The modified model is nonlinear since the δ_{t-k} are unknown and to be estimated iteratively.

3.0 On the Effects of Opening a New Freeway

3.1 Background

Highway 41 (HW 41), located in Fresno, California, was opened in September 1982. Its stated purpose was to remove traffic from congested urban arterials, to stimulate renewed interest in the downtown business district by providing improved access, and to provide for statewide traffic through Fresno to the mountains and national parks.

A study by federal and state agencies indicated that HW 41 would reduce accidents as well as air and noise pollution. Treating the highway opening as an intervention, our objective is to evaluate its effects on air quality as determined by a sampling station located 3 miles east of HW 41. Air quality is quantified in terms of the monthly mean of daily maximum ozone levels (measured in parts per hundred million).

3.2 Analysis Results: The Classical Model

The plot of the ozone data in Figure 13.1 demonstrates the seasonal fluctuations. Initial analyses are based on the following revision of model (13.1):

$$Y_t = \alpha_0 + \sum_h \alpha_h \cos(hct - \theta_h) + \sum_i \lambda_i t^i + \phi u$$
$$+ \sum_h \sum_i \omega_{hi} t^i \cos(hct - \theta_h) + \epsilon_t \qquad \textbf{(13.8)}$$

where ϕ is the effect of the intervention on Y_t: $u = 0$ for values of t before September 1982, and $u = 1$ for values of t after August 1982. The ω_{hi} quantify effects on Y_t of interactions between the harmonics and time. In $c = 2\pi/k$, $k = 12$ for the 12 monthly data points in the seasonal cycle.

Model (13.8) is linearized in the manner of model (13.3), and predictors are scanned for significance through stepwise regression. Results of this analysis are unambiguous in that only the first two harmonics and u are significant. With $R^2 = .897$ and standard errors in parentheses, the prediction equation for Y_t is given by

$$Y_t = 7.211 - 2.535 \cos(\pi t/6) - 2.077 \sin(\pi t/6) - 1.581u$$
$$ (.190) \qquad\qquad (.179) \qquad\qquad (.387)$$
$$- .488 \cos(\pi t/3) + .244 \sin(\pi t/3)$$
$$ (.181) \qquad\qquad (.180) \qquad\qquad\qquad \textbf{(13.9)}$$

This result indicates that HW 41 has reduced the mean ozone level by an average of 1.58 parts per million. A health official volunteered the opinion that such a drop is negligible in reducing air pollution and that "the opening of new freeways is not a means of reducing air pollution."

The next task is to give physical interpretations to the harmonics, which requires estimation of amplitudes and phase angles. For the first harmonic, α_1 is estimated by $(2.535^2 + 2.077^2)^{1/2} = 3.299$ (see [13.5]), θ_1 is estimated by 219.33 degrees. Converting the θ_1 estimate to a monthly figure, we have $(219.33/360)(12) = 7.31$. Hence, the maximum for the first harmonic occurs in mid-July and the minimum six months later in mid-January. This harmonic has an obvious climatic interpretation.

For the second harmonic, α_2 is estimated by $(.488^2 + .244^2)^{1/2} = .510$, while θ_2 is estimated by 151.97 degrees. Since the second harmonic completes two cycles per year, the first maximum occurs in mid-February (2.53 months) and the second in mid-August (8.53 months). Two explanations can be given for the second harmonic. (1) Because mid-February and mid-August correspond, approximately, to the beginning of the spring and summer university semesters, the influx of traffic degrades air quality (particularly since the sampling station is situated on campus). (2) The peak in mid-February corresponds to the coldest part of the year, when fireplaces are in maximum use. The peak in mid-August corresponds to the last tourist surge of the summer season.

3.3   Analysis Results: The Modified Classical Model

Identification of lagged shocks to be included in the modification in (13.6) is based on the sample autocorrelations between lagged residuals corresponding to model (13.9). Residual autocorrelations identify δ_{t-1} as the most recent lagged shock affecting Y_t. With δ_{t-1} included in the model, residual autocorrelations identify δ_{t-2} as the most recent lagged shock affecting Y_t. This process is continued until no residual autocorrelations are significant. The end result is that δ_{t-1}, δ_{t-2}, δ_{t-6}, and δ_{t-13} are included in the model as predictors along with the first two harmonics and u. BMDP2T[5] software provides backcasting estimates;[4] initial estimates in the iterative process are obtained from conditional least-squares estimation. Estimation results are as follows, where $\hat{Y}_t$ denotes the predicted value of Y_t, $\hat{\delta}_{t-k}$ denotes the estimate of δ_{t-k}, and $R^2 = .941$:

$$\hat{Y}_t = 7.266 - 2.517 \cos(\pi t/6) - 2.133 \sin(\pi t/6) - 1.855u$$
$$\phantom{\hat{Y}_t = 7.266}(.127)(.117)(.326)$$
$$\phantom{\hat{Y}_t = 7.266}- .284 \cos(\pi t/3) - .195 \sin(\pi t/3) - .264\delta_{t-1}$$
$$\phantom{\hat{Y}_t = 7.266-.28}(.023)(.027)(.107)$$

$$+ \quad .285\delta_{t-2} - \quad .331\delta_{t-6} - \quad .618\delta_{t-13}$$
$$(.107) \qquad (.115) \qquad (.094) \qquad\qquad \textbf{(13.10)}$$

Figure 13.2 presents a three-dimensional illustration of model (13.10) with $u = \delta_{t-2} = \delta_{t-6} = \delta_{t-13} = 0$; t ranges over the 48 months of the sample, while δ_{t-1} ranges from -3 to 3.

Comparison of like coefficients in models (13.9) and (13.10) shows minor changes in the first harmonic and somewhat larger changes in the second harmonic, which reflects correlations between the second harmonic and lagged shocks. The coefficient of $\hat{\delta}_{t-1}$ indicates that the ozone level will tend to be higher (lower) when it is below (above) its expectation in the previous month. Since the coefficient of $\hat{\delta}_{t-2}$ is opposite in sign to that of $\hat{\delta}_{t-1}$, an implication is that the agricultural "burn days" are reflected in the model; for example, if, in one period, agricultural burning reduces air quality below regulated standards, burning is disallowed or reduced in subsequent periods. (Fresno County ranks first among all U.S. counties in the gross value of its agricultural products.) While the first two lagged shocks reflect an attempted equilibrium imposed by human agency, the last two shocks may reflect a more natural equilibrium imposed by the weather; for example, if weather conditions led to worse-

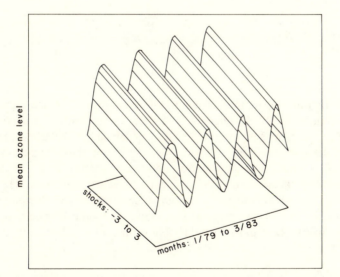

Figure 13.2. Model (13.10): mean ozone levels as a function of time (in months) and the first lagged shock.

than-expected air quality 6 and 13 months ago, conditions will tend to change and lead to better air quality in the present.

4.0   Modeling the Course of a Communicable Disease
4.1   Background

Data on the monthly log-incidence of poliomyelitis cover the period just prior to the demise of the disease through the Salk and Sabin vaccines. At the time the data were published, the classical analysis was the conventional method of modeling.[3] Here we reanalyze the data in terms of the modified classical model. The intent is to evaluate the conjecture that an excess of polio cases in one period portends an excess in the subsequent periods. If the conjecture is valid, then indicators may have existed for major outbreaks. Such a finding may be relevant to current seasonal outbreaks of influenza.

4.2   Analysis Results

As in the previous study, model (13.8) (excluding the intervention variable) is fitted to the data through stepwise regression. With $R^2 = .955$, the first two harmonics dominate the prediction. The fitted equation is

$$\hat{Y}_t = 2.046 - \underset{(.026)}{.769} \cos(\pi t/6) - \underset{(.026)}{.047} \sin(\pi t/6) + \underset{(.017)}{.038} \cos(\pi t/3)$$
$$- \underset{(.017)}{.017} \sin(\pi t/3)$$

$$\text{(13.11)}$$

For the first harmonic, the semiamplitude estimate is .771 and the phase angle estimate is 183.52 degrees. The latter corresponds to a maximum in early September and a minimum in early January. For the second harmonic, the semiamplitude estimate is .080 and the phase angle estimate is 300.57 degrees. The latter corresponds to maximums in early August and February; the minimums occur in early November and May. The first harmonic corresponds to the well-known epidemiological fluctuation of the disease. The interpretation of the second harmonic is uncertain.

Modification of model (13.11) follows the approach in section 3.3. With $R^2 = .975$, the modified prediction equation is given by

$$\hat{Y}_t = 2.042 - \underset{(.026)}{.775} \cos(\pi t/6) - \underset{(.026)}{.059} \sin(\pi t/6) + \underset{(.017)}{.033} \cos(\pi t/3)$$

$$- \ .066 \sin(\pi t/3) + \ .674\delta_{t-1} + \ .367\delta_{t-2} + \ .207\delta_{t-3}$$
$$(.017) \qquad\qquad (.096) \qquad (.113) \qquad (.095)$$
$$\tag{13.12}$$

Comparison of like coefficients in models (13.11) and (13.12) shows very small differences. All lagged shocks have positive coefficients, indicating, historically, that if the number of polio cases exceeded expectation in any of the previous three months, the number of cases tended to be higher in subsequent months. Based on these shock predictors, the implication is that major polio epidemics might have been predicted as much as three months in advance—knowledge that certainly would have benefited health officials. Because of interventions by the Salk and Sabin vaccines, data subsequent to those analyzed show a sharply decreasing, damped sine trend.

5.0 Modeling Sales and Effects of Advertising Outlays

5.1 Background

A study by Araki[6] provides the data on monthly sales for a chain of specialty stores offering half-size apparel for larger women. Modeling is intended to provide accurate, short-term forecasts of cash flow. Such forecasts form a basis for estimating the amount and maturity of short-term assets and borrowing portfolios and/or for signaling pending financial problems. Modeling also provides an evaluation of the effect of advertising intervention on sales.

5.2 A Forecasting Model

Application of Fourier analysis to the sales data is an exercise in futility. The significance of the first six harmonics—most with no physical interpretation—provides a model with no practical utility. In terms of an ARIMA analysis, a reasonable alternative is provided by the following multiplicative seasonal model:[4]

$$(1 - \alpha_1 B^1)(1 - \alpha_2 B^2)y_t = (1 - \gamma B^4)\delta_t + \phi(A_t/Y_{t-1} - \mu) \tag{13.13}$$

where B is a backshift operator (i.e., $B^k z_t = z_{t-k}$); α_1, α_2, γ, and ϕ are, respectively, the direct effects of y_{t-1}, y_{t-2}, δ_{t-4}, and $(A_t/Y_{t-1} - \mu)$ on y_t; δ_t is the model error (or the current shock); A_t is the dollar amount spent on advertising during time t; and μ is the average value of A_t/Y_{t-1}. In this modeling procedure, the sales data (denoted by the Y_t) are converted to a stationary series through first and twelfth differences:

$$y_t = (Y_t - Y_{t-1}) - (Y_{t-12} - Y_{t-13}) \tag{13.14}$$

The difference $Y_t - Y_{t-12}$ does not provide stationarity.

Model (13.13) is obtained in three stages. First, y_{t-1} and y_{t-2} are identified as predictors for y_t through examination of the sample auto-correlation and partial autocorrelation functions for y_t. Second, δ_{t-4} is identified as a predictor through the sample autocorrelation function of lagged residuals from the model obtained in stage 1. Finally, the advertising variable A_t/Y_{t-1} is identified through filtering[4] and then cross correlating the resulting residuals between time series (e.g., see the filter and cross correlation paragraphs of BMDP2T). The rationale for the ratio A_t/Y_{t-1} (as opposed to A_t and its lags) is that current advertising outlays (A_t) affect current sales (Y_t) in a relative (or interactive) sense—relative to last month's sales (Y_{t-1}). Lagged values of A_t/Y_{t-1} tend to be correlated with lagged values of both Y_t and δ_t. Such correlations are not surprising since one way of inducing a nonzero shock is through the intervention of advertising.

The result of fitting model (13.13) through backcasting estimation is as follows:

$$(1 + .549B^1)(1 + .743B^2)y_t = (1 - .917B^4)\delta_t + .457(A_t/Y_{t-1} - 23.7)$$
$$\;\;\;\;(.121)\;\;\;\;\;\;\;\;\;\;(.102)\;\;\;\;\;\;\;\;\;\;\;\;\;\;\;\;\;(.036)\;\;\;\;\;\;\;\;(.124)$$

$$\tag{13.15}$$

Monthly sales for the last 12 months of the sample are withheld from model estimation in evaluating the model's forecasting validity. Forecast results for these last 12 months are given in Table 13.1. All forecasts are reasonably close to observed sales except for January, where the forecast exceeds the observed sales by $65,692.

5.3 The Effects of Advertising

Effects of advertising are discussed in terms of the advertising variable in model (13.15). As A_t is increased, Y_t tends to increase so long as A_t/Y_{t-1} exceeds 23.7, the sample mean of A_t/Y_{t-1}. (In Figure 13.1 monthly sales figures are in thousands of dollars, while advertising outlays are in actual dollars.) The effect of A_t on Y_t is illustrated in Table 13.2 for each of five values of Y_{t-1}. For example, if $Y_{t-1} = \$150,000$, then A_t affects Y_t positively given that A_t exceeds $3,549.51—in which case the return

TABLE 13.1.   Monthly Sales and Forecasts Based on Model (13.15)

Month	Sales	Forecast	Standard error	Residual
Oct 85	$197,056	$171,452	24,080	25,604
Nov 85	207,520	183,638	26,420	23,882
Dec 85	379,504	380,436	26,420	−932
Jan 86	104,543	170,235	27,108	−65,692
Feb 86	142,765	158,653	27,747	−15,888
Mar 86	270,017	260,066	27,755	9,959
Apr 86	204,436	220,284	27,984	−15,848
May 86	230,373	226,450	28,053	3,923
Jun 86	285,715	297,305	28,124	−11,590
Jul 86	214,411	212,574	28,125	1,837
Aug 86	223,823	214,759	28,243	9,064
Sep 86	246,560	244,975	28,272	1,584

Source: S. Araki, "Sales Forecasting by Time Series Analysis for Village East Stores," unpublished graduate project, California State University, Fresno, 1986.

in sales per advertising dollar is $3.06. For Y_{t-1} = $250,000, the effect of A_t on Y_t is positive if A_t exceeds $5,915—in which case the return in sales per advertising dollar is $1.84. Clearly, as Y_{t-1} increases, A_t must also increase if A_t/Y_{t-1} is to affect Y_t positively; but by the same token, the return in sales per advertising dollar decreases. In general, the lower last month's sales, the greater the effect of this month's advertising outlay on this month's sales, assuming the advertising monies exceed a threshold value. Conversely, the higher last month's sales, the less the effect of this month's advertising outlay on this month's sales—again assuming advertising monies exceed a corresponding threshold.

These findings on advertising effects are specific to the product sold and probably to the retailer; for example, advertising dollars affect the purchase of clothing and grocery items differently. Because of data limitations, the effect of the advertising mode—television, radio, newspapers, etc.—is still to be studied.

TABLE 13.2.   Effects of Advertising Outlay (A_t) on Sales (Y_t) Based on Model (13.15)

Previous month's sales (Y_{t-1})	Advertising threshold: A_t value above which the advertising effect on sales is positive	Dollar return in sales per advertising dollar
$150,000	$3,550	$3.06
200,000	4,748	2.29
250,000	5,916	1.84
300,000	7,122	1.52
400,000	7,624	1.41

Source: S. Araki, "Sales Forecasting by Time Series Analysis for Villaga East Stores," unpublished graduate project, California State University, Fresno, 1986.

Exercise 1

Apply ARIMA methods to the poliomyelitis and pollution data and compare the results with those obtained through modified classical modeling. Can you provide arguments that second-order ARIMA modeling—as discussed in Chapter 12—should be considered?

References

1. Glass, G. V. "Estimating the Effects of Intervention into a Nonstationary Time Series." *American Education Research Journal* 9, no. 3 (1972): 463–77.

2. Box, G. E. P., and Tiao, G. C. "Intervention Analysis with Application to Economic and Environmental Problems." *Journal of the American Statistical Association* 70, no. 349 (1975): 70–80.

3. Bliss, C. I. "Periodic Regression in Biology and Climatology." *Connecticut Agricultural Experiment Station Bulletin,* no. 615 (1958).

4. Box, G. E. P., and Jenkins, G. M. *Time Series Analysis: Forecasting and Control.* Holden-Day: San Francisco, 1970.

5. Dixon, W. J., ed. *BMDP Statistical Software.* Berkeley and Los Angeles: University of California Press, 1985.

6. Araki, S. "Sales Forecasting by Time Series Analysis for Village East Stores." Unpublished graduate project, California State University, Fresno, 1986.

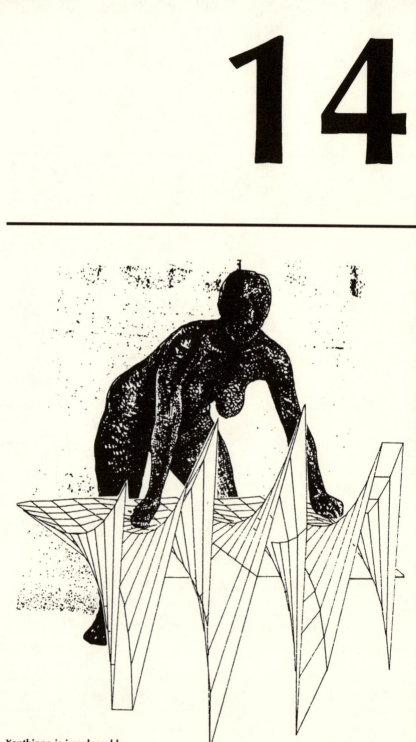

Xanthippe is irreplaceable.

ethodological Overview

1.0 Bayesian Discriminant Analysis

1.1 Categorical versus Continuous Predictions

Assume the experimental unit—the entity on which controls are imposed and from which variables are measured—is characterized by p variables and belongs, unbeknownst, to one of q known populations. The unit cannot be identified with any population directly, but only through the observed values of one or more of the p variables. The objectives are

1. to estimate the probability that the unit belongs to any particular population and/or
2. to classify the unit into one of the populations based on a statistical rule.

These objectives can often be addressed through Bayesian discriminant analysis, which complements regression analysis by providing predictions for categorical, rather than continuous, dependent variables. Such categorical predictions are in terms of objective (1) where probabilities are conditional on observed values of one or more of the p variables characterizing the unit.

Throughout this book, the assumption is that the populations are known in the sense that the data can be subdivided, a priori, according to these populations. This is in contrast to studies where the populations are unknown and to be defined; common recourses in such studies include factor[1] and cluster[2] analysis.

1.2 Prediction versus Decision Making

The first objective involves prediction and is addressed as follows. Let $\mathbf{y}' = (y_1, \ldots, y_i, \ldots, y_p)$ denote the row vector of p variables characterizing a unit belonging to population G_j, $j = 1, \ldots, q$. The probabilities $P(\mathbf{y}, G_j)$ and $P(G_j|\mathbf{y})$ denote, respectively, the joint probability of $\mathbf{y}$ and G_j and the conditional probability of G_j given $\mathbf{y}$. The joint probability function $P(\mathbf{y}, G_j)$ can be expressed in two ways:

$$P(\mathbf{y}, G_j) = P(\mathbf{y})P(G_j|\mathbf{y}) = P(G_j)P(\mathbf{y}|G_j)$$

Since

$$P(\mathbf{y}) = \sum_{j*=1}^{q} P(G_{j*})P(\mathbf{y}|G_{j*})$$

we have the results of Bayes's theorem:

$$P(G_j|\mathbf{y}) = \frac{P(G_j)P(\mathbf{y}|G_j)}{\displaystyle\sum_{j*=1}^{q} P(G_{j*})P(\mathbf{y}|G_{j*})} \tag{14.1}$$

The $P(G_j|\mathbf{y})$ are posterior probabilities, and the $P(G_j)$, prior probabilities. The difference in meaning between the two types of probability is that before observing $\mathbf{y}$, the unit belongs to G_j with probability $P(G_j)$. After examining the observed $\mathbf{y}$, say $\mathbf{y} = \mathbf{y}_0$, the unit belongs to G_j with probability $P(G_j|\mathbf{y}_0)$. Objective (1) is fulfilled by specifying $P(G_j)$ and a probability density function (pdf) for $P(\mathbf{y}|G_j)$.

The second objective shifts from prediction to decision making since the act of classifying a unit is a consequence of a decision rule. The rule can vary from the simple to the complex. A simple rule is to assign the unit to the population with the largest $P(G_j|\mathbf{y} = \mathbf{y}_0)$. A more complex statistical decision rule incorporates potential losses in terms of the costs of misclassification. Consider, for example, $q = 2$ populations and let $M(j|j*)$ denote the cost of misclassifying the unit into G_j when it actually belongs to G_{j*}. Assume a p-variate normal pdf[1] for $P(\mathbf{y}|G_j)$:

$$P(\mathbf{y}|G_j) = (2\pi)^{-p/2} |\Sigma_j|^{-1/2} \exp[-(\mathbf{y} - \boldsymbol{\mu}_j)' \Sigma_j^{-1} (\mathbf{y} - \boldsymbol{\mu}_j)/2] \tag{14.2}$$

where $E(\mathbf{y}|G_j) = \boldsymbol{\mu}_j$ denotes the expectation of $\mathbf{y}$ for population G_j and

$$\text{var}(\mathbf{y} \mid G_j) = \Sigma_j = E[\mathbf{y} - E(\mathbf{y} \mid G_j)][\mathbf{y} - E(\mathbf{y} \mid G_j)']$$

Under the assumptions that $\Sigma_1 = \Sigma_2 = \Sigma$ and that Σ and the $\boldsymbol{\mu}_j$ are known, Anderson[3] shows that the following rule minimizes the expected cost of misclassification. Assign the unit to the first population if

$$\mathbf{y}_0' \Sigma^{-1} (\boldsymbol{\mu}_1 - \boldsymbol{\mu}_2) \geq \left[\frac{(\boldsymbol{\mu}_1 - \boldsymbol{\mu}_2)' \Sigma^{-1} (\boldsymbol{\mu}_1 - \boldsymbol{\mu}_2)}{2} \right] \\ + \ln\left\{ \frac{[1 - P(G_1)]M(1 \mid 2)}{P(G_1)M(2 \mid 1)} \right\}$$

and to the second population otherwise. When unknown, $P(G_j)$ may be chosen such that the rule minimizes the maximum expected loss of misclassification.[4]

In practice, emphasis is primarily on prediction and simpler decision rules. Complex statistical rules tend to be avoided. Why? First, it is often difficult to devise credible costs of misclassification on a per case basis—at least under prevailing time and cost constraints. For example, what are the consequences—in terms of dollars—of convicting an innocent person or of acquitting a guilty person? Second, the individual making the decision is usually not the person providing the statistical prediction. When the latter individual proposes a complex decision rule as a "bottom line," he may cast himself in the role of a usurper. Thus, difficulties related to complex statistical rules can be both technical and political. A long-term remedy for such difficulties includes documentation of non-contrived applications of complex statistical decision rules that have proved successful.

1.3 The Conventional Analysis

Three assumptions underlie the conventional Bayesian discriminant analysis:

1. $P(G_j \mid \mathbf{y})$ is a p-variate normal pdf as given in (14.2).
2. The variances/covariances of elements of $\mathbf{y}$ are the same between populations; that is, $\text{var}(\mathbf{y} \mid G_j) = \Sigma_j = \Sigma$ for all j.
3. Observed values of $\mathbf{y}$ are independent between all experimental units.

Under these assumptions, (14.1) becomes

$$P(G_j|\mathbf{y}) = \left\{ 1 + \sum_{j*\neq j}^{q} [P(G_{j*})/P(G_j)]\exp(\beta_{0j*} + \boldsymbol{\beta}'_{j*}\mathbf{y}) \right\}^{-1} \qquad \textbf{(14.3)}$$

where

$$\beta_{0j*} = (\boldsymbol{\mu}'_j \Sigma^{-1} \boldsymbol{\mu}_j - \boldsymbol{\mu}'_{j*} \Sigma^{-1} \boldsymbol{\mu}_{j*})/2 \qquad \text{and} \qquad \boldsymbol{\beta}_{j*} = \Sigma^{-1}(\boldsymbol{\mu}_{j*} - \boldsymbol{\mu}_j)$$

The parameters $\boldsymbol{\mu}_j$ and Σ are usually unknown and estimated as follows. Let $\mathbf{y}_{jg}(p \times 1) = (y_{1jg}, \ldots, y_{ijg}, \ldots, y_{pjg})'$ denote the gth observation on $\mathbf{y}$ from population G_j; $g = 1, \ldots, n_j$. Then $\boldsymbol{\mu}_j$ and Σ are estimated by $\bar{\mathbf{y}}_j$ and S, respectively, where $\bar{\mathbf{y}}_j(p \times 1) = (\bar{y}_{ij})$; that is, $\bar{y}_{ij}$ is a typical element of the $p \times 1$ vector $\bar{\mathbf{y}}_j$;

$$\bar{y}_{ij} = \sum_{g=1} y_{ijg}/n_j$$

$$S_j(p \times p) = (S_{ijj*})$$

$$S_{ijj*} = \sum_{g=1} (y_{ijg} - \bar{y}_{ij})(y_{ij*g} - \bar{y}_{ij*})/(n_j - 1) \qquad \textbf{(14.4)}$$

Since it is assumed that $\Sigma_j = \Sigma$ for all j, Σ is estimated by

$$S = \sum_{j=1}^{q} (n_j - 1)S_j \Bigg/ \left(\sum_{j=1}^{q} n_j - q \right) \qquad \textbf{(14.5)}$$

$\boldsymbol{\beta}_{j*}$ by

$$\mathbf{b}_{j*} = S^{-1}(\bar{\mathbf{y}}_{j*} - \bar{\mathbf{y}}_j) \qquad \textbf{(14.6)}$$

and β_{0j*} by

$$\mathbf{b}_{0j*} = (\bar{\mathbf{y}}'_j S^{-1} \bar{\mathbf{y}}_j - \bar{\mathbf{y}}'_{j*} S^{-1} \bar{\mathbf{y}}_{j*})/2 \qquad \textbf{(14.7)}$$

For the case of two populations, $\mathbf{y}'\mathbf{b}_{j*}$ defines Fisher's linear discriminant function, which maximizes the variation between population samples relative to the within-sample variation.

The posterior probability is inversely proportional to

$$D_{0j}^2 = (\mathbf{y}_0 - \mathbf{y}_j)'S^{-1}(\mathbf{y}_0 - \mathbf{y}_j) \qquad \textbf{(14.8)}$$

the normalized distance from $\mathbf{y}_0$ to $\mathbf{y}_j$. (D_{0j}^2 is termed the Mahalanobis distance.) If all D_{0j}^2 are large for the observed $\mathbf{y}_0$, the implication is either that the model is inadequate or that the corresponding experimental unit belongs to none of the q populations under study.

For applications with $q \geq 2$, James-Stein estimation[5] of the $\boldsymbol{\mu}_j$ may improve results of the conventional analysis. This approach is illustrated in the reanalysis of Fisher's iris data in section 1.7.

When there is no information regarding the $P(G_j)$, uniform priors are assumed; that is, $P(G_j) = 1/q$, in which case (14.3) becomes

$$P(G_j|\mathbf{y}) = \left[1 + \sum_{j*=1}^{q} \exp(\beta_{0j*} + \boldsymbol{\beta}_{j*}'\mathbf{y}) \right]^{-1} \tag{14.9}$$

Nonuniform priors may be based on subjective judgment—such as the degree of rational belief—or on alternative data sources. Or, if each population is sampled in proportion to its size, $P(G_j)$ might be estimated by

$$n_j \Big/ \sum_{j*=1}^{q} n_{j*}$$

where n_j denotes the number of experimental units sampled from the jth population.

Problems of validity and/or ethics can arise when the $P(G_j)$ are chosen subjectively and are in marked contrast with the $P(G_j|y)$ based on uniform priors. Too many instances can be documented where the priors have been chosen to override the data simply because the data did not support the experimenter's viewpoint. In developing his theorem, the Reverend Mr. Bayes might have emphasized his vocation as well as his avocation.

1.4 Misclassification Probabilities

Consider the simple rule that classifies the unit into that population with the largest $P(G_j|\mathbf{y} = \mathbf{y}_0)$. What is the probability of misclassifying the unit into G_j when it actually belongs to G_{j*}? Under the conventional analysis, misclassification probabilities are estimated empirically as discussed below. Such estimates are valid if the sample sizes (the n_i) are large both in absolute value and relative to the value of p—in which case the parameters are closely approximated and thus replaced by corresponding sample estimates. If, however, the sample sizes are small or not large relative to p, the estimated misclassification probabilities may be misleading, depending on the empirical approach.

Several publications[6,7,8] show that the exact small sample properties of $b_{0j} + b_j' y$ are complex and unresolved, even for two populations. An alternative is through empirical approaches,[9,10,11] several of which are described as follows:

1. Classify each observation after using all the observations in estimating the posterior probabilities; then use the proportions of misclassified observations to estimate the misclassification probabilities.
2. Withhold one portion of the sample; use the other portion to estimate the $P(G_j|y)$; base the estimated misclassification probabilities on the withheld portion.
3. Apply the jackknife technique, where observations are deleted one at a time; the deleted observation is then classified by the estimated $P(G_j|y)$ based on all the other observations; all the observations are thus used to estimate the misclassification probabilities.

Note that in (2), there is independence between the estimated $P(G_j|y)$ and the withheld sample, which is not the case in (1). The jackknife amounts to withholding the entire sample while, at the same time, ensuring independence between the estimated $P(G_j|y)$ and the withheld sample. A Monte Carlo study[11] shows that option (3) performs well and that option (1) leads to biased estimates of misclassification probabilities unless the n_j are large. When the sample is small, (2) may not be valid. Options (1) and (3) are available in BMDP7M,[12] the routine for stepwise discriminant analysis.

1.5 Procedures under Heteroscedastic Data

In application, heteroscedastic data are common. It is likely that the assumed homogeneity of the Σ_j is violated as often as the assumed homogeneity of error variances in regression analysis. As such, the conventional analysis should be preceded with a test of

$$H_0 : \Sigma_j = \Sigma \text{ for all } j \qquad (14.10)$$

Anderson[3] and Box[13] provide tests of H_0 based on the statistic

$$L = \sum_{j=1}^{q} (n_j - 1)\ln|S| - \sum_{j=1}^{q} (n_j - 1)\ln|S_j| \qquad (14.11)$$

Box shows that, under H_0,

$$KL \qquad (14.12)$$

is, asymptotically, an approximate χ^2 variate with $(q - 1)p(p + 1)$ degrees of freedom:

$$K = 1 - \left(\sum_{j=1}^{q} \frac{1}{n_j - 1} - \frac{1}{\sum_{j=1}^{q} n_j - q}\right) \frac{2p + 3p - 1}{6(p + 1)(q - 1)} \tag{14.13}$$

The approximation appears good for p and q less than 4 or 5 and values of n greater than 18. For larger p and q and smaller n_j, Box develops approximations to the F pdf. It should be emphasized that these tests are based on the normality assumption and are not robust to departures from normality.

If H_0 is rejected and the n_j are large (both in absolute value and relative to p), sample estimates may be substituted for population parameters in the normal pdf in (14.2). The posterior probability $P(G_j|\mathbf{y})$ is then estimated by

$$\frac{P(G_j)|S_j|^{-1/2} \exp[(\mathbf{y} - \mathbf{y}_j)'S_j^{-1}(\mathbf{y} - \mathbf{y}_j)/2]}{\sum_{j*=1}^{q} P(G_{j*})|S_{j*}|^{-1/2} \exp[(\mathbf{y} - \mathbf{y}_{j*})'S_{j*}^{-1}(\mathbf{y} - \mathbf{y}_{j*})/2]} \tag{14.14}$$

This approach is termed quadratic discriminant analysis; that is, when the S_j differ, (14.14) contains second-order terms in elements of $\mathbf{y}$. However, when the sample sizes are small and the data are mildly heteroscedastic, Monte Carlo studies[14] have shown that more reliable results may be obtained through the conventional, rather than the quadratic, discriminant analysis.

The quadratic analysis is found to perform poorly when elements of $\mathbf{y}$ are heteroscedastic and nonnormal.[15] One recourse is to attempt normality-inducing transformations. (Similar to regression, such transformations may also relieve the heteroscedasticity.) If normality cannot be achieved through transformation, $P(\mathbf{y}|G_j)$ may be selected from a wide variety[16] of nonsymmetric multivariate pdf's that conform to the problem at hand.

If under the conventional assumptions the n_j are small, it may be reasonable to replace the p-variate normal pdf for $P(\mathbf{y}|G_j)$ with the p-variate Student t pdf:[16]

$$P(\mathbf{y}|G_j) = C_j[(n_j - 1) + (\mathbf{y} - \boldsymbol{\mu}_j)'S^{-1}(\mathbf{y} - \boldsymbol{\mu}_j)]^{-(p+n_j-1)/2} \tag{14.15}$$

where

$$C_j = \frac{(n_j - 1)^{(n_j-1)/2}[(p + n_j - 1)/2]|S|^{-1/2}}{\pi^{p/2}[(n_j - 1)/2]}$$

As the n_j increase, (14.15) approaches the multivariate normal pdf.

In applying (14.14), problems increase in severity when p, the number of elements in $\mathbf{y}$, is large relative to the n_j. Thus, one objective should be to keep the number of predictors small—especially in the heteroscedastic case relative to the homoscedastic case.[17] Under the conventional assumptions, BMDP7M[12] provides a scanning procedure for selecting a small subset of significant predictors. For the quadratic analysis, Fatti and Hawkins[18] provide a promising scanning procedure for selecting predictors.

1.6   Recourses for Categorical Predictors

When some or all of the p variables characterizing the experimental unit are discrete, the normality assumption in (14.2) is questionable. There are a number of recourses: (1) logistic regression may be utilized; (2) a discrete pdf may be assumed for the categorical predictors; (3) the variables may be transformed to linear combinations thereof through principal component or factor analysis; (4) the conventional analysis may be utilized, regardless of the assumed normality for the discrete variables, if prediction is paramount and predictive validity is established through, say, the jackknife technique.

The software program BMDPLR[12] provides the option of stepwise logistic regression. For two populations, the model

$$E(G_j|\mathbf{y}) = \exp(f_{0j} + \mathbf{f}_j'\mathbf{y})/[1 + \exp(f_{0j} + \mathbf{f}_j'\mathbf{y})] \tag{14.16}$$

is fitted to the data through maximum-likelihood estimation, where f_{0j} and the vector $\mathbf{f}_j$ are unknown parameters to be estimated. The discrete elements of $\mathbf{y}$ are converted to dummy variables as in analysis of variance. In the stepwise procedure, only those elements of $\mathbf{y}$ that significantly add to the discrimination between populations are included in the model. Note that model (14.16) can be written as

$$E(G_j|\mathbf{y}) = [1 + \exp(-f_{0j} - \mathbf{f}_j'\mathbf{y})]^{-1} \tag{14.17}$$

which is identical to model (14.9). Thus, for two populations and uniform priors in the conventional discriminant analysis, the model is identical to that for logistic regression. For this reason, the two approaches, very often, lead to nearly identical results.

In studies where **y** measures responses to numerous questions—such as in a psychological inventory—and where samples are large and representative of the populations under consideration, option (3) is often appropriate. (For small sample sizes, it may be inappropriate unless it is known that the sample eigenvectors defining the linear combinations are good approximations to the population eigenvectors.)[1] Reasons for this recourse are as follows. First, problems of multicollinearity[19] are avoided. Second, the principal components tend to be symmetrically distributed, which supports the normality assumption. Third, relevant discrete variables, when taken in linear combination, are included in the model even though they may have small weights. When scanned individually through stepwise procedures, these variables might not be statistically significant, especially if their number is large—as in human factor inventories. Fourth, principal components—or rotations thereof as in factor analysis—can often be given physical interpretation. Fifth, when the number of discrete variables is large, scanning interaction between relatively few principal components is a simple way of evaluating the significance of second-order terms. Anderson[3] presents a mathematical treatment of principal component analysis; Morrison[1] summarizes its development in connection with factor analysis.

In option (2), an appropriate selection of a discrete pdf for $P(\mathbf{y}|G_j)$ depends on the application. For experiments falling toward the controlled end of the spectrum, elements of **y** might follow a binomial or multinomial pdf. For the latter pdf, $P(\mathbf{y}|G_j)$ is chosen as

$$f(\mathbf{y}|\boldsymbol{\pi}_j) = N! \prod_{i=1}^{p} (\pi_{ij})^{y_{ij}}/y_{ij}! \tag{14.18}$$

where $N = \Sigma_{i=1}^{p} y_i$, $\boldsymbol{\pi}_j = (\pi_{1j}, \ldots, \pi_{ij}, \ldots, \pi_{pj})'$, $\Sigma_{i=1}^{p} \pi_{ij} = 1$, and $\boldsymbol{\pi}_j$ is assumed to remain constant for all experimental units belonging to population G_j. For more uncontrolled experiments—especially those in areas of operational test and evaluation where **y** is measured from an experimental unit in each of a number of field trials—$\boldsymbol{\pi}_j$ may vary between trials within population G_j. To develop a pdf that accounts for between-trial variation in the $\boldsymbol{\pi}_j$, it may be appropriate to assume that $\boldsymbol{\pi}_j$ follows a p-variate beta pdf between trials in population G_j:

$$g(\boldsymbol{\pi}_j|\boldsymbol{\alpha}_j) = \prod_{i=1}^{p} (\pi_{ij})^{\alpha_{ij}-1}/\beta(\boldsymbol{\alpha}_j) \tag{14.19}$$

where the parameter $\alpha_{ij} \geq 0$ is the ith element of the $p \times 1$ vector $\boldsymbol{\alpha}_j$, and

$$\beta(\boldsymbol{\alpha}_j) = \prod_{i=1}^{p} \Gamma(\alpha_{ij}) \Big/ \Gamma\left(\sum_{i=1}^{p} \alpha_{ij}\right)$$

Multiplying $f(\mathbf{y} \mid \boldsymbol{\pi}_j)$ and $g(\boldsymbol{\pi}_j \mid \boldsymbol{\alpha}_j)$ and integrating out $\boldsymbol{\pi}_j$ leads to the following compound pdf:

$$h(\mathbf{y} \mid N, \boldsymbol{\alpha}_j) = N!\,\beta(\alpha_{1j} + y_1, \ldots, \alpha_{pj} + y_p) \Big/ \left[\beta(\boldsymbol{\alpha}_j) \prod_{i=1}^{p} y_i!\right] \qquad \textbf{(14.20)}$$

Termed the multinomial-multivariate beta (MMB) pdf,[16] (14.20) is an extension of a result by Skellam,[20] who compounded the binomial and beta pdf's. Dropping the subscript j—which identifies population G_j—the first and second moments of the MMB pdf are as follows:

$$E(y_i/N) = \alpha_i \Big/ \sum_{i*=1}^{p} \alpha_{i*}$$

$$\mathrm{var}\left(\frac{y_i}{N}\right) = \frac{\alpha_i \left(\sum_{i*=1}^{p} \alpha_{i*} - \alpha_i\right)\left(N + \sum_{i=1}^{p} \alpha_i\right)^2}{\left(1 + \sum_{i=1}^{p} \alpha_i\right) N}$$

$$\mathrm{covar}\left(\frac{y_i}{N}, \frac{y_{i*}}{N}\right) = -\frac{\alpha_i \alpha_{i*}\left(\sum_{i=1}^{p} \alpha_i + N\right)}{\sum_{i=1}^{p} \alpha_i^2 \left(1 + \sum_{i=1}^{p} \alpha_i\right) N} \qquad \textbf{(14.21)}$$

In estimating the α_i iteratively through maximum-likelihood estimation, initial estimates can be obtained through the method of moments, as is illustrated in Chapter 10.

In option (2), the Poisson pdf,

$$f(y \mid \mu) = e^{-\mu} \mu^y / y! \qquad \textbf{(14.22)}$$

may also be a candidate for $P(y|G_j)$ in applications where y is measured in terms of count data. Though the subscript j is omitted on the Poisson parameter μ, it is understood that μ varies between, but not within, populations. If μ varies both within and between populations, alternative pdf's may be evaluated.[21] For example, suppose that, within each population, μ varies according to a gamma pdf. To account for this variation, we multiply (14.22) and the gamma pdf, integrate out μ from 0 to infinity, and obtain the negative binomial pdf:[21]

$$h(y|\alpha, \gamma) = (1 + \alpha)^{-\gamma/\alpha}\left(\frac{\alpha}{1 + \alpha}\right)^y \frac{\Gamma[(\gamma/\alpha) + y]}{y!\,\Gamma(\gamma/\alpha)} \tag{14.23}$$

where α and γ are parameters of the pdf,

$$E(y) = \gamma \quad \text{and} \quad \text{var}(y) = \gamma(1 + \alpha) \tag{14.24}$$

As an alternative, suppose that within populations, μ varies according to a Poisson pdf with $E(\mu) = \lambda$. Setting $\lambda = \gamma/\alpha$, multiplying (14.22) with the Poisson pdf for μ, and summing out μ leads to the Neyman type A (NTA) pdf:[21]

$$h(y|\alpha, \gamma) = (\alpha^y/y!\,e^{-\gamma/\alpha}) \sum_{k=0}^{\infty} (k^y/k!)(e^{-\alpha}\gamma/\alpha)^k \tag{14.25}$$

whose first two moments are identical to those in (14.24). As $\alpha \to 0$, both the negative binomial (NB) and NTA pdf's tend to the Poisson pdf.

The NB and NTA pdf's are commonly fitted to count data from plant and insect populations. It has been conjectured[21] that the NB pdf is more applicable to insect populations and the NTA pdf to plant populations— especially when reproduction of the plant species is generated by seeds or by offshoots of parent plants or by seeds carried by living creatures. The conjecture seems valid when there is less competition between the insects of the particular species and more competition and crowding between plants of the particular species. Fisher[22] fits the NB pdf to the number of ticks found on sheep, while the illustration in section 1.8 utilizes the NTA pdf to discriminate between plant species.

The question remains as to whether the chosen pdf, when fitted per species to count data, can adequately distinguish between species in a model based on Bayesian discriminant analysis. To do so, the pdf must fit each data set well, and the pdf parameters should differ between species. Even if these conditions are met, it may be necessary to introduce sufficient ad hoc information through the prior probabilities in order to avoid large misclassification probabilities.

1.7   Illustration: Fisher's Iris Data

In a taxonomic illustration by Fisher,[23] discrimination between *Iris setosa* (G_1), *I. versicolor* (G_2), and *I. virginica* (G_3) species of iris is in terms of the following plant characteristics: sepal length (SL), sepal width (SW), petal length (PL), and petal width (PW). Per species, there is a total of $n_j = 50$ plants, $j = 1, 2, 3$.

We begin by applying the conventional analysis (see sec. 1.3) with uniform priors; that is, $P(G_j) = 1/3$. The classification rule is to assign a plant to the species with the highest posterior probability. (If the Mahalanobis D^2 distances are excessively large for a certain prediction, the implication may be that the plant belongs to a species not under consideration.) Conventional analysis results are presented in BMDP7M.[12] For alternatives (1) and (3), classification results for this analysis are identical and given in the upper portion of Table 14.1. Note that the discrimination is nearly perfect even though, as will be shown, the Σ_j differ.

In more typical applications, predictions are not nearly as good. To degrade the discrimination, only sepal length and width are used as predictors under the conventional analysis. Based on (14.3) to (14.7), the posterior probabilities are estimated as follows:

$$P(G_3 \mid \text{SL, SW}) \approx \left[1 + \frac{P(G_1)}{P(G_3)} \exp(20.36 - 10.25\text{SL} + 12.14\text{SW}) \right.$$
$$\left. + \frac{P(G_2)}{P(G_3)} \exp(15.20 - 2.56\text{SL} + 0.35\text{SW}) \right]^{-1}$$

$$P(G_2 \mid \text{SL, SW}) \approx \left[1 + \frac{P(G_1)}{P(G_2)} \exp(-5.16 - 7.66\text{SL} + 11.85\text{SW}) \right.$$
$$\left. + \frac{P(G_3)}{P(G_2)} \exp(-15.20 + 2.56\text{SL} - .29\text{SW}) \right]^{-1}$$

$$P(G_1 \mid \text{SL, SW}) \approx 1 - P(G_2 \mid \text{SL, SW}) - P(G_3 \mid \text{SL, SW}) \quad \textbf{(14.26)}$$

where "is estimated by" is denoted by $\approx$. With the priors equal to $1/3$ in the above equations, alternatives (1) and (3) give identical classification results, as shown in the middle portion of Table 14.1. Note that the discrimination is not as perfect as that shown in the upper portion of Table

TABLE 14.1. Classification Results for Three Discriminant Analyses

Iris species	Number of plants assigned to—		
	setosa	*versicolor*	*virginica*
Conventional analysis: $y = (SL, SW, PL, PW)'$			
setosa	50	0	0
versicolor	0	48	2
virginica	0	1	49
Conventional analysis: $y = (SL, SW)'$			
setosa	49	1	0
versicolor	0	35	15
virginica	0	15	35
Quadratic discriminant analysis: $y = (SL, SW)'$			
setosa	49	1	0
versicolor	0	35	15
virginica	0	12	38

Source: The data analyzed here are from R. A. Fisher, "The Use of Multiple Measurements in Taxonomic Problems," *Annals of Eugenics* 7 (1936): 179–88.

14.1, though it is clear that *setosa* stands apart from the other two species.

Equation (14.26) is graphed in Figures 14.1 and 14.2. The first figure is based on uniform priors; on the horizontal axes, sepal length and width are varied over the ranges 45 to 75 cm and 25 to 40 cm, respectively. The posterior probability of *virginica*, given on the vertical axis, approaches unity for larger values of sepal length and width. Figure 14.2 fixes the prior probability of *setosa* at .1 and the sepal width at 30 cm.

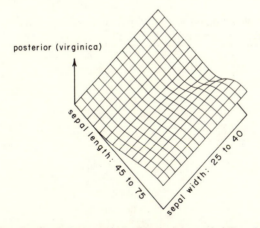

posterior (virginica)

Figure 14.1. Bayesian discriminant analysis: the posterior probability of *I. virginica* conditional on sepal length, sepal width, and uniform priors.

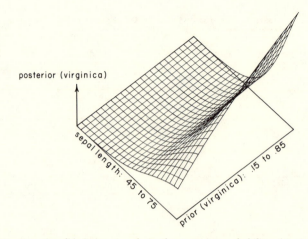

posterior (virginica)

sepal length: 45 to 75

prior (virginica): .15 to .85

Figure 14.2. Bayesian discriminant analysis: the posterior probability of *I. virginica* conditional on sepal length and the prior probability of *virginica;* sepal width = 30 cm and prior (*I. setosa*) = .1.

On the horizontal axes, sepal length is as in Figure 14.1, while the prior probability of *virginica* is varied over the range .15 to .85. For larger values of sepal length, Figure 14.2 illustrates the pronounced effect of the prior on the posterior probability. (In Figure 14.2, there is a threefold magnification of the posterior probabilities relative to Figure 14.1.)

Next, we test the hypothesis $H_0: \Sigma_1 = \Sigma_2 = \Sigma_3 = \Sigma$ for the case

TABLE 14.2   Individual and Pooled Variance/Covariance Matrices of (SL, SW) for *setosa, versicolor,* and *virginica* Species of *Iris*

setosa

$$S_1 = \begin{bmatrix} .1242 & .0992 \\ .0992 & .1437 \end{bmatrix}$$

versicolor

$$S_2 = \begin{bmatrix} .2664 & .0852 \\ .0852 & .0985 \end{bmatrix}$$

virginica

$$S_3 = \begin{bmatrix} .4043 & .0938 \\ .0938 & .1040 \end{bmatrix}$$

Pooled

$$S = \begin{bmatrix} .2650 & .0927 \\ .0927 & .1154 \end{bmatrix}$$

where SL and SW are used as predictors. Table 14.2 presents estimates of the three individual dispersion matrices and the pooled dispersion matrix. For (14.11) to (14.13), we have $L = 36.4178$, $K = .9804$, and $KL = 35.7022$ with 6 degrees of freedom. Since KL exceeds the critical χ^2 value—which, at the .05 level of significance equals 12.6—H_0 is rejected. Using quadratic discriminant analysis as in (14.14), we obtain the classification results for alternative (1) at the bottom of Table 14.1. Note that these classification results show a slight improvement for the *virginica* species relative to those in the middle portion of the table.

Classification results in Table 14.1 remain the same when the normal pdf is replaced with the Student t pdf—as one would expect with such large sample sizes.

For $\mathbf{y}' = (SL, SW)$, $\boldsymbol{\mu}_j$ is estimated by the unbiased estimator $\mathbf{y}_j$ for both the conventional and the quadratic discriminant analysis. As an alternative to $\mathbf{y}_j$, suppose we utilize a biased $\boldsymbol{\mu}_j$ estimator from the class of James-Stein[5] estimators:

$$\boldsymbol{\mu}_j \approx (1 - c/Q)\mathbf{y}_j \qquad \text{for} \qquad c > 0 \tag{14.27}$$

where

$$Q = \mathbf{y}_j' S_j^{-1} \mathbf{y}_j \tag{14.28}$$

Keating and Mason[24] propose the following adaptive estimators among those in (14.27): (1) Set $c = 0$ and choose the unbiased $\boldsymbol{\mu}_j$ estimator when $Q \leq q - 1$. (2) Set $c = q - 1$ and choose the biased $\boldsymbol{\mu}_j$ estimator when $Q > q - 1$.

Consider the adaptive estimator under the conventional analysis where S, the pooled covariance matrix in Table 14.2, is substituted for the S_j in (14.28). Values of Q are, respectively, 128.46, 138.77, and 169.19 for the three iris samples. Since corresponding values of $c/Q = 1/Q$ are quite small, the biased $\boldsymbol{\mu}_j$ estimators are very close to the unbiased estimators. Accordingly, classification results are almost identical to those in the middle portion of Table 14.1. (The only exception is that an additional *versicolor* plant is misclassified.) The same general result holds when the adaptive estimator is applied in the quadratic analysis; that is, values of Q are, respectively, 206.83, 142.92, and 132.76, which, again, lead to very small differences between biased and unbiased $\boldsymbol{\mu}_j$ estimators. Simulation studies would be of considerable value in determining conditions under which the biased estimators lead to better discrimination than unbiased estimators for smaller values of Q.

1.8   Illustration: On the Probability of "Dead on Arrival" for Cardiac Incidents

Data for this study are drawn from a master file of emergency medical services in Oahu, Hawaii, from 1975 to 1976. The heart attack victim, having entered the system of emergency medical services, will or will not arrive at the hospital alive. Our objective is to estimate the posterior probability that the victim will be dead on arrival (DOA). The probability is conditional on ad hoc information, as quantified through the prior probability, on victim demographics and on response times associated with elements of the emergency medical system (EMS).

Every day roughly 4,000 victims suffer heart attacks (*Wall Street Journal,* 28 May 1987). Statistical abstracts from the 1970s state that approximately 50%–70% of these individuals die at home or work, on the street, or on the way to the hospital. For individuals who survive the trip to the hospital, 10%–20% die within the hospital.[25] The objective of an EMS is to increase the chance of survival while, at the same time, to reduce the chance of temporary or permanent disability.

It is generally agreed that elements of an EMS include (1) detection, (2) notification, (3) communication, (4) transportation, (5) hospital care, and (6) the training of staff.[25] Each of these elements can be measured in terms of performance variables, many of which are either response or service times. Our analysis utilizes response times associated with the first four elements.

By the time the victim reaches the hospital, whether dead or alive, a sequence of events has transpired. First, the incident is detected. Second, a cognizant individual is notified. Third, an ambulance is dispatched. Fourth and fifth, the ambulance arrives on the scene and departs with the victim. Finally, the ambulance arrives at the hospital. Throughout this period, the victim may or may not receive varying types of aid, whether medical or paramedical.

Very few incidents in the master file contain information on detection times. Because of the circumstances of cardiac incidents, this is not surprising: (1) detection may occur from the onset of symptoms to when a full-fledged heart attack is in progress, and (2) the most reliable source of information, usually the victim, may not be in a condition to give the information.

The binary dependent variable—dead or alive on arrival—is modeled, exploratorily, through Bayesian discriminant analysis utilizing BMDP7M. Conventional assumptions are employed (see sec. 1.3), even though one of the predictors is categorical. Predictors, up through the second order, include the victim's age, sex, and the time between notification and arrival at the hospital. Key variables not considered include (1) time between detection and notification, (2) events associated with this and other time intervals such as the time and type of medical care, if any, and (3) the nature and severity of the cardiac incident. Per case, ad hoc information on the excluded variables may be incorporated in the model, subjectively, through the prior probability. It should be noted that, for the data analyzed, there is no way of identifying incidents in which the ambulance siren was turned off when the victim was obviously dead en route.

In the stepwise discriminant analysis, significant predictors include all first-order terms and two interactions: response time by age and age by sex. As estimated through the jackknife technique with uniform priors, misclassification probabilities are .24 for those DOA and .32 for those not DOA. (Thus, it seems likely that highly accurate predictions could be developed if reliable information on the omitted variables were available and utilized either subjectively in the prior probability or objectively by expanding the list of predictors.) Model exercises are presented in Table 14.3, which illustrates effects of age, sex, and response time on the probability of DOA.

It is seen that increased response times and age combine interactively to increase the chances of DOA. Females are seen to have lower probabilities than males, though this difference decreases with increasing age. An explanation of the gender effect may be that sex partially reflects the time between detection and notification—in that females may tend to react to their symptoms more quickly than males, at least for younger ages. However, these data are from the 1970s; in more recent times the difference in reactions of men and women toward their early symptoms might be minimal.

These results should be reevaluated by updating the data base and including variables excluded in this analysis. If the reanalysis shows comparable results, the implication is that increased monies should be allotted to public education and to decreasing response times.

TABLE 14.3 Cardiac Incidents: Posterior Probability of Dead on Arrival

	Response time			
	60 minutes		90 minutes	
Age	Male	Female	Male	Female
35	.38	.23	.41	.26
45	.47	.35	.51	.39
55	.57	.48	.64	.55
65	.68	.62	.79	.73

Note: Conditional on uniform priors, victim demographics, and the time between notification of the incident and arrival of victim at the hospital (response time).

1.9   Illustration: Distinguishing between Plant Species

In the two previous illustrations, a multivariate normal pdf is assumed for $P(\mathbf{y}|G_j)$ in (14.1). In this application, $\mathbf{y} = y$ is a single discrete variable—the number of plants of a particular species in a quadrant—and $P(y|G_j)$ is taken as the NTA pdf in (14.25).

Evans[26] fits several pdf's—the NTA, the NB, and the Polya-Aeppli (PA) pdf's—to count data on species of plants and insects. An earlier analysis of these data had clearly rejected the Poisson pdf. Evans concludes that the plant and insect counts are fairly well fitted by the NTA and NB pdf's, respectively, but not conversely and not by the PA pdf. He suggests that the difference in fits between the NTA and NB pdf's is due to the greater degree of overcrowding and competition in the case of the plants.

We will utilize a portion of Evans's results on the plant data. Plant counts are based on 40 quadrants, each 1 m square. (Evans notes the lack of experimental work on the effect of quadrant size on pdf's fitted to each of the plant species.) The quadrants under consideration were placed in vegetation described as "high prairie, non-grassy." Per quadrant, counts were made on the number of plants belonging to the following genera and species: *Psoralea floribunda* (G_1), *Erigeron ramosus* (G_2), *Helianthus scaberrimus* (G_3), and *Aster multiflorus* (G_4). Table 14.4 presents results of fitting the NTA pdf to count data per plant type. Observed and expected frequencies are in fairly close agreement. (Note that the χ^2 test is based on 1 degree of freedom since two parameters have been estimated.)[27]

The lower portion of the table contains the NTA pdf parameter estimates. Estimates are based on Evans's alternative procedure—which uses the mean and the proportion of zero counts—as opposed to method-of-moments estimation. The question arises as to whether the fitted pdf's differ significantly in shape. To answer this question, the null hypotheses

$$H_{0jj*}: (\alpha_j, \gamma_j) = (\alpha_{j*}, \gamma_{j*}) \qquad j \neq j* = 1, 2, 3, 4$$

are tested asymptotically;[3] in these tests, population variances/covariances are replaced by respective sample estimates given at the bottom of Table 14.5. (The tests are approximate since correlations of parameter estimates between species are ignored.) For adjacent species (G_1 vs. G_2, G_2 vs. G_3, G_3 vs. G_4), the H_{0jj*} are rejected only at the 10% level. For other species comparisons (G_1 vs. G_3, G_1 vs. G_4, G_2 vs. G_4), the H_{0jj*} are rejected at the 5% level. Based on these approximate tests, it cannot be said that the four fitted pdf's are highly distinguishable from one an-

TABLE 14.4. Results of Fitting the Neyman Type A Probability Density Function to Count Data from Four Plant Species

A. Observed frequencies (OF) and expected frequencies (EF)

No. of plants per quadrant	Species							
	G_1		G_2		G_3		G_4	
	OF	EF	OF	EF	OF	EF	OF	EF
0	6	6.0	15	15.0	20	20.0	24	24.0
1–2	19	15.5	12	10.5	11	7.4	9	6.6
3–4	7	11.2	7	7.9	4	6.8	2	5.6
≥ 5	8	7.3	6	6.6	5	5.8	5	3.8
Total	40	40.0	40	40.0	40	40.0	40	40.0
$\chi^2(1\ df)$		2.43		0.37		3.01		3.57

B. Parameter estimates

Parameter	Species			
	G_1	G_2	G_3	G_4
$\alpha \approx a$	.74	1.87	2.44	2.40
$E(y) = \approx c$	2.68	2.17	1.85	1.35
Variance (a)	.15	.20	.27	.21
Variance (c)	.12	.16	.16	.12
Covariance (a, c)	.02	.05	.06	.06

Source: The data analyzed here are from D. A. Evans, "Experimental Evidence concerning Contagious Distributions in Ecology," *Biometrika* 10 (1953): 186–211.

$$\text{Variance } (a) = \left[\frac{a^2}{c(1 + a)} + \frac{a^4}{c^2[(1 + a)\exp(-a) - 1]^2} \right.$$
$$\left. \times \left\{ \exp\frac{c[1 - \exp(-a)]}{a} - \frac{1 - c}{1 + a} \right\} \right] \Big/ N$$

Variance $(c) = c(1 + a)/N$
Covariance $(a, c) = a/N$
N = number of quadrants = 40

other. The implication is that substitution of the fitted pdf's for $P(G_j|y)$ in (14.1) will result in somewhat poor discrimination between species—assuming uniform priors. Based on the expected frequencies in Table 4, results of substituting the fitted NTA pdf's for $P(y|G_j)$ (14.1) are shown in Table 14.5. For example, the first row of posterior probabilities are found as follows: $P(G_1|y = 0) = (6/40)/D = .09$, where $D = 6/40 + 15/4 + 20/40 + 24/40 = 1.63$; similarly, $P(G_2|y = 0) = (15/40)/D = .23$, $P(G_3|y = 0) = (20/40)/D = .31$, and $P(G_4|y = 0) = (24/40)/D = .37$.

At this point, it seems questionable whether count data on reproduction can adequately distinguish between plant species in the absence of other information. For a better discriminatory model, recourses are to

TABLE 14.5. Posterior Probability of Belonging to Species G_j under
Uniform Prior Probabilities $[P(G_j) = 1/4]$

No. of plants per quadrant	Species			
	G_1	G_2	G_3	G_4
0	.09	.23	.31	.37
1–2	.39	.26	.19	.16
3–4	.35	.25	.22	.18
≥5	.31	.27	.25	.17

incorporate sufficient ad hoc information in the prior probabilities and/
or to measure other plant characteristics as in the illustration utilizing
Fisher's iris data.

2.0 Regression Systems

2.1 The Variables

Assume the experimental unit is characterized by p endogenous variables, y_h, $h = 1, \ldots, p$, and q exogenous variables, x_i, $i = 1, \ldots, q$.
The endogenous variables are a set of jointly dependent variables determined by events both external and internal to the unit. Exogenous variables are predetermined by events external to the unit and may include
(1) treatments that are deliberately manipulated to determine their effects
on endogenous variables of interest and (2) concomitants that are introduced to increase efficiency and reduce bias.

A distinction is made between two types of exogenous variables:
those that are deliberately manipulated (or are predetermined and controlled) and those that occur naturally (or are predetermined and uncontrolled). The former are termed *factors* and the latter *concomitants*. This
distinction becomes important when effects of exogenous variables are
interpreted.

2.2 Path Diagrams

The phrase *A affects B* means that a change in the variable B is
usually associated with a change in the variable A. The association may
be causal (in the sense that A is a mechanism through which B changes),
alias (in the sense that A is correlated with and a stand-in for the variable
C, which is a mechanism through which B changes), or spurious. Factors
are causal variables, while each concomitant may be causal, alias, or
spurious. Per experiment, opinions as to the nature of concomitants are
often varied.

The study of effects may focus on (1) the aggregate effect of each exogenous variable on each endogenous variable and/or (2) the mechanism through which each exogenous variable affects each endogenous variable as traced through the effects of endogenous variables on one another. Path diagrams—schematic arrays of hypothesized effects in mechanism (2)—underlie model specification, which will be limited to linear models.[28,29]

For purposes of illustration, let the unit be characterized by x, y_1, and y_2, where x is a factor. Suppose x affects y_2 and, in turn, y_2 affects y_1, as is depicted in the path diagram

$$x \rightarrow y_2 \rightarrow y_1 \qquad (14.27)$$

In this diagram, the effect of x on y_1 is indirect and through y_2. An indirect effect occurs whenever an intervening variable (necessarily endogenous) is directly affected by one variable and subsequently affects another variable. Individual arrows will denote direct effects, or the absence of intervening variables.

The following stochastic model (with equation intercepts omitted) is chosen to quantify effects in (14.27):

$$y_1 = \alpha y_2 + \delta_1 \qquad (14.28)$$

$$y_2 = \gamma x + \delta_2 \qquad (14.29)$$

where α and γ quantify the arrows in $y_2 \rightarrow y_1$ and $x \rightarrow y_2$, respectively; the δ's are random model errors. With appropriate model error assumptions, the above model is termed a *structural regression system*. In general, structural systems quantify all the direct effects in hypothesized path diagrams.

Regarding (1), the aggregate effect of x on y_1 is indirect and given by $\alpha\gamma$, the product of the two direct effects. Algebraically, this result can be obtained by substituting for y_2 in (14.28) the expression for y_2 in (14.29):

$$y_1 = (\alpha\gamma)x + (\delta_1 + \alpha\delta_2) \qquad (14.30)$$

The aggregate effect in (1) is termed an *overall effect*. In general, the overall effect of x_i on y_h is given by the sum of the direct and all indirect x_i effects on y_h. Under (14.27), the overall effect of x on y_1 is simply the indirect effect of x on y_1 because x has no direct effect on y_1; the overall x effect on y_2 is direct because x does not affect y_2 indirectly.

Equations (14.29) and (14.30) form the so-called *reduced regression system,* wherein all predictors are exogenous and all effects are strictly overall. The structural system will be shown to uniquely determine the reduced system though not conversely.

If x affects y_1 both directly and indirectly, diagram (14.27) is altered to include an additional arrow,

$$x \rightarrow y_2 \rightarrow y_1 \qquad\qquad\qquad (14.31)$$

and (14.28) is rewritten as

$$y_1 = \phi x + \alpha y_2 + \delta_1 \qquad\qquad\qquad (14.32)$$

where the coefficient ϕ quantifies the arrow in $x \rightarrow y_1$. The overall x effect on y_1, $\phi + \alpha\gamma$, is the sum of the direct and indirect x effects on y_1. Algebraically, this result is obtained from the reduced equation corresponding to (14.32); that is, the expression for y_2 in (14.29) is substituted for y_2 in (14.32):

$$y_1 = \phi x + \alpha(\gamma x + \delta_2) + \delta_1 = (\phi + \alpha\gamma)x + (\delta_1 + \alpha\delta_2) \qquad (14.33)$$

A causal feedback, denoted by $y_1 \leftrightarrow y_2$, is understood to mean that $y_2 \rightarrow y_1$ and $y_1 \rightarrow y_2$ during the course of the experiment. For the path diagram

$$x \rightarrow y_2 \leftrightarrow y_1 \qquad\qquad\qquad (14.34)$$

the structural system is written as

$$y_1 = \alpha_{12} y_2 + \delta_1 \qquad\qquad\qquad (14.35)$$
$$y_2 = \gamma x + \alpha_{21} y_1 + \delta_2 \qquad\qquad\qquad (14.36)$$

where α_{12} and α_{21} quantify the arrows in $y_2 \rightarrow y_1$ and $y_1 \rightarrow y_2$, respectively. The overall x effect on y_1, given by $\gamma\alpha_{12}/(1 - \alpha_{12}\alpha_{21})$, is obtained by substituting for y_2 in (14.35) the expression for y_2 in (14.36):

$$y_1 = \alpha_{12}(\gamma x + \alpha_{21} y_1 + \delta_2) + \delta_1$$

whereupon

$$y_1 = \frac{\gamma\alpha_{12}x}{1 - \alpha_{12}\alpha_{21}} + \frac{\delta_1 + \alpha_{12}}{1 - \alpha_{12}\alpha_{21}} \qquad\qquad (14.37)$$

It is instructive to derive the overall x effect on y_1 in (14.37) by depicting diagram (14.34) along a time axis as follows:

$$x \rightarrow y_2 \rightarrow y_1 \rightarrow y_2 \rightarrow y_1 \rightarrow y_2 \rightarrow y_1 \rightarrow$$

$$\text{---------}|\text{---------}|\text{---------}|\text{---------} \rightarrow \text{time}$$

$$t_1 \qquad\quad t_2 \qquad\quad t_3$$

At time t_1, the indirect x effect on y_1 is $\gamma\alpha_{12}$; at time t_2, it is $\gamma(\alpha_{12})^2\alpha_{21}$; at time t_3, it is $\gamma(\alpha_{12})^3(\alpha_{21})^2$, etc. Because there is no direct x effect on y_1, all indirect x effects on y_1 are added to obtain the following overall x effect on y_1:

$$\gamma\alpha_{12} + \gamma(\alpha_{12})^2\alpha_{21} + \gamma(\alpha_{12})^3(\alpha_{21})^2 + \gamma(\alpha_{12})^4(\alpha_{21})^3 + \ldots = \frac{\gamma\alpha_{12}}{1 - \alpha_{12}\alpha_{21}}$$

which is identically the coefficient of x in (14.37).

2.3 Direct Effects of Factors and Endogenous Variables: Caveats

In diagram (14.31), the direct y_2 effect on y_1 is with reference to the endogenous variables considered. Suppose another endogenous variable, say v, is introduced, where v is an intervening variable such that

$$\begin{array}{ccc}
 & v & \\
 & \nearrow \quad \searrow & \\
x & \uparrow & y_1 \\
 & \searrow \quad \nearrow & \\
 & y_2 & \\
\end{array} \qquad (14.38)$$

Relative to (14.31), the direct x effect on y_1 is replaced by an indirect effect through v. Moreover, the y_2 effect on y_1 is now both direct and indirect. Thus, the introduction of an additional endogenous variable (resulting, say, from a deeper probe into the unit's structure) may convert a direct effect into an indirect effect. This is in contrast to the overall x effect on y_1, which remains the same no matter how many intervening variables are introduced.

Under (14.32), the direct x effect on y_1 is the expected change in y_1 as x is deliberately changed from one level to another while y_2 is held fixed. The problem with such interpretations is that it may be impossible to control y_2. Or, the structure of the experimental unit may be altered if, in fact, the value of y_2 is manipulated. To address these difficulties, a key simplifying assumption is made regarding the stability of the unit's structure. When the unit's structure is disrupted, to the extent that an endogenous variable (say, y_h) is deliberately manipulated (either in reality or conceptually), it is assumed that all effects on y_h vanish, that no additional effects come into being, and that the remainder of the direct effects are unaltered; for example, if $x \rightarrow y_2 \rightarrow y_1$ becomes $x \rightarrow y_1 \leftarrow y_2$ when y_2 is deliberately manipulated, then structure is unstable and the stability assumption is violated.

In the presence of instability, a Bayesian analysis of the regression system offers greater options than the classical analysis. One may argue that (1) disruptions of the unit's structure portend varying degrees of instability and (2) that the effect of such disruptions is to cast regression coefficients in the role of random variables that follow a prior pdf. If the instability is not in conflict with diffuse (noninformative) priors, then results of classical analysis can be given Bayesian interpretations at least approximately.[30,31] When the unit instability is thought to be in conflict with the assumption of diffuse priors, varying forms of informative priors should be implemented as part of a sensitivity analysis.

2.4   A Historical Note

Path analysis was developed to estimate structural (direct and indirect) effects. Wright[32,33] originated path analysis during World War I, though he used correlation rather than regression to estimate structural effects. (Summary papers on path analysis are given by Wright[34,35,36] and Tukey.[28]) In the 1920s Frisch formulated Wright's concept in terms of regression. Frisch was partially motivated by other analysts' misuse of regression. In an early paper he cautioned against the use of a single equation when a system of equations is required for problem resolution:

> In . . . 1928 I drew attention to the fact that in statistical regression analysis there exists a great danger of obtaining nonsensical results whenever one includes in one and the same regression equation a set of variates that contain two or more subsets which are already—taken by themselves—highly intercorrelated. Suppose, for instance, that we have statistical variates x_1, x_2, x_3 (measured from their means), and that we know for a priori reasons that there exists not one but two independent linear equations between them (since the variates are measured from their means, we may assume the equations to be homogenous). Further, suppose that a great number of observations are made, each observation giving the values of the three variates and being represented as a point in the three dimensional (x_1, x_2, x_3) space. All these observation points would lie on a straight line

through the origin in (x_1, x_2, x_3) space. From the distribution of these set points it would be absurd to try to determine the coefficients of any of the two equations that we know a priori should exist between the variates. Indeed, a set of points lying on a line does not contain enough information to determine a plane.[37]

Frisch's comments merit renewed attention in view of multicollinearity and its proposed resolution through principal components[38] and ridge regression.[39,40]

2.5 Structural and Reduced Regression Systems

Let $y(p \times 1)$ and $x(q \times 1)$ denote the vectors of endogenous and exogenous variables, respectively. Subdivide x according to $x' = (x_f', x_c')$, where x_f and x_c are vectors of factors and concomitants, respectively. Let v denote a vector of excluded variables associated with the experimental unit. It is assumed that x_c is unaffected by x_f, that v may be affected by both x_f and x_c, and that both x_f and x_c are unaffected by v. (If elements of x_c are affected by x_f, an alternative may be to redefine such elements as endogenous variables.)

Conditions are now given for the existence of a linear structural regression system. Assume that y_h is linearly related to the other endogenous variables, x, and v according to the following system of deterministic equations:

$$Ay = Lx + L_v v = L_f x_f + L_c x_c + L_v v \qquad (14.39)$$

where the $p \times p$ matrix $A = (\alpha_{hH})$ quantifies direct effects among the endogenous variables; $h, H = 1, \ldots, p$; $\alpha_{hh} = 1$. Form the regression of v on x:

$$v = Mx + \Delta = M_f x_f + M_c x_c + \Delta \qquad (14.40)$$

where $M = (M_f | M_c)$ is a matrix of regression coefficients and Δ is the model error. Assume that the Δ are identically and independently distributed (i.i.d.) with $E(\Delta) = O$ and variance $(\Delta) = \Sigma_\Delta$; that is,

$$\Delta : \text{i.i.d.}(O, \Sigma_\Delta) \qquad (14.41)$$

Overall effects of x_f on v are given by elements of M_f. Overall effects in M_c are interpreted as alias effects if elements of x_c are alias variables.

Substitute for v in (14.39) the expression for v in (14.40):

$$\mathbf{A}\mathbf{y} = \Gamma\mathbf{x} + \boldsymbol{\delta} = \Gamma_f\mathbf{x}_f + \Gamma_c\mathbf{x}_c + \boldsymbol{\delta} \qquad (14.42)$$

where $\Gamma = L_v\mathbf{M}$, $\Gamma_f = (L_f + L_v\mathbf{M}_f)$, $\Gamma_c = (L_c + L_v\mathbf{M}_c)$, and

$$\boldsymbol{\delta} : \text{i.i.d.}(\mathbf{O}, \Sigma_\delta = L_v\,\Sigma_\Delta\,L_v') \qquad (14.43)$$

Note that $\mathbf{x}$ is independent of $\boldsymbol{\delta}$ and that $\boldsymbol{\delta}$ is not the joint effect of excluded variables but, rather, the remainder of $\mathbf{v}$ after effects of $\mathbf{x}$ have been subtracted out.[41] Under assumption (14.43), model (14.42) is the general form of a linear structural regression system. With respect to $\mathbf{y}$ and $\mathbf{x}$, the structural system quantifies all direct effects in the underlying path diagram.

It should be noted that with reference to $\mathbf{y}$ and $\mathbf{x}$, Γ_f is the direct $\mathbf{x}_f$ effect on $\mathbf{y}$. If all elements of $\mathbf{x}_c$ are alias variables, then $\Gamma_c = (L_c + L_v\mathbf{M}_c)$ is a matrix of conglomerate, direct effects; that is, L_c is the direct $\mathbf{x}_c$ effect on $\mathbf{y}$, while $L_v\mathbf{M}_c$ is the indirect alias effect on $\mathbf{y}$ through $\mathbf{v}$.

The reduced system corresponding to (14.42) is given by assuming $|\mathbf{A}| \neq 0$ and multiplying both sides of (14.42) by $\mathbf{A}^{-1}$:

$$\mathbf{y} = \mathbf{B}\mathbf{x} + \boldsymbol{\epsilon} = \mathbf{B}_f\mathbf{x}_f + \mathbf{B}_c\mathbf{x}_c + \boldsymbol{\epsilon} \qquad (14.44)$$

where

$$\mathbf{B} = \mathbf{A}^{-1}\Gamma \qquad \mathbf{B}_f = \mathbf{A}^{-1}\Gamma_f \qquad \mathbf{B}_c = \mathbf{A}^{-1}\Gamma_c \qquad (14.45)$$

and

$$\boldsymbol{\epsilon} = \mathbf{A}^{-1}\boldsymbol{\delta} : \text{i.i.d.}(\mathbf{O}, \Sigma_\epsilon = \mathbf{A}^{-1}\Sigma_\delta\,\mathbf{A}^{-1}) \qquad (14.46)$$

From (14.45) and (14.46), it is seen that $\mathbf{B}$ and Σ_ϵ are uniquely determined, given $\mathbf{A}$, Γ, and Σ_δ. Conversely, given $\mathbf{B}$ and Σ_ϵ, solutions for $\mathbf{A}$, Γ, and Σ_δ are non-unique—unless restrictive assumptions are imposed on $\mathbf{A}$, Γ, and Σ_δ.

Under assumption (14.46), ordinary least-squares (OLS) estimation provides consistent estimates of reduced system parameters.[42] Such estimates may be termed *objective* since they are obtained without reference to a structural system (which is usually based on a subjective specification of the path diagram). Because of this "objectivity," the analysis of overall effects tends to receive primary emphasis; for example, in his analysis of overall treatment effects through multivariate analysis of variance (MANOVA), Roy[43] makes no reference to structural systems. (In his lectures on MANOVA in the early 1960s, Roy rejected consideration of structural systems because of their subjective basis.) Though the analysis of overall effects is obligatory, it is merely a first step. Why? (1) Sooner or later, scientific inquiry almost always turns to structural effects after beginning with aggregate effects. (2) Analysis of the structural system may provide an alternative when assumptions underlying conventional analyses are invalid (see sec. 2.12). (3) The structural system may lead to a restricted reduced system (see secs. 2.10–2.11) where treatment contrast precision can be increased relative to the unrestricted systems of MANOVA (see sec. 2.13).

2.6 Identification

Consider the identification of A and Γ based on knowledge of B, where, from (14.45), $B = A^{-1}\Gamma$. Three illustrations are given to facilitate an understanding of just-, over-, and underidentification.

The reduced system corresponding to the structural system in (14.35) and (14.36) is $y_1 = \beta_{11}x + \epsilon_1$ and $y_2 = \beta_{21}x + \epsilon_2$, where $\beta_{11} = \alpha\gamma$ and $\beta_{21} = \gamma$. Knowledge of the β's leads to two equations in two unknown structural parameters. Solutions for α and γ are $\gamma = \beta_{21}$ and $\alpha = \beta_{11}/\beta_{21}$. This example illustrates just-identification of structural parameters; that is, knowledge of B in $B = A^{-1}\Gamma$ defines the same number of equations as unknowns.

The reduced system corresponding to the structural system in (14.29) and (14.32) is $y_1 = \beta_{11}x + \epsilon_1$ and $y_2 = \beta_{21}x + \epsilon_2$, where $\beta_{11} = \phi + \alpha\gamma$ and $\beta_{21} = \gamma$. Knowledge of these β's leads to two equations in three unknown structural parameters. Although parameters of (14.29) are just-identified, those of (14.32) are underidentified; that is, knowledge of B in $B = A^{-1}\Gamma$ defines fewer equations than unknowns.

Finally, take $y_1 = \alpha y_2 + \delta_1$ and $y_2 = \gamma_1 x_1 + \gamma_2 x_2 + \delta_2$ as the structural model for the path diagram

$$
\begin{array}{c}
x_1 \\
\searrow \\
y_2 \rightarrow y_1 \\
\nearrow \\
x_2
\end{array}
$$

The corresponding reduced system is $y_1 = \beta_{11}x_1 + \beta_{12}x_2 + \delta_1$ and $y_2 = \beta_{21}x_1 + \beta_{22}x_2 + \delta_2$, where $\beta_{11} = \alpha\gamma_1$, $\beta_{12} = \alpha\gamma_2$, $\beta_{21} = \gamma_1$, and $\beta_{22} = \gamma_2$. Knowledge of these β's leads to four equations in three unknown structural parameters with multiple solutions for α; that is, $\alpha = \beta_{11}/\beta_{21}$ and $\alpha = \beta_{12}/\beta_{22}$. Structural parameters in the first structural equation are overidentified, while those in the second are just-identified; that is, knowledge of B in $B = A^{-1}\Gamma$ defines more equations than unknowns.

The following can be shown for the general case of p structural equations. For the hth equation to be just- or overidentified, it is necessary that the number of variables in the hth equation (excluding y_h and δ_h) be less than or equal to the number of exogenous variables in the structural system.[42]

Because knowledge of the parameter matrix B is not usually available, why is the concept of identification important? In application, it is usually desirable to obtain consistent estimates of reduced and structural parameters (assuming one does not sacrifice too much efficiency in the process of obtaining consistent estimates). As mentioned earlier, OLS estimation in the reduced system provides a consistent B estimate under assumption (14.46). The problem lies in estimating A and Γ. Except under very restrictive assumptions (such as those leading to diagonally recursive systems[42]), OLS estimation in the structural system does not provide consistent estimates of A and Γ because the model errors are usually correlated with the endogenous predictors. If, however, the consistent B estimate is substituted for B in $B = A^{-1}\Gamma$, then the resulting estimates of A and Γ are consistent (because, under very general conditions, a function of consistent estimators is also consistent[42]). For underidentified equations, the alternatives are (1) to impose additional restrictions in the path diagram, (2) to utilize inconsistent estimators that may have smaller mean square error, or (3) to settle for estimated overall effects.

2.7   Indirect Estimation of Structural Effects

With $\mathbf{y}_h$ and $\mathbf{x}_i$ denoting $n \times 1$ vectors of observations on y_h and x_i, respectively, the hth reduced equation in (14.44) is written as

$$\mathbf{y}_h = X\boldsymbol{\beta}_h + \boldsymbol{\epsilon}_h \qquad\qquad (14.47)$$

where X is the $n \times q$ matrix of observations on all exogenous variables, $\boldsymbol{\beta}'_h$ is the hth row of B, and $\boldsymbol{\epsilon}_h = (\epsilon_{h1}, \ldots, \epsilon_{hn})'$. From (14.46), we have

$$E(\boldsymbol{\epsilon}_h) = \mathbf{O} \qquad \text{and} \qquad \text{cov}(\boldsymbol{\epsilon}_h, \boldsymbol{\epsilon}_H) = I_n \sigma_{\epsilon hH} \qquad (14.48)$$

where $\sigma_{\epsilon hH}$ is a typical element of Σ_ϵ.

The OLS estimate of $\boldsymbol{\beta}_h$ is

$$\mathbf{b}_h = (X'X)^{-1} X' \mathbf{y}_h \qquad\qquad (14.49)$$

$$\text{covar}(\mathbf{b}_h, \mathbf{b}_H) = (X'X)^{-1}\sigma_{\epsilon hH} \tag{14.50}$$

Σ_ϵ is estimated by $S_\epsilon = (s_{\epsilon hH})$, where

$$s_{\epsilon hH} = (\mathbf{y}_h - X\mathbf{b}_h)'(\mathbf{y}_H - X\mathbf{b}_H)'/(n - q) \tag{14.51}$$

Next, consider utilization of prior information on $\boldsymbol{\beta}_h$—in the sense that

$$\boldsymbol{\beta}_{hp} = \boldsymbol{\beta}_h + \boldsymbol{\epsilon}_{hp} \tag{14.52}$$

is a prior estimate of $\boldsymbol{\beta}_h$ with $E(\boldsymbol{\epsilon}_{hp}) = \mathbf{o}$ and $\text{var}(\boldsymbol{\epsilon}_{hp}) = \Sigma_{\epsilon hp}$. The results in (14.47) and (14.52) can be combined according to

$$\begin{bmatrix} \mathbf{y}_h \\ \boldsymbol{\beta}_{hp} \end{bmatrix} = \begin{bmatrix} X \\ I_q \end{bmatrix} \boldsymbol{\beta}_\eta + \begin{bmatrix} \boldsymbol{\epsilon}_h \\ \boldsymbol{\epsilon}_{hp} \end{bmatrix} \tag{14.53}$$

or

$$\mathbf{u}_h = T_h\boldsymbol{\beta}_h + \boldsymbol{\zeta}_h \tag{14.54}$$

where the correspondence between terms in (14.53) and (14.54) is obvious. For $\boldsymbol{\zeta}_h$, we have

$$\text{var}(\boldsymbol{\zeta}_h) = \begin{bmatrix} I_n\sigma_{\epsilon hh} & K_{\epsilon h} \\ K_{\epsilon h} & \Sigma_{\epsilon hp} \end{bmatrix} = W_{\epsilon h} \tag{14.55}$$

where $K_{\epsilon h} = \text{cov}(\boldsymbol{\epsilon}_h, \boldsymbol{\epsilon}_{hp})$.

The following weighted least-squares estimate of $\boldsymbol{\beta}_h$ is obtained by assuming $|W_{\epsilon h}| \neq 0$ and minimizing $\boldsymbol{\zeta}_h' W_{\epsilon h}^{-1} \boldsymbol{\zeta}_h$ with respect to $\boldsymbol{\beta}_h$:

$$\mathbf{B}_h = (T_h' W_{\epsilon h}^{-1} T_h)^{-1} T_h' W_{\epsilon h}^{-1} \mathbf{u}_h \tag{14.56}$$

The result in (14.56) reduces to the following Goldberger-Theil estimator[44] when $K_{\epsilon h} = 0$:

$$\mathbf{B}_h = (X'X\sigma_{\epsilon hh} + \Sigma_{\epsilon hp}^{-1})^{-1}(X'X\mathbf{b}_h\sigma_{\epsilon hh} + \Sigma_{\epsilon hp}^{-1}\boldsymbol{\beta}_{hp}) \tag{14.57}$$

In a Bayesian context, $\mathbf{B}_h$ is the mean of the posterior pdf on $\boldsymbol{\beta}_h$ assuming (1) $\boldsymbol{\beta}_h$: normal $(\boldsymbol{\beta}_{hp}, \Sigma_{\epsilon hp})$ and (2) a diffuse prior pdf for $\sigma_{\epsilon hh}$.[31] Regarding (14.57), the following conditions should be noted: $\mathbf{B}_h$ approaches $\boldsymbol{\beta}_{hp}$ as diagonal elements of $\Sigma_{\epsilon hp}$ become infinite; $\mathbf{B}_h$ approaches $\mathbf{b}_h$ if either diagonal elements of $\Sigma_{\epsilon h p}$ approach infinity or β_{hp} approaches b_h.

The indirect method of estimating direct effects (by substituting either [14.49] or [14.57] for rows of B in $B = A^{-1}\Gamma$ and solving for A and Γ) is usually conceptual. In practice, direct methods of estimation are the usual recourse. Nonetheless, the estimation of B is relevant as an end in itself and/or as a diagnostic of misspecified structural effects (see sec. 2.12).

2.8   Direct Estimation of Structural Effects

The hth structural equation in (14.42) is written as

$$y_h = Y_h\alpha_h + X_h\gamma_h + \delta_h = Z_h\theta_h + \delta_h \qquad (14.58)$$

where $Y_h(n \times p_h)$ and $X_h(n \times q_h)$ are, respectively, matrices of observations on endogenous and exogenous variables affecting y_h; $\alpha_h'(1 \times p_h)$ and $\gamma_h'(1 \times q_h)$ are, respectively, vectors of nonzero elements of the hth row of A and Γ; $p_h \le p$, $q_h \le q$, and $p + q < n$; $\delta_h = (\delta_{h1}, \ldots, \delta_{hn})$; and $Z_h = (X_h|Y_h)$; $\theta_h = (\alpha_h', \gamma_h')$. From (14.43), we have

$$E(\delta_h) = O \qquad \text{and} \qquad \text{cov}(\delta_h, \delta_H) = I_n\sigma_{\delta hH} \qquad (14.59)$$

where $\sigma_{\delta hH}$ is a typical element of Σ_δ.

The vector θ_h can be estimated through either limited-information or full-information estimation techniques.[42] Two-stage least-squares (2SLS) estimation, a special case of Theil's k-class estimation, and limited-information maximum-likelihood estimation are limited-information techniques. Three-stage least-squares (3SLS) and full-information maximum-likelihood estimation are full-information techniques. Through limited-information techniques, each equation is fitted without reference to the other equations. Such is not the case for full-information techniques. The choice between techniques depends on the level of assurance with which the structural model is hypothesized. Higher levels may justify a full-information method, and lower levels, a limited-information method. When different from the limited-information estimator, the full-information estimator has greater asymptotic efficiency. The increased efficiency is due to adjustments for intrasample biases (see sec. 2.11). If, however, a particular equation is misspecified, such adjustments may severely bias estimates in other equations.

As derived in section 2.9, the 2SLS estimator for θ_h is

$$\theta_h(2S) = T_h^{-1}(Z_h'X)(X'X)^{-1}X'y_h \qquad (14.60)$$

where $T_h = (Z_h'X)(X'X)^{-1}(X'Z_h)$. When the hth equation is just-identified, $Z_h'X$ is square and (14.60) becomes

$$\theta_h(2S) = (Z_h'X)^{-1}X'y_h \tag{14.61}$$

(The 2SLS estimator derives its name from a conceptual, twofold application of OLS estimation. In the first application, Y_h in [14.58] is estimated by its reduced-form estimate, XB_h, where columns of B_h are given by the b_h in [14.49]. The second application of OLS estimation is in $y_h = (XB_h)\alpha_h + X_h\gamma_h + \delta_h$, where Y_h has been replaced by its reduced-form estimate, XB_h. The resulting estimate of $\theta_h = (\alpha_h', \gamma_h')'$ is precisely $\theta_h(2S)$ in [14.60]. In this conceptual, two-stage process, the endogenous matrix Y_h is replaced by a consistent estimator, XB_h, which is treated, statistically, as if it were exogenous.)

Compared with the indirect estimation of structural effects, (14.60) is computationally convenient and optimally combines multiple solutions for overidentified parameters. Asymptotically,

$$\text{cov}[\theta_h(2S), \theta_H(2S)] = T_h^{-1}(Z_h'X)(X'X)^{-1}(X'Z_H)T_H^{-1'}\sigma_{\delta hH} \tag{14.62}$$

Elements of Σ_δ are estimated by

$$s_{\delta hH} = [y_h - Z_h\theta_h(2S)]'[y_H - Z_H\theta_H(2S)]/m_{hH} \tag{14.63}$$

where $m_{hH} = \text{minimum}(n - p_h - q_h, n - p_H - q_H)$. Since (14.62) is an asymptotic result, the customary divisor on the right-hand side of (14.63) is n rather than m_{hH}. Reasons for our divisor are that (1) $s_{\delta hH}$ is unbiased for $\sigma_{\delta hH}$ when all predictors in the hth and Hth equations are exogenous and (2) division of the residual sum of squares by m_{hH} may tend to compensate for the fact that asymptotic variances underestimate small sample variances.

Approximate tests[3] of the null hypothesis $H_0: \theta_h = \theta_{ho}$ can be based on the asymptotic result in (14.62). An exact test of H_0 is as follows: Regress δ_h in (14.58) on X:

$$E(\delta_h|X) = X_{\psi h}$$

where ψ_h is a $q \times 1$ vector of regression coefficients. The OLS estimate of ψ_h is $\psi_h^* = (X'X)^{-1}X'\delta_h$, the regression sum of squares is SSR $= \delta_h'X(X'X)^{-1}X'\delta_h$, and the residual sum of squares is SSE $= \delta_h'\delta_h - \text{SSR}$. Since $E(\delta_h'X) = O'$ implies that $\psi_h = O$, it follows that

$$F = \frac{SSR/q}{SSE/(n-q)} \tag{14.64}$$

follows the central F pdf with q and $n-q$ degrees of freedom. The substitution of θ_{ho} for θ_h and $y_h - Z_h\theta_{ho}$ for δ_h in (14.64) provides an exact test of H_0. Equating F with the tabular F defines an exact confidence region for θ_h.

For 3SLS estimation, the structural system is written as

$$y = D(Z_h)\theta + \delta \tag{14.65}$$

where the $(np \times 1)$ vector $y = (y_1', \ldots, y_h', \ldots, y_p')'$; $D(Z_h)$, of order $(np) \times [\Sigma_h(p_h + q_h)]$, is a pseudodiagonal matrix with typical element Z_h; the $[\Sigma_h(p_h + q_h)] \times 1$ vector $\theta = (\theta_1', \ldots, \theta_h', \ldots, \theta_p')'$; and the $np \times 1$ vector $\delta = (\delta_1', \ldots, \delta_h', \ldots, \delta_p')$. The 3SLS estimator for θ is

$$\theta(3S) = T^{-1}D(Z_h'X)[(X'X)^{-1} \circledR \Sigma_\delta^{-1}]D(X')y \tag{14.66}$$

where $D(Z_h'X) = D(Z_h')D(X)$,

$$T = D(Z_h'X)[(X'X)^{-1} \circledR \Sigma_\delta^{-1}]D(X'Z_h) \tag{14.67}$$

and $\circledR$ denotes the direct product of two matrices. Asymptotically,

$$\text{var}[\theta(3S)] = T^{-1} \tag{14.68}$$

In (14.67), elements of Σ_δ can be estimated by the $s_{\delta hH}$ in (14.63).

In application, structural estimation techniques can lead to inefficient estimates. Consider, for example, a two-equation structural system with a causal feedback. Let $X = (X_h | X_h^*)$, where X_h^* contains columns of X not included in the hth equation. Assume that columns of X are orthogonal. Then from (14.62),

$$\text{var}[\alpha_{hH}(2S)] = \sigma_{\delta hh}/(y_H'y_H)\{\Sigma_J [r(H, J)]\}^2 \tag{14.69}$$

where α_{hH} is the direct y_H effect on y_h, and $r(H, J)$ is the sample correlation between y_H and the Jth exogenous variable. If these correlations are small, (14.69) can be large. In this case one should consider OLS estimation as applied per structural equation. Though usually inconsistent, the resulting estimates may have smaller mean square error.

2.9 Utilization of Prior Information in Estimating Structural Effects

Analogous to (14.52), suppose that

$$\boldsymbol{\theta}_{hp} = \boldsymbol{\theta}_h + \boldsymbol{\delta}_{hp} \tag{14.70}$$

is a prior estimate of $\boldsymbol{\theta}_h$, where $p_h + q_h = r_h \leq q$, $E(\boldsymbol{\delta}_{hp}) = \mathbf{O}$, and $\text{var}(\boldsymbol{\delta}_{hp}) = \Sigma_{\delta hp}$. Combining (14.70) and (14.58), we have

$$\begin{bmatrix} \mathbf{y}_h \\ \boldsymbol{\theta}_{hp} \end{bmatrix} = \begin{bmatrix} Z_h \\ I_h \end{bmatrix} \boldsymbol{\theta}_h + \begin{bmatrix} \boldsymbol{\delta}_h \\ \boldsymbol{\delta}_{hp} \end{bmatrix} \tag{14.71}$$

or

$$\mathbf{w}_h = U_h \boldsymbol{\theta}_h + \boldsymbol{\xi}_h \tag{14.72}$$

where I_h denotes the $r_h \times r_h$ identity matrix; the correspondence between terms in (14.71) and (14.72) is obvious. For $\boldsymbol{\xi}_h$, we have

$$\text{var}(\boldsymbol{\xi}_h) = \begin{bmatrix} I_n \sigma_{\delta hh} & K_{\delta hp} \\ K'_{\delta hp} & \Sigma_{\delta hp} \end{bmatrix} = W_{\delta h} \tag{14.73}$$

where $K_{\delta hp} = E(\boldsymbol{\delta}_h \boldsymbol{\delta}'_{hp})$.

Since $E(Z'_h \boldsymbol{\delta}_h) \neq \mathbf{O}$, assuming $|W_{\delta h}| \neq 0$ and minimizing $\boldsymbol{\xi}'_h W_{\delta h}^{-1} \boldsymbol{\delta}_h$ with respect to $\boldsymbol{\theta}_h$ lead to an inconsistent $\boldsymbol{\theta}_h$ estimator. An alternative estimation approach is through instrumental variable estimation[42] as follows. Multiply both sides of (14.72) by M'_h,

$$M'_h \mathbf{w}_h = M'_h U_h \boldsymbol{\theta}_h + M'_h \boldsymbol{\xi}_h \tag{14.74}$$

where the instrumental variable matrix M_h is defined as follows:

$$M'_h = (X' \,|\, J'_h) \tag{14.75}$$

where $X(n \times q)$ is defined in (14.47) and

$$J_h = [\Sigma_{\delta hp}^{-1} \,|\, 0] \tag{14.76}$$

and the null matrix 0 is of order $r_h \times (q - r_h)$. Although $E(U'_h \boldsymbol{\xi}_h) \neq \mathbf{O}$, $M'_h U_h$ and $M'_h \boldsymbol{\xi}_h$ are uncorrelated in the sense that

$$\text{plim } E[(\xi_h' M_h)(M_h' U_h)] = O \qquad (n \to \infty)$$

Applying weighted least-squares estimation in (14.74) by minimizing $(\xi_h' M_h)(M_h' W_{\delta h} M_h)^{-1}(M_h' \xi_h)$ with respect to θ_h, we obtain the following θ_h estimator.

$$\theta_h^* = [(U_h' M_h)(M_h' W_{\delta h} M_h)^{-1}(M_h' U_h)]^{-1}(U_h' M_h)(M_h' W_{\delta h} M_h)^{-1} M_h' w_h \tag{14.77}$$

When $K_{\delta hp} = 0$, (14.77) reduces to

$$\theta_h^* = [(Z_h' X + J_h)(X'X\sigma_{\delta hh} + J_h' \Sigma_{\delta hp} J_h)^{-1}(X'Z_h + J_h')]^{-1}$$
$$\times (Z_h' X + J_h)(X'X\sigma_{\delta hh} + J_h' \Sigma_{\delta hp} J_h)^{-1}(X'w_h + J_h'\theta_{hp}) \tag{14.78}$$

In a Bayesian context, θ_h^* is the mean of the posterior pdf of θ_h assuming (1) θ_h : normal $(\theta_{hp}, \Sigma_{\delta hp})$ and (2) a diffuse prior pdf for $\sigma_{\delta hh}$. As diagonal elements of $\Sigma_{\delta hp}$ approach 0, θ_h^* approaches θ_{hp}. As elements of $\Sigma_{\delta hp}$ become infinite, θ_h^* approaches the 2SLS estimator in (14.60).

2.10 Restricted versus Unrestricted Reduced Systems

Restricted systems were introduced by the writer[45] in 1961. In 1962 Zellner[46] published the same concept, though he termed restricted systems "seemingly unrelated regressions."

When the hth reduced equation is written as in (14.47), the system is termed *unrestricted* because all q exogenous variables are included in each equation; that is, $X_h = X$ for all h. When (1) the number of predictors is less than q for at least one equation and (2) model errors are correlated within experimental units, then the reduced system is termed *restricted*:

$$y_h = X_h \beta_h + \epsilon_h \tag{14.79}$$

where $X_h(n \times Q_h)$ contains $Q_h \leq q$ columns of $X(n \times q)$, $\beta_h(Q_h \times 1)$ denotes the overall effects of exogenous variables in the hth equation, and $E(\epsilon_h \epsilon_H') = I_n \sigma_{\epsilon hH} \neq 0$.

Analogous to (14.64), the reduced system is written as

$$y = D(X_h)\beta + \epsilon \tag{14.80}$$

where $D(X_h)$, of order $(np) \times (\Sigma_h Q_h)$, is a pseudodiagonal matrix with typical diagonal element X_h, and $\beta = (\beta_1', \ldots, \beta_h', \ldots, \beta_p')'$. From (14.48), we have

$$\boldsymbol{\epsilon} : (\mathbf{O}, I_n \circledR \Sigma_\epsilon) \tag{14.81}$$

The generalized least-squares (GLS) estimator (also known as the Aitken[47] estimator) for $\boldsymbol{\beta}$, obtained by minimizing $\boldsymbol{\epsilon}'(I_n \circledR \Sigma_\epsilon)^{-1}\boldsymbol{\epsilon}$ with respect to $\boldsymbol{\beta}$, is

$$\mathbf{b} = \{D(X'_h)(I_n \circledR \Sigma_\epsilon^{-1})[D(X_h)]\}^{-1}D(X'_h)(I_n \circledR \Sigma_\epsilon^{-1})\mathbf{y} \tag{14.82}$$

$$\text{var}(\mathbf{b}) = \{D(X'_h)(I_n \circledR \Sigma_\epsilon^{-1})[D(X_h)]\}^{-1} \tag{14.83}$$

When the system is unrestricted, the right-hand sides of (14.82) and (14.83) reduce to (14.48) and (14.49), respectively. When equations of the restricted system are fitted singly through OLS estimation, $\boldsymbol{\beta}_h$ is estimated by

$$\mathbf{b}_h^* = (X'_h X_h)^{-1} X'_h \mathbf{y}_h \tag{14.84}$$

$$\text{var}(\mathbf{b}_h^*) = (X'_h X_h)^{-1}\sigma_{\epsilon h h} \tag{14.85}$$

When it is unknown and has nonzero off-diagonal elements, Σ_ϵ is a nuisance parameter matrix in (14.82). There are no nuisance parameters in (14.48) and (14.84), which is one argument for fitting unrestricted systems or estimating equations of the restricted system singly. However, we will show that the estimators in (14.48) and (14.84) are inefficient, at least asymptotically, relative to the estimator in (14.82).

Prior to the illustration, we complete the estimation of $\boldsymbol{\beta}$ in (14.82) by substituting S_ϵ in (14.50) for the unknown Σ_ϵ. This substitution provides a consistent $\boldsymbol{\beta}$ estimator, denoted by $\mathbf{b}(S_\epsilon)$, since S_ϵ is a consistent estimator for Σ_ϵ. The asymptotic variance or $\mathbf{b}(S_\epsilon)$ is estimated by the substitution of S_ϵ for Σ_ϵ in (14.83).

If normality is assumed in (14.81) and maximum-likelihood estimation is applied in estimating $\boldsymbol{\beta}$, $\mathbf{b}(S_\epsilon)$ can be taken as an initial estimator in the iterative process. This initial estimator and the maximum-likelihood estimator have the same asymptotic properties. An advantage of $\mathbf{b}(S_\epsilon)$ is that some of its small sample properties are known.[48]

2.11 Adjustments for Intrasample Biases in Restricted Systems

For purposes of illustration, consider the restricted system

$$y_{1g} = \beta_{10} + \beta_1 x_g + \epsilon_1 \quad \text{and} \quad y_{2g} = \beta_{20} + \epsilon_2 \tag{14.86}$$

where (x_g, y_{hg}) denotes the gth observation of n observations on (x, y_h). The error assumptions follow those in (14.81). Assume Σ_ϵ is known and let $\Sigma_g x_g = 0$. Then from (14.82), β_{10} and β_{20} are estimated by sample averages for y_1 and y_2, respectively, and β_1 is estimated by (excluding the subscript g on the variables and summation symbol)

$$b_1 = \frac{\sum xy_1}{\sum x^2} - \frac{(\sigma_{\epsilon 12}/\sigma_{\epsilon 22}) \sum xy_2}{\sum x^2} \tag{14.87}$$

From (14.83),

$$\text{var}(b_1) = \sigma_{\epsilon 11} \bigg/ \sum x^2 (1 - \rho^2) \tag{14.88}$$

where $\rho = \sigma_{\epsilon 12}/(\sigma_{\epsilon 11}\sigma_{\epsilon 22})^{1/2}$ is the correlation between ϵ_1 and ϵ_2. If the second equation in (14.86) is written as

$$y_{2g} = \beta_{20} + \beta_2 x_g + \epsilon_{2g} \tag{14.89}$$

(so that the system is unrestricted) or if the first equation is estimated singly through OLS estimation, then β_1 is estimated by

$$b_1^* = \sum xy_1 \bigg/ \sum x^2 \qquad \text{var}(b_1^*) = \sigma_{\epsilon 11} \bigg/ \sum x^2 \tag{14.90}$$

To explain the difference between b_1 in (14.87) and b_1^* in (14.90), we first distinguish between within-sample biases—termed *w-biases*—and the conventional between-sample biases. Between samples, the OLS estimator $b_2^* = \Sigma xy_2/\Sigma x^2$ is unbiased for β_2 in (14.89): $E(b_2^*) = \beta_2$. However, given the knowledge that $\beta_2 = 0$, $b_2^* \neq 0$ is a w-bias. Because of the correlation between ϵ_1 and ϵ_2 in (14.86), this w-bias becomes part of the OLS estimate of β_1 in (14.90). The adjustment of b_1^* for the w-bias follows from the conditional expectation of b_1^* given b_2^* in a normal pdf. Specifically, $E(b_1^* | b_2^*) = \beta_1 - (\sigma_{\epsilon 12}/\sigma_{\epsilon 22})\beta_2 = \beta_1$ since $\beta_2 = 0$; but $E(b_1^* | b_2^*)$ is estimated by $b_1^* - (\sigma_{\epsilon 12}/\sigma_{\epsilon 22})b_2^*$, which is precisely the estimator b_1 in (14.87). The variance of b_1 in (14.88) follows directly from $\text{var}(b_1^* | b_2^*)$. Adjustment for the w-bias leads to increased efficiency; that is, $\text{var}(b_1) \leq \text{var}(b_1^*)$, where the equality holds only when $\rho = 0$. General results are presented elsewhere.[45,46]

GLS estimation applied to reduced systems and 3SLS estimation applied to structural systems can be viewed as identical techniques that adjust for w-biases. When the reduced system is unrestricted, w-biases are not estimable—in which case OLS and GLS estimation lead to identical estimates. When the structural system is just-identified (and/or when all structural model errors are uncorrelated), 2SLS and 3SLS estimators are identical. When the two estimators differ, the 3SLS estimator adjusts for w-biases in the following sense. In the first of the three stages of least-squares estimation, Y_h in (14.58) is estimated by its reduced-form estimator XB_h. When Y_h is replaced by XB_h, the structural system can be viewed, asymptotically, as a reduced restricted system—assuming over-identification for at least one equation. The second and third stages of least-squares estimation simply complete the application of GLS estimation; that is, in the second stage, 2SLS is applied in estimating Σ_δ by S_δ (in the same way that OLS estimation in the unrestricted system can be applied in estimating Σ_ϵ by S_ϵ), while the third stage is GLS estimation after S_δ replaces Σ_δ.

2.12 Illustration: Reanalysis of Snedecor's Data

Snedecor[49] presents an illustration of a randomized block design. The objective is to evaluate effects of fertilizers (treatments) on the yield (y_1) of sugar beets. Standard covariance analysis (SCA) is applied with stand (y_2) as the concomitant. With y_2 ignored, effects of treatments on yield are highly significant. When yield is adjusted for stand, treatment effects on y_1 are not significant. The implication is that treatment effects on y_1 are through y_2, which invalidates the usual interpretation of SCA.

The problem is reformulated in terms of structural regression with y_1 and y_2 as endogenous variables and treatments and blocks as exogenous variables. Comments are in order regarding blocks, whether fixed or random. Relative to their usual quantification through dummy variables, blocks can and should be quantified by concomitants measuring soil fertility; for example, Cady et al.[50] quantify blocks in terms of 10 variables, including depth of rooting zone, soil slope, and soil texture. Such improved quantification leads to more viable predictions and to explanations of significant block by treatment interactions.

Direct effects are illustrated in the path diagram

$$\begin{array}{ccc} \text{treatment} & & \text{yield } (y_1) \\ & \searrow & \uparrow \\ \text{block} & \rightarrow & \text{stand } (y_2) \end{array}$$

and quantified in terms of the structural system

$$y_{1k\mathcal{L}} = \gamma_{10} + \gamma_{1k} + \alpha y_{2k\mathcal{L}} + \delta_{1k\mathcal{L}}$$
$$y_{2k\mathcal{L}} = \gamma_{20} + \gamma_{2k} + \tau_{2\mathcal{L}} + \delta_{2k\mathcal{L}} \tag{14.91}$$

γ_{h0} and $\delta_{hk\mathcal{L}}$ are, respectively, the intercept and error for the hth equation, $h = 1, 2$; γ_{hk} is the direct kth block effect on y_h, $k = 1, \ldots, 6$; α is the direct effect of y_2 on y_1; and $\tau_{2\mathcal{L}}$ is the direct effect of the $\mathcal{L}$th treatment on y_2, $\mathcal{L} = 1, \ldots, 7$. In the corresponding reduced system, the first equation is $y_{1k\mathcal{L}} = (\gamma_{10} + \alpha\gamma_{20}) + (\gamma_{1k} + \alpha\gamma_{2k}) + \alpha\tau_{2\mathcal{L}} + (\delta_{1k\mathcal{L}} + \alpha\delta_{2k\mathcal{L}})$; the second equation is identical to the second structural equation.

Because treatments have no direct effect on y_1 and the number of treatments is greater than two, the first structural equation meets the necessary conditions for overidentification. To illustrate the multiple estimates for α, we apply OLS estimation in the reduced system. In the second equation, the contrast $\tau_{2\mathcal{L}} - \tau_{2\mathcal{L}*}$ is estimated by $\Sigma_k(y_{2k\mathcal{L}} - y_{2k\mathcal{L}*})/6$, while in the second equation $\alpha(\tau_{2\mathcal{L}} - \tau_{2\mathcal{L}*})$ is estimated by $\Sigma_k(y_{1k\mathcal{L}} - y_{1k\mathcal{L}*})/6$. Thus α can be estimated by any of the six estimates $\Sigma_k(y_{1k\mathcal{L}} - y_{1k\mathcal{L}*})/\Sigma_k(y_{2k\mathcal{L}} - y_{2k\mathcal{L}*})$, $\mathcal{L} \neq \mathcal{L}*$.

The 2SLS and 3SLS estimates are given in Table 14.6, where *blk* and *trt* abbreviate block and treatment, respectively. Relative to the re-

TABLE 14.6. Reanalysis of Snedecor's Data

Dependent variable	Predictors	Estimated by 2SLS			Estimated by 3SLS		
		Coefficient estimate	Standard error	$|t|$	Coefficient estimate	Standard error	$|t|$
Stand (y_2)	Intercept	286.000	—	—			
	Blk 1	1.857	12.315	.15	Same as		
	2	−6.143	12.315	.50	2SLS results		
	3	18.714	12.315	1.52			
	4	−11.000	12.315	.89			
	5	−18.286	12.315	1.48			
	Trt 1	−56.333	13.491	4.18	−60.275	12.546	4.80
	2	9.667	13.491	.72	10.594	12.395	.85
	3	−57.500	13.491	4.26	−56.227	12.552	4.48
	4	27.667	13.491	2.05	34.916	12.428	2.81
	5	65.333	13.491	4.84	60.407	12.599	4.79
	6	−56.333	13.491	4.18	−56.356	12.546	4.49
Yield (y_1)	Intercept	−3.583	—	—			
	Blk 1	−.344	.192	1.79	Same as		
	2	−.053	.192	−.28	2SLS results		
	3	−1.165	.195	5.97			
	4	.700	.193	3.63			
	5	.988	.194	5.09			
	Stand	.031	.002	15.50			

Source: The data reanalyzed here are from G. W. Snedecor, *Statistical Methods*, 4th ed. (Ames: Iowa State College Press, 1946), p. 303.

sults of 2SLS estimation, the standard errors of the 3SLS treatment estimates are decreased owing to adjustments for w-biases.

Through 2SLS estimation, the covariance matrix of the structural model errors is estimated by

$$\begin{bmatrix} 0.2711 & -6.5642 \\ -6.5642 & 955.5033 \end{bmatrix}$$

The negative correlation between δ_1 and δ_2, estimated by $-6.5033/(.2711)(955.5033) = -.408$, implies that when y_2 is above its expectation, y_1 tends to be below its expectation. This might be interpreted to mean that when stand is higher than usual, there is greater competition between plants for food and moisture. Because of this competition, the yield tends to be lower than usual.

Since model (14.91) may be inadequate, it is subjected to a diagnostic test. Several reasons may be given for model inadequacy. First, the restrictions leading to just- or overidentification are incorrect if the path diagram is incorrectly specified. Second, the model may be invalid if, say, a nonlinear,[28,29] rather than a linear, model is appropriate. Third, the error assumptions may be erroneous; for example, the errors may be correlated not only within but between experimental units.

Given that the model and error assumptions are valid, Baseman[51] provides a test of the restrictions leading to overidentification. For the hth structural equation, the restrictions are rejected if

$$(n - q)/(R_h - 1)/(q - q_h - p_h) > F_\alpha \qquad (14.92)$$

where F_α is the α-level critical value of Fisher's F pdf with $q - q_h - p_h$ and $n - q$ degrees of freedom;

$$R_h = (1, \mathbf{a}_h')(SSE_h)(1, \mathbf{a}_h')'/(1, \mathbf{a}_h')(SSE)(1, \mathbf{a}_h') \qquad (14.93)$$

$\mathbf{a}_h$ is the 2SLS estimator of α_h (14.58); $SSE_h = \boldsymbol{\mu}_h'\boldsymbol{\mu}_h - \boldsymbol{\mu}_h'X_h(X_h'X_h)^{-1}$ $\times X_h'\boldsymbol{\mu}_h$ and $SSE = \boldsymbol{\mu}_h'\boldsymbol{\mu}_h - \boldsymbol{\mu}_h'X(X'X)^{-1}X'\boldsymbol{\mu}_h$ are, respectively, $(q_h + 1)$ $\times (q_h + 1)$ matrices of residual sums of squares and cross products of the regressions of $\boldsymbol{\mu}_h = (\mathbf{y}_h|Y_h)$ on X_h and $\boldsymbol{\mu}_h$ on X.

Application of the diagnostic test to equation (14.91) leads to the following values for terms on the right-hand side of (14.93): $\mathbf{a}_h$ is a single element whose value (from Table 14.6) is .031;

$$SSE_1 = \begin{bmatrix} 29.55 & 565.64 \\ 565.64 & 36137.67 \end{bmatrix}$$

$$SSE = \begin{bmatrix} 23.23 & 682.20 \\ 682.20 & 28665.10 \end{bmatrix}$$

For the left-hand side of (14.93), we have $R_1 = 1.067$. Substituting these values in (14.92), we have $(42 - 12)(1.067 - 1)/(12 - 7) = .40 < F(\alpha = .05; 5, 30) = 2.57$. Hence, restrictions leading to overidentification in (14.91) are not rejected.

2.13 Illustration: Reanalysis of Scheffe's Data

Scheffe[52] discusses an experiment on the effects of three feeding treatments on growth rates for pigs. Six young pigs, three males and three females, were selected from each of five litters and assigned to one of five pens. Each of the treatments, containing increasing amounts of protein, was given to one male and one female in each pen. After weighing the pigs individually in each of 16 weeks, a growth rate was established in terms of the OLS slope estimate, y_1. (There is no evidence of heterogenous variances among slope estimates.) The weight of each pig prior to treatment is denoted by y_2.

Scheffe utilizes the model

$$y_{1k\mathscr{L}m} = \gamma_0 + s_k + f_{\mathscr{L}} + (sf)_{k\mathscr{L}} + p_m + \alpha y_{2k\mathscr{L}m} + \delta_{k\mathscr{L}m} \tag{14.94}$$

to illustrate SCA. The first term and the last term on the right-hand side of (14.94) are intercept and model error, respectively. With y_2 considered exogenous, the other terms are overall effects on y_1: s_k is the effect of the kth sex, $k = 1, 2$; $f_{\mathscr{L}}$ is the effect of the $\mathscr{L}$th treatment, $\mathscr{L} = 1, \ldots, 3$; $(sf)_{k\mathscr{L}}$ is the effect of the $(k, \mathscr{L})$th interaction; p_m is the effect of the mth pen, $m = 1, \ldots, 5$; and α is the y_2 effect on y_1. As opposed to Snedecor's illustration, treatments have no effect on the covariable y_2.

Scheffe's model is altered by including sex by pen interaction effects, denoted by $(sp)_{km}$, in model (14.94). Analysis results are given in Table 14.7 under the heading "standard covariance analysis." No interaction is significant under SCA.

Next, consider a structural interpretation of the problem where y_1 and y_2 are endogenous, while sex, treatments, and pens are exogenous. (Comments regarding blocks in Snedecor's data apply to pens in Scheffe's data; i.e., the pen is largely a reflection of the litter, while the litter can be quantified in terms of concomitants such as litter size, gestation period, and birth weights. Dummy variable quantification of pens should be replaced by the concomitants if possible.) Direct effects are identified in the path diagram

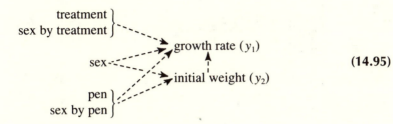

$$(14.95)$$

and quantified in the structural system

$$y_{1k\mathscr{L}m} = \gamma_{10} + s_{1k} + f_{1\mathscr{L}} + (sf)_{1k\mathscr{L}} + p_{1m}$$
$$+ (sp)_{1km} + \alpha y_{2k\mathscr{L}m} + \delta_{1k\mathscr{L}m} \qquad (14.96)$$

$$y_{2k\mathscr{L}m} = \gamma_{20} + s_{2k} + p_{2m} + (sp)_{2km} + \delta_{2k\mathscr{L}m}$$

First and last terms on the right-hand side of these equations are intercepts and model errors, respectively. Direct effects are defined as follows: s_{hk} is the kth sex effect on y_h, $h = 1, 2$; $f_{1\mathscr{L}}$ is the $\mathscr{L}$th treatment effect on y_1; $(sf)_{1k\mathscr{L}}$ is the effect of the $(k, \mathscr{L})$th interaction on y_1; $(sp)_{hkm}$ is the (k, m)th interaction effect on y_h; and α is the direct y_2 effect on y_1.

Because the first structural equation is underidentified, consistent estimates of its parameters are not available unless additional restrictions are imposed in the path diagram. However, since primary interest is in overall treatment effects, consistent estimates of these effects are available either through SCA or through the reduced system corresponding to structural system (14.96). The reduced system, given by

$$y_{hk\mathscr{L}m} = \beta_{h0} + {}_0s_{hk} + {}_0f_{h\mathscr{L}} + {}_0(sf)_{hk\mathscr{L}} \qquad (14.97)$$
$$+ {}_0p_{hm} + {}_0(sp)_{hkm} + \epsilon_{hk\mathscr{L}m}$$

is restricted since treatment effects do not appear in the second reduced equation. Overall effects in (14.97) are defined as follows: $\beta_{10} = \gamma_{10} + \alpha\gamma_{20}$, $\beta_{20} = \gamma_{20}$, ${}_0s_{1k} = s_{1k} + \alpha s_{2k}$, ${}_0s_{2k} = s_{2k}$, ${}_0f_{1\mathscr{L}} = f_{1\mathscr{L}}$, ${}_0f_{2\mathscr{L}} = 0$, ${}_0(sf)_{1k\mathscr{L}} = (sf)_{1k\mathscr{L}}$, ${}_0(sf)_{2k\mathscr{L}} = 0$, ${}_0p_{1m} = p_{1m} + \alpha p_{2m}$, ${}_0p_{2m} = p_{2m}$, ${}_0(sp)_{1km} = (sp)_{1km} + \alpha(sp)_{2km}$, ${}_0(sp)_{2km} = (sp)_{2km}$, $\epsilon_{1k\mathscr{L}m} = \delta_{1k\mathscr{L}m} + \alpha\delta_{2k\mathscr{L}m}$, and $\epsilon_{2k\mathscr{L}m} = \delta_{2k\mathscr{L}m}$. Through GLS estimation in the restricted system, adjustments are made for w-biases. Resulting treatment estimates are more efficient relative to those obtained through SCA or through OLS estimation in the unrestricted system. (The unrestricted system is obtained by augmenting the second reduced equation in [14.97]; i.e., ${}_0f_{2\mathscr{L}}$ and ${}_0(sf)_{2k\mathscr{L}}$ are included in the second reduced equation even though they are known to be 0.)

TABLE 14.7 Reanalysis of Scheffe's Data

Dependent variable →	Restricted system: estimated by GLS						Standard covariance analysis: estimated by OLS			Structural eq. for y_i; $(sp)_{1hm} = 0$: estimated by 2SLS		
	Growth rate			Initial weight			Growth rate			Growth rate		
Predictor	Coef. est.	Stand. error	|t|	Coef. est.	Stand. error	|t|	Coef. est.	Stand. error	|t|	Coef. est.	Stand. error	|t|
Intercept	9.399	—	—	40.100	—	—	4.883	—	—	6.296	—	—
Male (sex)	−.120	.117	1.03	1.033	.602	1.72	−.234	.108	2.17	−.198	.123	1.52
Trt 1	.378	.136	2.78	(−.300)	.852	.35	.378	.142	2.66	.367	.165	2.22
2	−.082	.136	.60	(.600)	.852	.70	−.082	.143	.57	−.061	.166	.37
Pen 1	.167	.234	.71	4.733	1.205	3.93	−.355	.279	1.27	−.188	.297	.63
2	−.298	.234	1.27	−6.433	1.205	5.34	.411	.333	1.23	.185	.342	.54
3	−.481	.234	2.06	−.433	1.205	.36	−.433	.200	2.17	−.449	.234	1.92
4	.676	.234	2.89	5.233	1.205	4.34	.099	.294	.34	.283	.309	.92
Male × trt 1	.059	.124	.48	(−.167)	.852	.20	.059	.141	.42	.065	.165	.39
× trt 2	−.053	.124	.43	(−1.133)	.852	1.33	−.053	.149	.36	−.092	.171	.54
Male × pen 1	−.305	.234	1.30	−4.200	1.205	3.49	−.158	.264	.60	—	—	—
× pen 2	.000	.234	.00	1.967	1.205	1.63	−.217	.215	1.01	—	—	—
× pen 3	.180	.234	.77	2.300	1.205	1.91	−.073	.221	.33	—	—	—
× pen 4	−.216	.254	.85	−3.033	1.205	2.52	.118	.236	.50	—	—	—
Initial weight	—	—	—	—	—	—	.110	.041	2.68	.075	.039	1.92
Error df	16			16			15			19		

Source: The data reanalyzed here are from H. Scheffe, *The Analyses of Variance* (New York: Wiley, 1961), p. 217.

Table 14.7 presents GLS estimates of reduced system parameters. Estimates in parentheses in the initial weight equation are those obtained by augmenting the reduced system so that it becomes unrestricted. Note that the sample estimates support the restrictions that the $_0f_{2\mathscr{L}}$ and the $_0(sf)_{2k\mathscr{L}}$ are 0. Note also that the estimated treatment effects on y_1 are identical for both the restricted system analysis and SCA; that is, for both analyses, the formula for an estimated treatment contrast is $[\Sigma_{k,m}(y_{1k\mathscr{L}m} - y_{1k\mathscr{L}*m})/10] - (s_{12}/s_{22})[\Sigma_{k,m}(y_{2k\mathscr{L}m} - y_{2k\mathscr{L}*m})/10]$, where the s_{hH} denote estimated variances/covariances of reduced model errors. Variances, however, differ as a result of adjustments for w-biases. (See Mallios[53] for a general discussion on structural experimental design.)

In the SCA, effects of sex by pen are not significant, while in the reduced equation for y_2, these effects are highly significant. The implication is that the sex by pen effects on y_1 are not direct but through y_2; that is, the $(sp)_{1km} = 0$. If these restrictions were known a priori, the first structural equation meets the necessary condition for overidentification. With the $(sp)_{1km}$ deleted from the first structural equation, results of 2SLS estimation are presented in Table 14.7. (Results for the second structural equation are identical to those for the second reduced equation.) Results of 3SLS estimation would be identical to applying GLS estimation in the system $y_{1k\mathscr{L}m} = \gamma_{10} + s_{1k} + f_{1\mathscr{L}} + (sf)_{1k\mathscr{L}} + p_{1m} + \alpha\Pi_{2k\mathscr{L}m} + \delta_{1k\mathscr{L}m}$ and $y_{2k\mathscr{L}m} = \gamma_{20} + s_{2k} + p_{2m} + (sp)_{2km} + \delta_{2k\mathscr{L}m}$, where $\Pi_{2k\mathscr{L}m}$ is the predicted value of $y_{2k\mathscr{L}m}$ obtained through OLS estimation in the regression of y_2 on all the exogenous variables.

Exercise 1

In the 5 December 1985 issue of the *New England Journal of Medicine*, researchers at the National Cancer Institute reported that certain untreatable tumors could be shrunk by using a technique that boosts the immune system with interleukin-2 (IL-2), a protein the body uses naturally in its defense against disease. The technique is said to be especially effective in shrinking tumors caused by advanced kidney and skin cancer and tumors of lymphoid tissue (blood-related cancers).

The so-called immunodoptive therapy relies on a two-step technique in which the patient's white blood cells are extracted and treated with IL-2. This causes the white blood cells to produce lymphokine-activated killer cells (LAK cells), which can destroy malignant cells. These LAK cells, plus more IL-2, are then injected periodically into the patient over a period of days—depending on the patient's ability to tolerate the LAK cell infusion.

Treatment results for 25 cancer patients are given in Table 14.8. Perform a discriminant analysis on these data using no response versus partial or complete

TABLE 14.8. Results of Treatment with Lymphokine-Activated Killer (LAK) Cells and Recombinant Interleukin-2 in 25 Patients with Cancer

Patient no.	Diagnosis	Age	IL-2 Infusion No. of doses	IL-2 Infusion Total units (10^{-3} kg)	LAK-Cell Infusion No. of doses	LAK-Cell Infusion Cells (10^{-10})	Result
1	Melanoma	33	47	790	9	4.2	Complete regression of subcutaneous metastases
2	Rectal cancer	41	35	510	9	4.3	Partial regression of pulmonary metastases
3	Melanoma	33	40	800	13	12.6	No response
4	Osteosarcoma	24	90	1,340	14	7.4	No response
5	Melanoma	42	70	700	13	11.6	No response
6	Synovial-cell sarcoma	36	76	760	9	6.6	No response
7	Melanoma	23	68	680	10	5.9	Partial regression of pulmonary metastases
8	Colon cancer	59	42	280	10	6.4	Partial regression of hepatic metastases
9	Melanoma	35	65	1,490	10	7.9	No response
10	Colon cancer	54	51	510	5	2.9	No response
11	Colon cancer	59	76	760	10	18.4	No response
12	Colon cancer	35	71	1,830	10	9.7	No response
13	Colon cancer	47	48	1,180	10	7.9	No response
14	Malignant fibrous histiocytoma	35	66	940	10	12.6	No response
15	Esophageal cancer	59	68	1,200	9	10.1	No response
16	Renal-cell cancer	54	27	2,280	5	9.9	Partial regression of pulmonary metastases
17	Colon cancer	48	14	1,400	4	1.8	No response
18	Colon cancer	57	36	2,200	5	5.0	No response
19	Lung adenocarcinoma	40	12	1,200	5	5.1	Partial regression of primary pulmonary tumor
20	Neurofibrosarcoma	28	37	2,670	9	11.7	No response
21	Renal-cell cancer	45	35	2,500	9	8.4	Partial regression of pulmonary metastases
22	Melanoma	43	22	1,840	5	4.4	Partial regression of pulmonary and mediastinal metastases
23	Melanoma	49	44	3,320	10	9.8	Partial regression of pulmonary metastases
24	Colon cancer	42	24	1,950	5	3.1	Partial regression of pulmonary metastases
25	Renal-cell cancer	59	21	1,470	5	3.1	Partial regression of pulmonary metastases

Source: S. A. Rosenberg et al., "Observations on the Systemic Administration of Autologous Lymphokine-Activated Killer Cells and Recombinant Interleukin-2 to Patients with Metastatic Cancer," *New England Journal of Medicine*, 5 Decembmer 1985, table 1.

response as the binary dependent variable. Explain why the number of doses of IL-2 infusion is a significant predictor.

Exercise 2

A newspaper article (*Fresno Bee*, 9 August 1984) reported that a psychology professor analyzed data on participants in the modern Olympics (from 1896 to 1965). He found that the frequency with which a nation goes to war is related to the number of athletes it sends to the games. The relation between national belligerence and athletes engaged in contact sports was even stronger. The study concluded that the modern Olympic games do nothing to reduce international conflict and may actually foster national belligerence. Are the associations described in this study causal, alias, or spurious? Would you agree or disagree with the conclusion and why?

Exercise 3

Two researchers claim to have found an association between military spending and infant mortality around the world. Their report (*Lancet*, June 1985), based on data from 141 countries, shows that the larger the percentage of gross national product a country spends on weapons, the higher its infant death rate. What is the nature of the association under discussion? Give reasons for its existence.

Exercise 4

At the 1985 meeting of the American Association for the Advancement of Science, a researcher reported that the greater the number of children and the shorter the intervals between successive births, the less the average intellectual attainment per child. Comment on the type of association and give reasons for its existence.

Exercise 5

In a study, Vietnam veterans who were in heavy combat were compared with Vietnam era veterans who served elsewhere. The analysis provided evidence of an association between wartime stress and subsequent financial and/or marital problems. The combat veterans earned an average of $3,000 less annually than their noncombat counterparts and had a higher divorce rate. For each veteran in the study, let $ denote present salary, L the combat time in the Vietnam era, R

the individual's race, and S the individual's socioeconomic status prior to entering the service. An implication of the study is that the negative effect in $L \to \$$ is causal. If, however, the true path diagram is

then L is simply an alias for R and S. If the path diagram is

the L becomes more causal, depending on the strength of the effect in $L \to \$$. Finally, if the diagram is

then W is a factor. Give a rationale for each diagram.

Exercise 6

An association was detected between the winner of the Super Bowl (as determined early in the year) and the percentage change in the Standard and Poor 500 index during the course of the year. The data are presented below. With the exception of two years, 1970 and 1984, the change in the index is positive if the winner is from the old NFL conference (before the NFL-AFL merger) and negative if the winner is from the old AFL conference. (Note that the association holds even with the October Crash of 1987.) How would you characterize this association? Give reasons for its existence. How would the results change if the index changes are adjusted for inflation?

Super Bowl	Year	Winner	Conference	% change (S&P 500)
I	1967	Green Bay	Old NFL	20.1
II	1968	Green Bay	Old NFL	7.7
III	1969	N.Y. Jets	Old AFL	−11.4

Super Bowl	Year	Winner	Conference	% change (S&P 500)
IV	1970	Kansas City	Old AFL	0.1
V	1971	Baltimore	Old NFL	10.8
VI	1972	Dallas	Old NFL	15.6
VII	1973	Miami	Old AFL	−17.4
VIII	1974	Miami	Old AFL	−29.7
IX	1975	Pittsburgh	Old NFL	31.5
X	1976	Pittsburgh	Old NFL	19.1
XI	1977	Oakland	Old AFL	−11.5
XII	1978	Dallas	Old NFL	1.1
XIII	1979	Pittsburgh	Old NFL	12.3
XIV	1980	Pittsburgh	Old NFL	25.8
XV	1981	Oakland	Old AFL	−9.7
XVI	1982	San Francisco	Old NFL	14.8
XVII	1983	Washington	Old NFL	17.3
XVIII	1984	L.A. Raiders	Old AFL	1.4
XIX	1985	San Francisco	Old NFL	24.9
XX	1986	Chicago	Old NFL	14.6
XXI	1987	N.Y. Giants	Old NFL	2.0

Exercise 7

Rao[54] discusses results of a United Nations study where agrricultural output (O) was predicted in terms of gross domestic product (G) and per capita income (G/N); N denotes the population of the particular country. Based on OLS estimation, the fitted equations are as follows:

$$\hat{O} = 34.322 + .402G \qquad R^2 = .94$$
$$(.036)$$
$$\hat{O} = -8.001 + 5.698(G/N) \qquad R^2 = .96$$
$$(.397)$$
$$\hat{O} = -131.716 - 1.266G + 22.816(G/N) \qquad R^2 = .99$$
$$(.239) \qquad (3.345)$$

where $\hat{O}$ denotes the predicted value of O, R^2 is the coefficient of determination, and standard errors of estimates are given in parentheses. There is a sign discrepancy in the coefficients of G in the first and third equations, which should not be ascribed to chance. Attributing the discrepancy to multicollinearity (the correlation between G and G/N is .9985) is unsatisfactory without further explanation. Use the following path diagram to explain the negative coefficient of G in the third equation.

$$G \leftarrow\rightarrow O$$
$$\nwarrow \quad \nearrow$$
$$\diagdown \; \diagup$$
$$N$$

References

1. Morrison, D. F. *Multivariate Statistical Methods*. New York: McGraw Hill, 1967.

2. Hartigan, J. A. *Clustering Algorithms*. New York: Wiley, 1975.

3. Anderson, T. W. *An Introduction to Multivariate Statistical Analysis*. New York: Wiley, 1958.

4. Blackwell, D., and Girshick, M. A. *Theory of Games and Statistical Decisions*. New York: Wiley, 1954.

5. Vinod, H. D., and Ullah, A. *Recent Advances in Regression Analysis*. New York: Dekker, 1981.

6. Anderson, T. W. "Classification by Multivariate Analysis." *Psychometrica* 16 (1951): 31–50.

7. Sitgreaves, R. "On the Distribution of Two Random Matrices Used in Classification Procedures." *Annals of Mathematical Statistics* 23 (1952): 263–70.

8. Wald, A. "On a Statistical Problem Arising in the Classification of an Individual into One of Two Groups." *Annals of Mathematical Statistics* 15 (1944): 145–62.

9. Lachenbruch, P. A. "An Almost Unbiased Method of Obtaining Confidence Intervals for the Probability of Misclassification in Discriminant Analysis." *Biometrics* 23 (1967): 639–45.

10. Lachenbruch, P. A., and Mickey, M. R. "Estimation of Error Rates in Discriminant Analysis." *Technometrics* 10 (1968): 1–11.

11. Lachenbruch, P. A. "On Expected Probabilities of Misclassification in Discriminant Analysis, Necessary Sample Size, and a Relation with the Multiple Correlation Coefficient." *Biometrics* 24 (1968): 823–34.

12. Dixon, W. J., ed. *BMDP Statistical Software*. Berkeley and Los Angeles: University of California Press, 1985.

13. Box, G. E. P. "A Generalized Distribution Theory for a Class of Likelihood Criteria." *Biometrika* 36 (1949): 317–46.

14. Marks, S., and Dunn, O. J. "Discriminant Functions when Covariance Matrices Are Unequal." *Journal of the American Statistical Association* 69 (1974): 356, 555–59.

15. Lachenbruch, P. A., Sneeringer, C., and Revo, L. T. "Robustness of the Linear and Quadratic Discriminant Function to Certain Types of Nonnormality." *Communications in Statistics,* no. 1, (1973): 39–56.

16. Johnson, N. L., and Kotz, J. S. *Continuous Multivariate Distributions*. New York: Wiley, 1972.

17. Van Ness, J. W. "On the Effects of Dimension in Discriminant Analysis for Unequal Covariance Populations." *Technometrics* 21 (1979): 119–28.

18. Fatti, L. P., and Hawkins, D. M. "Variable Selection in Heteroscedastic Discriminant Analysis." *Journal of the American Statistical Association* 81 (1986): 394, 494–500.

19. Gunst, R. F., and Mason, R. L. "Advantages of Examining Multicollinearities in Regression Analysis." *Biometrics* 33 (1977): 249–60.

20. Skellam, J. G. "A Probability Distribution Derived from the Binomial Distribution by Regarding the Probability of Success as Variable between Sets of Trials." *Journal of the Royal Statistical Society,* series B, 10, (1948): 257–61.

21. Johnson, N. L., and Kotz, J. S. *Discrete Distributions.* Boston: Houghton Mifflin, 1969.

22. Fisher, R. A. "The Negative Binomial Distribution." *Annals of Eugenics* 11 (1941): 182–87.

23. Fisher, R. A. "The Use of Multiple Measurements in Taxonomic Problems." *Annals of Eugenics* 7 (1936): 179–88.

24. Keating, J. P. and Mason, R. L. "James-Stern Estimation from an alternative perspective." *American Statistician* 42 (1988): 2.

25. Flagle, C. D., ed. *Advanced Medical Systems: Issues and Challenges.* Sixth Annual Meeting of the Society for Advanced Medical Systems. New York: Symposia Specialists, 1975.

26. Evans, D. A. "Experimental Evidence Concerning Contagious Distributions in Ecology." *Biometrika* 10 (1953): 186–211.

27. Cramer, H. *Mathematical Methods of Statistics.* Princeton: Princeton University Press, 1957.

28. Tukey, J. W. "Causation, regression, and path analysis." In *Statistics and Mathematics in Biology,* ed. O. Kempthorne, T. Bancroft, J. Gowen, and J. Lush. Ames: Iowa State College Press, 1954.

29. Turner, M. E., Monroe, R., and Lucas, H. L. "Generalized Asymptotic Regression and Path Analysis." *Biometrics* 17 (1961): 120–43.

30. Chow, G. C. *Analysis and Control of Dynamic Economic Systems.* New York: Wiley, 1975.

31. Zellner, A. *An Introduction to Bayesian Inference in Econometrics.* New York: Wiley, 1971.

32. Wright, S. "On the Nature of Size Factors." *Genetics* 3 (1918): 367–74.

33. Wright, S. "Causation and Correlation." *Journal of Agricultural Research* 20 (1921): 557–85.

34. Wright, S. "The Method of Path Coefficients." *Annals of Mathematical Statistics* 5, (1934): 161–215.

35. Wright, S. "The Genetic Structure of Populations." *Annals of Eugenics* 15 (1951): 323–54.

36. Wright, S. "The Interpretation of Multivariate Systems." In ref. 27.

37. Frisch, R. *Statistical Confluence Analysis by Means of Complete Regression Systems.* Universitetets Økonomiske Institutt (Oslo), 1934.

38. Webster, J., Gunst, R., and Mason, R. "Latent Root Regression Analysis." *Technometrics* 16 (1974): 513–22.

39. Hoerl, A., and Kennard, R. W. "Ridge Regression: Biased Estimation for Non-Orthogonal Problems." *Technometrics* 12 (1970): 55–67.

40. Marquardt, D., and Snee, R. "Ridge Regression in Practice." *American Statistician* 29 (1975): 3–20.

41. Pratt, J. W., and Schlaifer, R. "On the Nature and Discovery of Struc-

ture." *Journal of the American Statistical Association* 79 (1984): 9–33.

42. Goldberger, A. S. *Econometric Theory*. New York: Wiley, 1964.

43. Roy, S. N. *Some Aspects of Multivariate Analysis*. New York: Wiley, 1957.

44. Toutenburg, H. *Prior Information in Linear Models*. New York: Wiley, 1982.

45. Mallios, W. S. "On Linear Regression Systems." *Proceedings of the Seventh Conference on the Design of Experiments in Army Research, Development, and Testing*. Durham: U.S. Army Research Office, 1961.

46. Zellner, A. "An Efficient Method of Estimating Seemingly Unrelated Regressions and Tests for Aggregation Bias." *Journal of the American Statistical Association* 57 (1962): 348–68.

47. Aitken, A. C. "On Least Squares and Linear Combinations of Observations." *Proceedings of the Royal Society of Edinburgh* 55 42–48 (1934–35).

48. Zellner, A. "Estimators for Seemingly Unrelated Regression Equations: Some Finite Sample Results." *Journal of the American Statistical Association* 58 (1963): 977–93.

49. Snedecor, G. W. *Statistical Methods*. 4th ed. Ames: Iowa State College Press, 1946.

50. Cady, F. B., Anderson, R. L., and Allen, D. M. "Analyzing a Series of Soil Fertility Experiments." In *Exploring Data Analysis*, ed. W. J. Dixon and W. L. Nicholson. Los Angeles: University of California Press, 1974.

51. Baseman, R. L. "On Finite Sample Distributions of Generalized Classical Linear Identifiability Test Statistics." *Journal of the American Statistical Association* 55 (1960): 650–59.

52. Scheffe, H. *The Analysis of Variance*. New York: Wiley, 1961.

53. Mallios, W. S. "The Analysis of Structural Effects in Experimental Design." *Journal of the American Statistical Association* 55 (1970): 650–59.

54. Rao, C. R. "Some Thoughts on Regression and Prediction." *Sankhya*, series C, 37 (1975): 102–20.

INDEX